NEW YORK REVIEW BOOKS
CLASSICS

THE UNCOLLECTED ESSAYS OF ELIZABETH HARDWICK

ELIZABETH HARDWICK (1916–2007) was born in Lexington, Kentucky, and educated at the University of Kentucky and Columbia University. A recipient of a Gold Medal from the American Academy of Arts and Letters, she was the author of three novels, a biography of Herman Melville, and four collections of essays. A co-founder and advisory editor of *The New York Review of Books*, she contributed more than one hundred reviews, articles, reflections, and letters to the magazine. NYRB Classics publishes *Sleepless Nights*, a novel; *Seduction and Betrayal*, a study of women in literature; *The New York Stories of Elizabeth Hardwick*; and *The Collected Essays of Elizabeth Hardwick*.

ALEX ANDRIESSE was born in Cedar Rapids, Iowa, in 1985. His stories, essays, and poems have appeared in *Granta*, *Prodigal*, *The Review of Contemporary Fiction*, and *Literary Imagination*. He is the translator of Roberto Bazlen's *Notes Without a Text* and François-René de Chateaubriand's *Memoirs from Beyond the Grave, 1768–1800* (an NYRB Classic). He lives in the Netherlands.

THE UNCOLLECTED ESSAYS
OF ELIZABETH HARDWICK

Edited by

ALEX ANDRIESSE

NEW YORK REVIEW BOOKS

New York

THIS IS A NEW YORK REVIEW BOOK
PUBLISHED BY THE NEW YORK REVIEW OF BOOKS
435 Hudson Street, New York, NY 10014
www.nyrb.com

First published as a New York Review Books Classic in 2022.

Library of Congress Cataloging-in-Publication Data
Names: Hardwick, Elizabeth, author. | Andriesse, Alex, editor.
Title: The uncollected essays of Elizabeth Hardwick / edited and introduced by
    Alex Andriesse.
Description: New York: New York Review Books, [2022] | Series: New York
    Review Books classics |
Identifiers: LCCN 2021027768 (print) | LCCN 2021027769 (ebook) |
    ISBN 9781681376233 (paperback) | ISBN 9781681376240 (ebook)
Subjects: LCGFT: Essays.
Classification: LCC PS3515.A5672 U53 2022 (print) | LCC PS3515.A5672 (ebook) |
    DDC 814/.52—dc23
LC record available at https://lccn.loc.gov/2021027768
LC ebook record available at https://lccn.loc.gov/2021027769

ISBN 978-1-68137-623-3
Available as an electronic book; ISBN 978-1-68137-624-0

Printed in the United States of America on acid-free paper.
10 9 8 7 6 5 4 3 2 1

CONTENTS

FEMININE PRINCIPLE

READINGS

MUSINGS

INTRODUCTION

YOU MIGHT think *The Uncollected Essays of Elizabeth Hardwick* would be a simple sequel to *The Collected Essays* edited by Darryl Pinckney—a gleaning of what remained in the field after that rich harvest. Indeed, a selection more representative of Hardwick than Pinckney's is difficult to imagine. Merely assembling the essays, reviews, introductions, and eulogies he omitted would have been a worthwhile endeavor. It also would have made for a disjointed book, less a companion volume to *The Collected* than an appendage, incapable of standing on its own.

The thirty-five pieces I have gathered here are meant to make a case for Hardwick as an essayist in the word's widest, wildest, oldest sense. I don't think this will provoke much controversy. Readers are aware of Hardwick's nonfictional forays beyond the bounds of criticism—in "Boston," "In Maine," "The Apotheosis of Martin Luther King"—although they may not be aware of how many of these forays she left out of the books published during her lifetime. Most of these Hardwick probably considered too topical or eccentric, or just too short. About one-third of the thirty-five collected here were written for glossy magazines (*Vogue*, *Vanity Fair*) where every word was counted, and it is easy to understand why she would not have wanted to juxtapose these pieces with longer essays composed for *The New York Review of Books* or *Partisan Review*. Besides, as Pinckney has said, Hardwick "never liked publishing a book." Her ambition took the form of perfectionism rather than productivity; the quality of the writing she left to hibernate in back issues is proof, among other things, of a genuine, now nearly bygone, modesty.

Not to clutter this portrait of the artist as an essayist, I have excluded all of Hardwick's reviews of fiction, theater, and movies, and almost all of her prefaces and introductions. In doing so, my intention was to foreground the imaginative prose that perhaps best represents her own definition of the essay as "nothing less than the reflection of all there is: art, personal experience, places, literature, portraiture, politics, science, music, education—and just thought itself in orbit." To impose *some* sense of order on "all there is," I have imitated Hardwick's habit of grouping her essays into sections—as in the Letters, Lives, and Locations of *A View of My Own*—though I recognize these sections are relatively arbitrary. Hardwick's interests, like everyone's, tend to blend together.

The one introduction I have included, written for *Best American Essays, 1986*, serves as a kind of keynote. Beginning with one of Hardwick's characteristic questions ("The essay?"), it proceeds to describe a few features of this most protean form. Essays, Hardwick finds, are "addressed to a public in which some degree of equity exists between the writer and the reader"; they are "about something, something we may not have had reason to study and master, often matters about which we are quite ignorant"; and they make a "contribution to the cultural life." Formally speaking, they are exercises in style as a vehicle for ideas, with the result that a collection of essays becomes, in her words, "a collection of variations" very much in the musical sense.

The first of the themed sections in this book, "Places, People, Things," is self-explanatory. "New York City: Crash Course" approaches Hardwick's adopted home from the air, zigzagging through the boroughs in time and space, from the first Dutch settlers to the Dead Rabbits and Plug Uglies, from Melville at his desk to Captain Kidd on the stand. "Lexington, Kentucky" returns us to the city that was "truly home" ("not just a birthplace") to Hardwick, before "Puritanical Pleasures" takes us up north to the small town of Castine, Maine, where she spent some forty or so summers. As for people— Hardwick's preferred subject whatever she happened to be writing—

there are émigrés (Einstein, Balanchine, Nabokov), friends (Sontag and Porter), and at least one movie star (Faye Dunaway). The inclusion of "Things," with its canny assessment of possessions ("a threat to the soul and a solace to the senses"), was irresistible.

"Piety and Politics," the second section, is more the sort of grouping Hardwick herself might have made. A short meditation on election years sets the tone for these essays on the Union's abiding love of spectacle and change. "The landscape of America seems often like one of those endangered kingdoms in old sagas," she writes, in a lucid, visionary prose one can scarcely believe was once printed in *Vogue*:

> Nightly, Grendel steals upon the knights sleeping in the hall and slays the fairest and the weakest alike. The siege, chronic, of change is one that we live with—and so we are never quite sure what has come upon us. Are we in the midst of destruction or renewal? Have we been blessed with something better: or have we, instead, merely a replacement?

Hardwick's reflections on politicians, criminals, and other popular American figures—George Wallace, Jimmy Carter, the Kennedy and Menendez brothers, O. J. Simpson, Bill Clinton, Monica Lewinsky—are often simultaneously reflections on how the explosion of television altered American life forever, exposing to the public what had previously been private and, in the process, making a mockery of both dignity and shame.

A satirical but deadly serious piece proposing a male celibacy amendment to round out Republican lawmakers' antiabortion platform—"a sort of balancing of the human budget"—leads in to "Feminine Principle," the third section, which chronicles Hardwick's engagement with feminism from what Robert Lowell called the "tranquilized fifties" through the early seventies, when Hardwick's life was transformed by her divorce from Lowell and the magazines she was writing for were filled to the gills with talk of "liberation."* These are extraordinary essays, the majority of which were composed in the same years as the literary criticism contained in *Seduction and Betrayal* (and the correspondence contained in *The Dolphin Letters*). They make clear how different Hardwick's reaction to second-wave feminism was from some of her coevals, such as her close friend Mary McCarthy, who once called feminism "bad for women in its self-pity, shrillness, and greed." Hardwick, for her part, was not at all dismissive either of the fight for equal pay or of the sight of naked babies riding "papooselike on the backs of mother and father and friend"; the women's movement she found "quite serious" in all its facets. Yet she found the loosening of contracts between people, and the resultant pressure on the fragile individual, unsettling. If liberation was a sign of social progress, it was also, frequently, a source of personal pain. "One of the purposes of a more conscious and independent existence for women," Hardwick wrote in 1973, "is to relieve them of their conviction that they will always be safe."

The "Readings" section of this book might have gone on for hundreds of pages if I had let in reviews and introductions. I limited it instead to three of Hardwick's essays on the subject of reading and the cultural assumptions we bring to this "almost free pleasure." One gets a sense from these pieces of some of the lesser-known figures in her personal canon (Kay Boyle, Elizabeth Madox Roberts) as well as her admirable unwillingness to insist, to anyone already reading, on the importance of reading.

The last section, "Musings," is frankly miscellaneous. Here are Hardwick's thoughts on opera, summer, Southern food, and Christmas music, opening with a very funny medley of quotations from her summer reading. If there *is* a theme in these pieces, it may be Hardwick's lifelong interest in what valuable elements of the past—about which she harbored few sentimental notions—had been sacrificed to

---

*It's worth noting that the one time Hardwick quotes Lowell in print (in "The Heart of the Seasons"), she misquotes him, writing "Heaven is something with a girl in summer" for "All life's grandeur / is something with a girl in summer." Considering her enduring affection for Lowell and his work, I'd call this a sign of familiarity, rather than indifference.

bring the present into being. *"Parsifal"* finds in the experience of attending a four-plus-hour performance of Wagner's opera profound insights into the loss of time that has come with material progress, and "Notes on Leonardo and the Future of the Past," about popping in to an exhibition of Da Vinci's inventions in 1966, may be one of the most farseeing of Hardwick's uncollected writings. Its skepticism about "miracles of technology" that don't pay off in "happiness, leisure, and health" emerges from its own postwar, pre-internet era. But it speaks directly to the miracles we grapple with today.

Hardwick often speaks directly to us. Her compassion and fair-mindedness have something to do with this, as does the poise of her prose, its repudiation of generalities and jargon. Like Virginia Woolf before her, she deliberately addressed herself not to critics or scholars but to common readers—those mythical creatures whom even critics and scholars may incarnate, if they can ease the death grip of their expertise.

This collection emphasizes the variety of Hardwick's writing, but it also testifies to her writing's remarkable consistency. Whether visiting subjects taken up for a single occasion (Dunaway, grits souf-flé) or revisiting subjects taken on before (Katherine Anne Porter, the coast of Maine), Hardwick never hurries. She is never simplistic for the sake of convenience or hyperbolic for the sake of being heard. She is sublime at describing a deliveryman's high-top hairstyle, circa 1990, as well as the age-old beauties of the nocturnal fabric over Mount Monadnock: "a storm of stars in the heavens, a pattern of gorgeous gleaming dots on the dark blue silk of the sky, all spreading down like a huge soft cloak to the edge of the field." Always, she shows herself alert to the conditions of the poor, the exploitation of women and workers and people of color, the coarse-grained language of the powerful—and, always, she communicates this alertness in a graceful, idiosyncratic style that owes more to reactionary De Quincey and Whiggish Macaulay than to any of her contemporaries.

If someone ever gets around to compiling another anthology of English prose chosen for its distinguished style, Hardwick should have a prominent place within it. The shape of her sentences, the wisdom of her elisions, the unexpectedness of her adjectives, are utterly unique. A few of Hardwick's favorite words ("accommodation," "astonishment") and favorite quotations ("What I always thought the finest thing in the theater...is the *chandelier*") turn up more than once in these pages. But even these chance repetitions are charming—and telling, too. Whatever Hardwick approaches, she approaches as herself. Is there a more civilized companion on this barbarous road?

—ALEX ANDRIESSE

THE UNCOLLECTED ESSAYS
OF ELIZABETH HARDWICK

THE ART OF THE ESSAY

THE ESSAY? Thousands of pages of prose are published each month and not many of them are given to fiction. Perhaps most of the pages are information about the events of the day or the week and are not to be thought of as essays. What is this thunder and hail of newsprint felling the forests of the world? Journalism? Not quite, not nowadays. The knowing would not restrict the word "journalism" to mere information, if information can be thought of as *mere*. Nowadays journalism is a restless and predatory engagement, having established its imperial mandate under the phrase "new journalism," established its claim with such occupying force that the phrase itself is no longer needed, no longer defining.

If we cannot be sure we are reading journalism according to the rules of the professional schools, we are even less certain that we are reading the elevated essay. Still, there is something called the essay, and volumes by individual writers are published under the title. Even then the term does not provide a serenity of precision; it is not altogether genuine in its shape, like fiction or poetry. It does not even have the advantage of pointing to scale, since some essays are short and many are long and most incline to a condition of unexpressed hyphenation: the critical essay, the autobiographical essay, the travel essay, the political—and so on and so on.

There is a self-congratulatory sense in the word "essay." It wants to signify that what has been offered is not a lesser offering, not just a review, a sketch, a "piece"—odd, useful word—summoned to feed the hungry space of periodicals. Sometimes the vagrant coinage "essayistic" appears in the press, and this is bad news for the language, since it indicates an extension of murky similarity to what is itself more than a little cloudy. Of course, we always know what a barbarism is trying to say; its nature is to indicate the struggle for definition.

To be like an essay, if not quite the real thing, means that, in a practical bit of prose, attention has been paid to expressiveness and that to gain expressiveness certain freedoms have been exercised, freedoms illicit in the minds of some readers, freedoms not so much exercised as seized over the border. Essays are aggressive even if the mind from which they come is fair, humane, and, when it is to the point, disinterested. Hazlitt, in an essay on the poets living in his own time, writes: "Mrs. Hannah More is another celebrated modern poetess, and I believe still living. She has written a great deal which I have never read." It might take Mrs. More, if indeed she lived still, some time to figure out just what was being said.

The aggressiveness of the essay is the assumption of the authority to speak in one's own voice, and usually the authority is earned by previous performance. We see a name on the cover or inside the pages and we submit to the reading with some eagerness, which may be friendly eagerness or not. One of the assumptions of the essayist is the right to make his own mistakes, since he speaks only for himself, allowing for the philosopher's cunning observation that "in my opinion" actually asserts "all reasonable men will agree." This claim is sometimes disputed by an elected authority, the editor, who may think too many villages have been overrun by the marauder. Since the freedom of the open spaces is the condition of the essay, too much correction and surgical intervention turns the composition into something else, perhaps an article, that fertile source of profit and sometimes pleasure in the cultural landscape.

William Gass, in what must be called an essay, a brilliant one, about Emerson, an essayist destined from the cradle, makes a distinction between the article and the essay. Having been employed by the university and having heard so many of his colleagues "doing an article on," Mr. Gass has come to think of the article as "that awful object" because it is under the command of defensiveness in footnote, reference, coverage, and would also pretend that all must be useful and certain, even if it is "very likely a veritable Michelin of misdirection." If the article has a certain sheen and professional polish, it is the polish of "the scrubbed step"—practical economy and neatness. The essay, in Mr. Gass's view, is a great meadow of style and personal manner, freed from the need for defense except that provided by an individual intelligence and sparkle. We consent to watch a mind at work, without agreement often, but only for pleasure. Knowledge hereby attained, great indeed, is again wanted for the pleasure of itself.

We would not want to think of the essay as the country of old men, but it is doubtful that the slithery form, wearisomely vague and as chancy as trying to catch a fish in the open hand, can be taught. Already existing knowledge is so often required. Having had mothers and fathers and the usual miserable battering of the sense of self by life may arouse the emotional pulsations of a story or a poem; but feeling is not sufficient for the essay. Comparisons roam about it, familiarity with those who have plowed the field before, shrewdness concerning the little corner or big corner that may remain for the intrusion of one's own thoughts. Tact and appropriateness play a part. How often we read a beginner's review that compares a thin thing to a fat one. "John Smith, like Tolstoy, is very interested in the way men interact under the conditions of battle." Well, no.

Fortunately, the essay is not a closed shop, and the pages do vibrate again and again with the appearance of a new name with no credentials admired or despised. An unknown practitioner of the peculiar animation of the prose of an essay takes up the cause. It is an occasion for happiness since it is always astonishing that anyone will write an essay. Some write them not once but more or less regularly. To wake up in the morning under a command to animate the stones of an idea, the clouds of research, the uncertainty of memory, is the punishment of the vocation. And all to be done without the aid of end rhyme and off rhyme and buried assonance; without an imagined character putting on a hat and going into the street.

Those with the least gift are the most anxious to receive a commission. It seems to them that there lies waiting a topic, a new book, a performance, and that this is known as material. The true prose writer knows there is nothing given, no idea, no text or play seen last evening until an assault has taken place, the forced domination that we call "putting it in your own words." Talking about, thinking about a project bears little relation to the composition; enthusiasm boils down with distressing speed to a paragraph, often one of mischievous banality. To proceed from musing to writing is to feel a robbery has taken place. And certainly there has been a loss; the loss of the smiles and ramblings and discussions so much friendlier to ambition than the cold hardship of writing.

Essays are addressed to a public in which some degree of equity exists between the writer and the reader. Shared knowledge is a necessity, although the information need not be concrete. Perhaps it is more to be thought of as a sharing of the experience of reading certain kinds of texts, texts with omissions and elisions, leaps. The essayist does not stop to identify the common ground; he will not write, "Picasso, the great Spanish painter who lived long in France." On the other hand, essays are about something, something we may not have had reason to study and master, often matters about which we are quite ignorant. Elegance of presentation, reflection made interesting and significant, easily lead us to engage our reading minds with Zulus, herbaceous borders in the English garden, marriage records in eighteenth-century France, Japanese scrolls.

In the contemporary essay, as in contemporary fiction, the use of the first-person narrator or expositor has become so widespread it must be seen as a convenience. This is a puzzle having to do, perhaps, not with self-assertion to fill every available silence, but with modesty, a fear of presumption. In fiction a loss of movement is accepted by the choice of "I" in order to gain relief from knowing and imagining without the possibility of being there to know. That at least may be one of the aesthetic considerations. Also, the dominance of the first-person narrator in current fiction seems to reflect uncertainty about the classical conception of character; often the contemporary psyche is not seen as a lump of traits so much as a mist of inconsistencies, flights, constant improvisations. It is more agreeable to this sense of things to write "It seemed to me" rather than "It was."

In the essay we find the intrusion of the "I" even where little is autobiographical. In my mind I imagine a quite obscure reflection beginning, "I pulled into the filling station with my wife in the front seat and the kids restless and hungry in the back, and there I saw an interesting commercial logo, a sort of unicorn-horse that recalled to me certain medieval illuminated texts." What will follow is as it is, learned, perhaps difficult. How to account for the filling station, except as a fear of presumption about the subject, a search for immediacy, a loosening of the boundaries of prose? Of course it doesn't always work. There are many things worth knowing that cannot be made familiar. De Quincey in his memoir about the Lake Poets tells of a Mr. Wedgwood, a gifted, loved, quite rich young man, patron of Samuel Coleridge, the tormented genius who very much needed a patron. Mr. Wedgwood sought to distract himself from feelings of depression and lassitude by buying a butcher shop, where the wrangling abuse would force him to a high level of response. The experiment was not happy. There is a certain kind of polemical essay around that is a butcher shop of raw, hacked opinion which arouses a sure relief from torpor by encouraging dissent and violent rebuttal.

Intemperance in political writing has its hacks and its celebrated practitioners. As Trevor-Roper writes in his introduction to a volume of essays by the great Macaulay, "Macaulay could be very unjust to persons. He could also be vindictive. His essay on Boswell's *Life of Johnson* is both. He is unjust to Johnson, unjust to Boswell, and positively vindictive to the editor, Croker, who was not only a Tory but a member of parliament who enraged Macaulay by opposing him in the debates on parliamentary reform." Macaulay was a Whig. It is nearly always useful to be aware of the mind-set of essayists because a determined coloration of belief may spread itself far and wide and land not only on the political field but on the head of the novelist, the filmmaker, the historian. So it has been; so it is yet. The mastery of expository prose, the rhythm of sentences, the pacing, the sudden flash of unexpected vocabulary, redeem polemic, and, in any case, no one is obliged to agree. But ill-written, pompously self-righteous, lamely jocular forays offend because an air of immature certainty surrounds them. Too great a degree of exhortation and corrective insistence makes us wish for the tones of the earlier English "familiar essay," with its calm love of nature and tolerance of human frailty.

The essay form exists in so many shapes and sizes and is directed to every point of the compass. It is nothing less than the reflection of all there is: art, personal experience, places, literature, portraiture, politics, science, music, education—and just thought itself in orbit. Roland Barthes has written an essay on wrestling, the spectacle of it; Hazlitt composed "The Fight": "Reader, have you ever seen a fight? If not you have pleasure to come, at least if it is a fight between the Gas-man and Bill Neate." Proust wrote an essay "On Reading"; Sartre has written two essays on Faulkner and thousands have been written on Proust and Sartre and again on Faulkner.

There is nearly always a time when the novelist and poet will stand aside to create something other. This will be an imaginative essay, and often among the most beautiful and arresting we know. Such essays tend to be offhand and intuitive, flashing and yet exacting— D. H. Lawrence's, for example. Knowing how to write—there is no substitute for that. The writer may be said to precede the material, and that is why academic writing, where the material is the fundamental capital, is so often like hoeing a hard field in winter. However, being a professor and knowing a good deal about some things does not make one an academic writer. Only the withholding gods can accomplish that.

So there is no end to the essay, and no beginning. Walter Benjamin makes a visit to Moscow: "Each thought, each day, each life lies here as on a laboratory table." The poet Jules Laforgue goes to Berlin to be in the service of the Empress: "She has been bored, she is still bored, and she still dreams." Joan Didion has been to Alcatraz in California: "Alcatraz Island is covered with flowers now: orange and yellow nasturtiums, geraniums, sweet grass, blue iris, black-eyed Susans. Candytuft springs up through the cracked concrete in the exercise yard."

The essay, at least in reduction, is to be thought of as popular. Think of the number published. In the lightest examples—short sentences, short altogether, with photographs surrounding the shortness—it appears that words here and there about celebrities are gratifying in the gross. This cannot be the search for information, since there is little information in them. Libel is the handmaiden of information about the living. The appeal of celebrity journalism seems to rest upon a promise and the acceptance of the fact that the promise will again and again be unfilled. To know the sanitized items, in almost infinite repetition, about the famous indicates an overwhelming appetite. Born somewhere, lives somewhere, may have a "wonderful" child, possibly a mate to whom, for the time being, everything is owed. Parents somewhere and, nearer, the career itself. "I want to improve my acting." All of this is prose of some kind, a commission arranged and concluded.

The true essay, making as it does a contribution to the cultural life, is not so simple. Its celebrities are likely to be long-dead painters, writers, and thinkers; living ones not memorable in photographs, and not in a synopsis. Insofar as essays give information, and of course they do in their way, a peculiar condition of reciprocity, reader participation, prevails. Wit, the abrupt reversal, needs to strike a receptive ear or eye or else the surprise is erased, struck down. Expressiveness is an addition to statement, and hidden in its clauses is an intelligence uncomfortable with dogmatism, wanting to make allowances for the otherwise case, the emendation.

A well-filled mind itself makes the composition of essays more thorny rather than more smooth, with everything readily available. There is seldom absolute true assertion unless one is unaware. Words and phrases, ideas and opinions, invading the vast area of even the narrowest topic must fall back on a fluency of reference, reference sometimes merely hinted, if the convincing is to be achieved. Conviction itself is partial and the case is never decided. The essay is not the ground of verdicts. It rests on singularity rather than consensus.

Montaigne: can there be a reflection upon the essay without the dropping of this sacred name? Emerson finds Montaigne a "representative man" under the description the skeptic, as Shakespeare is the poet. A close reading of the essay will show that Emerson writes around Montaigne rather than about him. However much he may admire the French master's candor and "uncanonical levity," the men are not attuned, differences in temperament being too great. Gass, in his essay on Emerson, slides into a diversion on Montaigne and notes, "Have we digressed, however? I hope so." Hannah Arendt in her writing on the great modern essayist, Walter Benjamin, remarks upon the difference in the social station of the modern essayist when compared with the world of the classical European man of letters.

The world of the American essay is a democratic one, a meritocracy. And much more so now than in the time of Emerson, a man from the old Harvard, well educated in a nation commonly much less so. The tones of "Self-Reliance" and even of "Compensation" would not appear to be suitable orchestration today. Confidence it has, if very different from the given, worldly self-confidence of Montaigne. Emerson's confidence, his attraction to enlightened sermonizing, is addressed to an audience still small enough for instruction. "The man must be so much, that he must make all circumstances indifferent."

Modes of conduct—except for that of foreign policy, which is impersonal in spite of pleas to view it as a burning pan on the stove in the kitchen of every citizen—commend themselves as a subject mostly to cranks and uplifters and health fiends. If we would in the manner of Lord Chesterfield tell a young gentleman how to behave, the pages might take the form of case histories of drug addicts, dropouts, and statistics on earning power. The American essay, the contemporary one, is personal in its manners, as a display, and also as a wrestling with means, how to shape the exposition. Little is proposed as a model. The personality of the literary critic is sharp and—with the most gifted—eccentric, but it wishes to reveal a difference in itself, not to promote imitation in manner, but only imitation in opinion, since every opinion loves a follower.

A collection of essays is a collection of variations. The theme or the plot is not an imaginary construction, as in the novel, but arises from some factuality of history, culture, politics, personal experience, and above all from general ideas. Yet the most interesting will have the self-propelled interior life of imaginative literature, and this is true even when they are responses to an occasion. Expertise, an acquisition promoted by usefulness, is less cogent to the essay than passion, less to the point than is the soloist's personal signature flowing through the text. Such is the art of the essay.

1986

PLACES, PEOPLE, THINGS

NEW YORK CITY: CRASH COURSE

THE OLD New York airport was once called Idlewild, a pastoral welcome to the gate of a zoological garden of free-ranging species. Or so it seemed to say before the names were changed to those of politicians, those who won. Kennedy Airport, international arrival to our hysterical, battered and battering, pot-holed, bankrupt metropolis. A spectacular warehouse this city is; folk from anywhere, especially from those sunny sovereignties to the south of us, coming to peer out of blackened windows, each one in his shelter of sorts.

In 1879 a curious urban structure called the "dumb-bell tenement" won a prize as the most imaginative and useful design for the hordes seeking shelter. Windows looked out upon a rubbish-strewn courtyard, black and empty, giving neither light nor air but surely an improvement on something not previously thought of. Shelter, beautiful word, like dwelling. "Wuthering Heights is the name of Mr. Heathcliff's dwelling." But utter not the word "shelter" just now, here where it has acquired or grown a scrofulous hide.

Will you not come with me to the Shelter on this icy evening, dear, old homeless one, stuffed into your bag of rags and surrounded by up-standing pieces of cardboard, making as it were a sort of private room on the freeze of concrete near a corner or before a storefront? No, you f---ing little, rat-faced volunteer on vacation from the country club of Wellesley College or piling up credit at the Fordham School of Social Work. I'll die before I'll take my bag upon bag of nameless litter, my mangy head, my own, my leprous legs, purple, scabbed, and swollen, my numbed, crooked fingers, myself, to the City Shelter, or flophouse, whatever you call it.

It's a battle and the blue and white salvation van makes off slowly, idly offering in the gloom of perplexity the wide, public, rectangular barns, the dormitories with their rows of iron beds, muslin sheets, and flattened pillow, and somewhere down a corridor a lukewarm shower. The trouble is, among others, that if you nod off, what you're there for, you might become separated from your wealth of trash, robbed of your cache of mementos—an old key, a newspaper item perhaps of some paranoid interest, a safety pin, an arcane Welfare Department communication without name or number—things folded into layers of astounding clothing; and worst of all to be with others.

The 1990 Census is trying to take note of them, on the streets, in the tunnels of the subways, hiding behind a bush in the park, or on the lonesome late nights of the West Side Highway in the traffic dividing center, standing by a metal can burning trash for warmth . . . Well, there's no news in that, not here in New York . . . When you get right down to it, the van driver said, the homeless people are just a bunch of clichés. Are they ever, said the volunteer girl.

In our antiquity, not so many hundred years ago, this place was lying here, entrance to the dreaming acres north, south, and west, lying here waiting for something to happen for what's new? Waiting for the worn-down explorers trying to get to the Orient, waiting for them to alight from their obdurate, temperamental ships, waiting for a sort of opening night in Manhattan. At last they paddled ashore to our Bay and didn't find much, indeed "no indigenous civilization," or so they said. Not much except the usual basking verdure, several dozen or so small wind-rattled shelters made of tree bark, and "the poor Indian." (Columbus, around Santo Domingo or thereabout, took several of these solemn, long-faced, reddish-brown bodies back to Europe for the curiosity of it and perhaps to amuse his wife, "the well-born Doña Filipa Perestrello e Moniz"; and as a sort of wampum offering the transported native stock was to receive Christian baptism, to implant in innocent minds the Happy Hunting Ground complexities of the Resurrection.)

It was to be New Amsterdam with the Dutch putting up lots for sale and beginning to imagine our fate-laden checkerboard destiny. They bought, in a manner of speaking, the place and strangely the straggling settlers from the Zuider Zee, or IJsselmeer, initiated by a squatter's rights over the succeeding English, our aristocracy, "old New York," born in the memory perhaps of the murdered William the Silent. Van Rensselaer, Schuyler, and Schermerhorn, names with a somewhat heraldic resonance, supplanted the Oneida and the Algonquin. And were themselves supplanted in the porous atmosphere of New York which will, by a vivacious regicide, crown more kings and queens in a year than history knows of.

A gray Sunday afternoon, smoky light, and a sanctified drowsing between our rivers East and West, a quiet except for the sacrificial athleticism of the joggers, running or preparing to run in the park, as a rabbit out of its hutch will surely hop off. And some comfortable cows still lolling in their stalls on Central Park West. All of this before the tiny white lights come on, a cheerful, if unnatural, decoration strung on the winter tree branches. Cottony brilliant leaves they are as the grinding bus, with a few Sunday evening travelers, makes its way through the underpass in the soft, waxy beauty of the urban evening.

At the Lincoln Center Opera House, papier-mâché stone battlements by the ineffable Zeffirelli, worth, or cost, a couple of million, a piece of the rock. Baudelaire said that what he liked best about the opera was the *chandelier* and here some invisible hand lowers the large bunch of little globes and raises them before dimming in a pretty display of mechanical superfluity. In 1849, at the Astor Place Opera House, there was a ferocious outbreak of riot, one of peculiar import. On the heath, thunder and lightning, torches and baseball bats "hover through the fog and filthy air." The occasion was a performance of Shakespeare's *Macbeth*, in the theater which was then a shrine for the patroons who would trip in satin slippers through the horse droppings at the curb, having emerged from the carriage to leave the coachman in chimney-sweep black outfittings to rust in the long wait for the final curtain. And then it would be off to the houses, the mansions, edging ever upward from the thirties streets near Madison to the fifties on Fifth Avenue, the way things were going. In the old postcards of the city everything appears gay, small, empty, and tranquil. The swish of long skirts and the gothic ascension of many wonderful hats, worthy people treading the streets, down Broadway, and keeping away from the Plug Uglies, the Dead Rabbits, citizen gangs with their own rancorous claims.

For the *Macbeth* performance the Anglophiles had brought across the Atlantic a star, William Macready, an innocent elocutionist, on tour. This was seen as an insult to our own master of fustian, Edwin Forrest, and the mob mounted a patriotic stone-throwing, window-smashing, outraged, red-faced, beer-encouraged assault. Poor Macready, eloquence trembling through the dagger irresolution and the pacing melancholy of tomorrow and tomorrow, and at last having surrendered his head to Macduff, was to slink through the back door with a cortège, front and back, of high prestige, among them Washington Irving and John Jacob Astor. Still, the contract was in place and at a later performance thousands gathered to storm the building, stones flying like some hellish hailstorm of local resentment. The rioters were met with three hundred policemen and two hundred state militia who fired into the crowd, killing almost two dozen of the rebels. Macbeth Macready decamped on the next boat to England but the theatrical criticism of the populace, the class gap, the canals of separation, already impassable, represented by the rioters and the merchant class, represented by the point-blank fire, occasioned the usual bitter civic debate, howls ending in a draw.

Herman Melville, home from the cannibals and acquainted with mutiny, getting on fairly well with *Omoo* and *Typee*, signed like a good PEN member the first petition favoring the appearance of Macready on the boards. This was before the militia assault and what he might have thought about the state's forceful, explosive protection of the right to speechifying is not certain. Melville's mother was a Gansevoort, an "old New Yorker."

The emergency ambulance shrills through the night—or is it a fire truck, all glistening red and burnished brass shining in the murk, arriving in multiplication like a tank parade, the men in their black and yellow rubber mantles and their smart, brim-back hats, pirate hats, answering with good fortune this time only a wastebasket conflagration in the banal, sleepless interiors of ABC-TV. As early as seven in the morning, in the winds of winter or the breathless air of summer, the crowds gather outside the building to see great Pompey pass the streets of Rome, that is to see whoever might be interviewed on the morning show.

In 1838, on an arctic evening with temperatures sliding down to seventeen below zero, as if in the brush-strewn fields of Minnesota under a high, cold moon, there was a four-alarm flaming that swept through the stone and timber of the financial district. Thirteen acres turned to frozen rubble. They were soon back on the trading floor, as they are ever to be, mysterious men, *condottieri*, nowadays tanned from battle in the financing trenches, trim from the rigors of the conference call, nervous and powerful on their steeds, lances drawn, rulers of principalities in the Hamptons or in Beverly Hills. Should they be thrown from their horses they will be bathed in unguents, the precious oils of severance pay and bankruptcy bonuses, settlements. "Day after day the columns of the press revealed fresh scandals to the astonished public, which at last grew indifferent to such revelations. Beneath all the wrangling of the courts, however, while the popular attention was distracted by the clatter of lawyers' tongues, the leaders in the controversy were quietly approaching a settlement." (Charles Francis Adams on the Erie Railroad scandals of 1868.) A golden age it has been the last few years and about some of the financiers, soon to be tried and those tried before, you might say they wrote the script and played all the parts.

The men make and the wives spend, indeed are chosen for their talents in consumption, a contract historical, imitative, and pleasurable as the sunshine. But, think what an occupation it is to fill the cathedrals, the vaults and domes on Park Avenue and Fifth. Ten coats of paint on the glaze of the walls and even then, so often, not quite right. A burdensome eclecticism of track lighting and electrified ceiling ornamentations transported from the castles of Europe. In an entrance hall, four or five eighteenth-century Dutch interiors; up higher on the avenue the collector is, as we say, "into" contemporary and thus a Jasper Johns, bought yesterday, hangs over a leather sofa. Everywhere, gregarious tables to hold quaint miniatures, inlaid boxes, Georgian silver items; grand carpets from Xanadu, chairs from France, desks from England, and in the dining hall, large enough for the knights in a saga, rare, fragile practicalities in lots of twenty-four for receiving food and drink. Unassuaged longings, and who would imagine there was so much provenance left or waiting to be sold or traded. "Stone by stone we shall remove the Alhambra, the Kremlin and the Louvre and build them anew on the banks of the Hudson." (Benjamin de Casseres, *Mirrors of New York*.) A billion dollars is buying, arranging, dusting and polishing and insuring.

As for a mere million or two: Nothing much came forth from the red lips, the lithe, stalky, skin and bone woman in a mink tent getting out of the long, black, hired car. She emerges from the tomb and from the defiant optics of the black limousine windows, opaque as death on the outside, but from which she, inside, can look out to see a white poodle on its leash. I wish I had one, she says, and he, from the hearse in which they are driven, says, If you want one, buy one, for God's sake.

The black tube waits at the curb while they enter and loll for an hour or so, as if in a sudden resurrection, among the tropical plants of the lead-paned restaurant. The little French lamps on the table reveal luscious cakes waiting for the knife. But not for them. Perhaps for the two plump wage-earners from the "boroughs," maliciously defining address, perhaps for them the infantile fatality of the gorgeous concoctions, all cream and gurgle and clog, life-threatening and shaming. The tomb-dwellers look on from their decaf espressos.

The delivery boy from the Food Emporium is at the door. Theatrical youth, delivery youth, scarcely a boy. High-top running shoes with the laces slack, in the fashion, hair, also in the fashion, shaved from the nape of the neck to end in a pile at the top of the head beaming straight up as if struck by a thunderbolt—some name-brand mousse or spray helping to defy gravity. Around the streets they go, pushing their archival load: low-sodium seltzer water, kosher hot dogs, low-cholesterol mayo, Perdue chicken breasts, Weight Watchers margarine, four-grain bread, Ben and Jerry's Chocolate Cherry Ice Cream, Paul Newman's marinara sauce . . . What the deliverer gets from the $2.50 charge for service is a corporate secret, but here he is, deer-fleet, smelling briskly of cologne, on the job.

Slavery came to the Manhattan shores with great promptitude, came to New Amsterdam with black souls gathered up by the prudent Dutch at Curaçao, another of the country's far-flung "interests." And more were to arrive later, after Amsterdam gave way to New York. A pitiful insurrection among the slaves of the city took place in 1712, a dream-heavy insufficiency of Black Power it was. A few dozen from Africa, with a musket here and there, went on a rampage, set a few fires, killed a few whites. You see the insurrectionists glistening and trembling, large, agonized, bewildered figures like the Emperor Jones, trying to run for cover up a tree, in a swamp, and soon overcome by the city militia. And taught a lesson, yes, strung up for public viewing, burned, tortured on the wheel. Consequent fear on the streets, in the houses, no place is safe, muggers (derivation unknown) on every corner, too many of them . . . and so on and so on.

There appeared in the fearful city a most extraordinary white lunatic, one Mary Burton, indentured, that is, a citizen from the British Isles working to pay off the cost of the passage to the New World, pay on the credit card more or less, many of them of course declining in clever ways after reaching their destination, here. When fires and robberies broke out, Mary B. began to offer her inside dope gained in taverns, her dense knowledge of barroom alliances for felony. She took her interesting, fevered tales to the courts and thus set the slaveholders on edge for protection and revenge. Slaves hanged, burned at the stake, sent off somewhere, until Mary, wonderfully alert to the great industry of New York, alert to publicity, the magic of it, went astray, far afield, accusing respectable whites, whoever, and at last that was that for Mary. Slavery abolished in New York in 1799, too risky, not worth the bother, bottom-line.

City of journalism, the lone suitable literary art to catch up, take in this treasure island, open-faced, each street a logo, Fifth Avenue or Tenth Avenue, Duke Ellington Boulevard or Gramercy Park. East Side and West Side, the Village, a transparency, laid out, as easy to read as an advertisement, nothing hidden. You know where you are and who will be there with you, a sort of suburbanism in the air. Someone must be doing the work, coming in of a morning, double-parking, arriving over the bridges and expressways to fix the leaking pipe, to paint the high-gloss walls, lay the Italian tiles, scrape the floors in a gas mask, deliver the heating oil flowing in the long, fat coils. They run the elevators, stand importantly in their tuxedos in the old-fashioned restaurants, and at midnight take the subway train back to Brooklyn or Queens or Flushing or some other stop.

Nothing here in the brilliant inner city for the family man, place of torture and bankruptcy for the guards of the flaking, tedious columns of the Temple of Dendur at the Metropolitan Museum, for the news dealers, the movie ushers, the night workers with their pails and Dustbusters neatening at Rockefeller Center. The old shops in the West Thirties on Seventh Avenue with their filthy windows announcing WHOLESALE—dusty ribbons for unwanted hats, plastic flowers, buttons and buttonholes, bolts of figured cotton for the homemade house dress, thread for the Singer Sewing Machine, guitar strings: establishments sitting on prime real estate, a joke, you might say, of maladaptation and swept away in a quick fluid movement, as if by the hose from the Sanitation truck.

The Italo-Americans on the street where the deputed mobster lives in a small bungalow with a Mercedes equal in size out front and little sign here of melting in the pot. The Salvadorans, the Dominicans, the Koreans in their fruit stores, the Asian Indians at the newspaper kiosk, hot dog vendors from Greece, huddling together somewhere, each one a secret, inviolable clan, getting by, offering product but, off the income bracket, unAmericanized, still breathing in the hills of home.

The Irish and many of the German immigrants to the city were not attracted to fighting for the Union and in honor of the Emancipation Proclamation. So, when the Conscription Act was passed in 1863, falling largely on the working classes and the unemployed whites without the money to buy off, the great Draft Riots broke out. The Irish, objects of contempt in New York and Boston, did not always share the Yankee high-minded grief for the stain of slavery on the national psyche. The Rainbow Coalition of Protestant, well-to-do abolitionists and the black population was the same as it is now at the reign of our first black mayor. A horror of class and race war fell on the streets of Manhattan in 1863 as the rioters attacked the police, set fire to the Colored Orphan Asylum, lynched, broke into white abolitionist homes, set upon Horace Greeley's left-wing paper, the *Tribune*, and sent him flying out the back door or hiding under a table in fear of his life. "It was the women who inflicted the most fiendish tortures upon Negroes, soldiers, and policemen captured by the mob, slicing their flesh with butcher knives, ripping out eyes and tongues, and applying the torch after victims had been sprayed with oil and hanged on a tree." (*The Gangs of New York*, by Herbert Asbury.)

The explorers seldom came to a good end. Columbus died in want, ignorant of the fame that would attach his name to New York City banks, avenues, universities, restaurants, dry-cleaning establishments, video centers, delis—and many more. Sir Walter Raleigh, after smoking tobacco and eating the corn of the New World in Virginia, got into trouble with the Spanish and was beheaded in London. "What a head fell there," said the executioner. Verrazano was killed by the natives in the West Indies. Henry Hudson and his son, after a leveraged buyout of the Hudson Bay Company, were cast adrift to die up near Labrador, never to see the Palisades again.

The truest New Yorker among the great seamen was Captain Kidd, who, in his span of years, kept going and coming here, married a respectable and prosperous widow, Sarah Oort, and had a daughter, built himself a brick house and gathered up other properties. In the colonial period, Captain Kidd could be said to know everyone worth knowing; he knew the legislator Robert Livingston and the colonial governor of New England, Lord Bellomont, both of whom were mixed up in his affairs and maritime assignments and both abandoned him. Captain Kidd, sent out to hunt pirates, was accused of turning pirate himself and of murdering a troublesome seaman during a quarrel. The captain left some treasure from the legal looting of captured ships at Gardiner's Island on Long Island and left in romantic minds the possibilities of hidden treasure elsewhere. Like our own, finally sentenced to death or long imprisonment, he has had his defenders, investigative reporters telling a different story. As for him, his defense is familiar to New York ears: "I am the innocentest person of them all, only I have been sworn against by perjured persons."

The noble mariners of old, taking off without a space suit and nobody back in Europe on Mission Control, endured great suffering and often with little profit to themselves. But, of course, they would discover this America and the other America, South. And yet imagine the United States at last, each state with its boundaries and climate, mountains or flatlands for wheat; imagine all the states with their borders and squawking pride without the immense, obstinate, unassimilable, violently fluent New York City. Imagine the sulky provinciality of a vast country freed from this "unAmerican" city with its intimidating statistics of bodies, crimes, dope, guns, homicide records, robberies, illiterates, poverty, its blank towers, mausoleums hanging over the edge of the two rivers and blighting the rigid intersections in between, and its turbulent campaigns of consumption in the imperial mode.

From where have you come and why are you here? Why does the hummingbird return to the north? A puzzle, each resident of the recalcitrant city a puzzle. Once here a lingering infection seems to set in and the streets are filled with the complaints and whines of the hypochondriac who will not budge, will not face a fertile pasture.

Here it is, that's all, the place itself, shadowy, ever promising and ever withholding, a bad mother, queen of the double-bind . . . Nevertheless.

> Keep your fields of clover and timothy, and your cornfields
>   and orchards,
> Keep the blossoming buckwheat fields where the Ninth-
>   month bees hum;
> Give me faces and streets—give me these phantoms
>   incessant and endless along the trottoirs!
>
> Whitman

The constellations are not visible in the evening sky because of our impressive interference. Perhaps there, suddenly, is the red star, Deneb, United Airlines coming into port, edging down so gracefully with its rosy flickering lights, an everlasting beacon in the overloaded sky, saying, *prepare for landing.*

1990

LEXINGTON, KENTUCKY

This was, is, truly home to me, not just a birthplace. I was born here and educated here, left when I was twenty-three, but have always returned, even though my visits have been less frequent in recent years. Mama and Papa are dead, but my brothers and sisters remain, and a few friends. And Lexington? The mud of the present years flows peacefully over the mud of the past. That which remains the same is the most altered. The bird returns and finds the old nest, rotting, but still shaped by the dusty brown twigs. In the distance there are strange, new trees, never seen before, full of pink and blue and aqua feathers and rainproof straw and chirpy little birdlings whose will and wishes are a mystery. The bright unknown somehow casts a pall over the squat memorials, those things even more than fifty years ago thought to be comfortably antique, warm with time. I am astonished, gazing out over the rooftops of bank buildings, at the peculiarity of my feelings, the oddity of my passions, the meagerness of the landscape that I singled out for myself, like a surveyor pacing off a plot of stony soil, the rocks appearing like diamonds, constituting a chosen claim. I loved only Main Street, the ten-cent store, the old cigar store, where newspapers and magazines were sold, the Ben Ali, the Strand, and the State movie theaters, the lobbies of the Lafayette and Phoenix Hotel, Liggett's, the sandwiches on soft, white Kleenexy bread at Morford's Drug, the July dress sales at Embry's and Wolf-Wile's.

A crescendo of anxiety accompanies the past, and the new is only boredom on the surface, incomprehensible to me in its true nature, its unvarying plants and shoots flowering to their fate, its structures square and double-storied or stretched out in the way acceptable to our time, acceptable everywhere, in every city, each state, according to investment. Who can read *that* history—the history of now? Only some awkward boy or girl sweating in the playroom, swept on by the electrified jarrings and groanings of the house, will return to tell us what it has been—whether about Lexington or not is hard to say, for the glory of the place is a certain vault-like unreality, deadening to the lilt of the questioner's voice, since you have only to ask to be told what the Bluegrass is all about, what Lexington means.

In any part of the South, the mind struggles, wondering whether to lie under the blanket of the past or to endure the chill of the present. It is a difficult place, the enemy of the concrete and the particular. "How can you be from here, and think like you do?" What can I answer except to say that I have been, according to my limits, always skeptical, and that I have, always, since my first breath, "been from Kentucky." So much that is mean and unworthy in our country is appearance: people are always acting a part, banal, tacky, unfelt, inauthentic. Social wickedness and follies are "received" just as the emotion we feel sometimes about the flag in a breeze; they seem to unite the one with the many. They *imagine* themselves Southern, *imagine* themselves white people: imagine that this is definition, that the equation will have a certain solution, that the answer is their own. They are like the Aztecs with their bird god; prophecies that brought unceasing pain were nevertheless a daily consolation. There is a dreamlike, piercing pleasure in whiteness whenever it stands, even on a precipice, within sight of blackness. Poor people have lived on that alone, amidst every diminishment and insult, returning to it, as to the awakening sun in the morning.

Old families; no, our ancestors are horses. I would have gone to the ends of the earth to escape from ashtrays with horses on them, from the holy frescoes of turf scenes, winding around barrooms. And yet I store up in memory one or two rural treasures. The old Elmendorf horse farm lives on in me, like some beautiful, leafy, vine-laden Piranesi landscape. I seem to remember the damp, dark olive green of its lawns, the shaded black trees, the paths rolling, here and there brushed with sunshine, and yet closed, forest-dense, and only the pillars of the old mansion standing. Calumet Farm, with its Derby winners, its white fences and milky barns, trimmed with red, bathed in cheer and hope, always seemed to me a bit Californian. These are our cathedrals and abbeys.

Heroes. Man o' War ("a strapping fellow, in color a dark chestnut") was on view in the old days. There was a grandeur of muscle and a splendor of coat; memories of many a costly stand as stud seemed to linger in his coffee-brown eyes. Still an interview with this old Adam was of a singularly unresonant kind; you came away only with what you had brought with you. The thud of hooves, the highly bred, valuable thoroughbreds, were felt to bring honor to citizen and wanderer. Wizened, stunted jockey and luckless, strapped bettor took his place, each in his niche, engaged in a special pageantry.

1788: *The Kentucky Gazette*:

The famous horse Pilgarlic, of a beautiful color, full fourteen hands three inches high, rising ten years old, will stand the ensuing season at the head of Salt River at Captain Ave Irvins, Mercer County, and will cover mares at the very low price of ten shillings a leap...

What does the occasion of return call for? Description, comparison? Truth to oneself or to them? There is something gainful in being from a middle-sized, admired place, a place with an overbearing mythology. When I was in graduate school at Columbia, I met a girl who had grown up on a great rich person's estate in Long Island. Her father was a gardener and her mother a cook. It seemed to me that this was a fate sweet with possibilities, a sort of lighthouse, from which you could see a great deal that was meant to be hidden. It is easy to reach an ironical wisdom from a low spot, especially if you are disinclined to hopeless feats of emulation and not easily moved to admiration. But this girl, her whole life scarred by a brilliant and somehow unaccommodating intelligence, was inarticulate and bitter and wild with rage. In her twisted little heart the blood beat with hatred when cars drove up the driveway. She, with her eternal reading of James and Proust, hated the very smell of the evening air, filled with the unsettling drawl of debutantes; but true hatred came to rest in the sound of her father's gardening shears at the hedge and the swish, swish of her mother in rubber-soled nurse's shoes and a hairnet, bending forward with a bowl of vegetables resting expertly on her open palm. In truth, here was a great spirit destroyed by feudalism— a knotty little peasant reared in a Southampton cottage.

And so the horse farms were a sort of estate and, previously, people spoke of them almost in a hushed voice, but the owners, mostly well-known, immensely rich sportsmen, were absentees, like the old landowners of Russia who lived in Petersburg and often went years without visiting the estates. The horse was supreme, but the great owners hardly existed in our folklore, fortunately. Our golden stallion, standing on the courthouse as a weathervane, was our emblem, and the prince came from afar not for our graceful Lexington ways and our beautiful girls, but for our creatures, chewing limestone to perpetuate a dynasty of swift bones. It is said that certain of the rich farm owners now spend a part of the year in residence. "When the W—s put their children in school here, the teachers were afraid to correct them." How close to the surface, like the capillaries of a vein, are the traditions of local life. A glimpse of the truly rich, and the diseased relentlessness of their consumption, diminishes the claims of the local gentry. The prestige of "old families"—based upon what forgotten legacies beyond simple endurance in a more or less solvent condition?—cannot stand up to those bodies decorated with the precious minerals of the earth, covered with the skins of the most astonishing animals, seeking comfort and pleasures from the possession of every offering of the ground and the manufacturing imagination. Indeed who is old Dr. So and So, and Miss Somebody, with her garden and her silver cups? A blooded horse could buy and sell the lot of them.

Tobacco—that is truly more local, but I know nothing about it except that I would rather see the full-grown plants in a field than the quivering, wavering beauty of a new foal. The old warehouses and the tobacco sales, with the gossip of prices, the farmhands, the grading of the leaves—there is still something of a century ago, something of the country scenes in George Eliot. The memory of function, of sowing and reaping and selling and sowing and reaping again. Allotments and methods and machinery and bargains with tenants and country agents and rage at the government. But all I know about planting, all that I remember, are the violets and lilies of the valley at Castlewood, or is it called Loudoun—a brownish-gray stone Gothic Revival house —where we wandered; and tomato plants in our own resistant garden, and gladiola bulbs, yielding after effort, finally, their pinkish-orange goblets; and the difficult dahlia, forever procrastinating, heavily blooming at last, a liverish purple, or fuchsia. How I wish I could remember the names of the strains: weren't they Eleanor Roosevelt or Martha Washington? Papa at six in the morning, smoking a cigarette, staring at the staked tomato plant, the staked dahlia, the staked gladiola. Never anything you could put in a vase.

Winter visits from New York on the George Washington of the C & O, wearing a putative mink from the Ritz Thrift Shop on 57th Street. The train passed through mining towns in West Virginia, down through Ashland, Kentucky, through Olive Hill and Morehead, a stinging, green stillness along the way, the hills rising up on either side, to cradle the train as it slipped through the valley. Square, leaning cabins, clinging like mountain goats, ribbons of wood smoke stabbing the air. Trail of the Lonesome Pine, Little Shepherd of Kingdom Come ... I often felt guilty later, a fraud, that I knew nothing about the mountains except their songs, nothing firsthand of Appalachia, the martyrdom of Floyd Collins, of exhausted mine strips, of miners and their shy and resigned families, of the company stores, the rapacious mineowners. I read all that in *The Nation* and *The New Republic* and grieved and fumed like an idealist from the Bronx, but somehow I never met anyone who was going up that way, although I knew many who had come down from there, bringing the disreputable vowels of Harlan County, of London and Hazard, into the Bluegrass.

Beyond the business streets, there was nothing that held me except the older section of town, just north of Main. The newer "East End" with its 1920 stuccos and colonials, its nice tree-lined strips, its Drives and Ways and Avenues, its complacent children, its new Episcopalians and Christian Scientists: all of this was handsome and prosperous and comfortable and yet it lacked any compromising hint of history, seemed an elaborate defense against all the sufferings except alcoholism. There were, out there, no Negroes just around the corner, no truck routes to Ohio, no bums in cheap hotels, or country people arriving on Saturday. There was not a town of a similar size in the land that did not have its own nearly identical houses and laurel bushes, which told in their own hieroglyph the same story. Real Lexington was, to me, the old central core. It was Gratz Park and the Public Library, Morrison Chapel at Transylvania College, the John Hunt Morgan House, Dr. Buckner's house, called Rose Hill, and surviving amidst the rusty oilcans of a filling station, backed by the peeling frames of poor people, a fine old garden facing an adjoining rectangle of old pipes, broken clothesline, Coke bottles, and the debris of hope—those unchurning washing machines, discarded toilet bowls, rusting tire rims. In the North End, poor and rich, black and white, lived together blankly and, on the part of the white people, regretfully; but there it was, a certain tradition attaching to the serene old houses on Broadway, on Second and Third, on Limestone and Mill. Alas, neither group could be thought of as enlarged or ennobled by the forced coupling; blankness, yes blankness, rather than blindness, an absence, a Sahara, with its caravans of Fords and Chevrolets looking straight ahead toward the beckoning oases, those divisions and subdivisions, developments and superdevelopments.

In all our decades in Lexington, we lived in only two houses, both of them modest indeed; the first surrounded by black people and the second, somewhat "nicer," a few blocks away. It was in this North End of town, this mixture of the unlikely, among the races and classes, flung together by time and accident rather than by design worked out by building contractors. Negroes, the ill-lighted, rather darkly protected streets around the Public Library, Transylvania, where my two older sisters graduated, the dilapidated alleys, the race fights on Fifth Street, the depressing red-light district to the east, where the offerings on the porches or in the windows usually seemed to be missing some limb or another, the "bad black men" in their saloons on, yes, Race Street, where you didn't walk, but often drove through, quickly, in a car, vaguely troubled by the flash of knives, the siren of the police wagon in the night. The most interesting thing was to be witness day in and day out to the mystery of the behavior in your own neighborhood, to the side-by-side psychodramas of the decent and wage-earning, and the anarchic and bill-owing, to the drunken husband and the prayer-meeting couple. Of course that is just "life" and the monk in his cell, the tycoon at the golf links cannot escape these contraries. Still, the individual existence must take place somewhere and you live under the illusion of the particular, caught up in the spell of the setting.

The old Lexington race track burned down. The horses screamed all night. This meant that during the season, fall and spring, we would, from the sidewalk, no longer see the cars streaming by, the pedestrians hurrying, nor have bedded down all around us, on cots in the neighbors' living rooms, the old-monkey-faced jockeys. I remember little of this, but an image remains, as of an ancient troll; it was an old jockey, drunk, wanting us to play "Funiculì Funiculà" on the piano, while he sobbed, for joy and sadness.... Harken, harken, music sounds afar.... In the 1930s, under Roosevelt, one of the first housing projects went up on the site of the destroyed racing course. This place absolutely fascinated me, with its rules and its applications, its neat little plots, and there was always a good deal of talk about who was "in the project" and who was trying to get into it. Why should these uniform structures inflame the imagination that was repelled by subdivisions? No doubt it was the sway of sheer idea, of reclamation, even of a sort of socialism, of planning, price, and accommodation brought into a reasonable harmony. The project endures, looking a little quaint and small and subdued, but still bringing to mind Roosevelt's first term.

Autumn nights, the maul and jar of Halloween, fear as I ran alone, at eight o'clock down the little lane beside our house, with only an old streetlight, like a distant moon, to lighten these last steps. Everyone in his house, cool wind, working people thinking of going to bed soon. A few years later, across town, at Henry Clay High School, I remember best a light rain splashing the windows of cars, and the hours and hours and hours, the eternity, of students parked outside Saloshin's Drug, drinking Cokes. They are all married and some have been dead for a long time. "Drinking himself to death" is not a mere phrase. It was the fate of quite a few that I have known, gone in their youth, and the ones thus seized quite unexpected. It seemed to fall upon them, the blackness of night. Peace be with you all—Earl and Billy and Bobby and Betty and Sammy and Lutie!

A cold snap in the winter, japonica in the spring, the trees arching overhead on Bryan Station Pike. Teeth pulled early, the nuns at the old St. Joseph Hospital. The mind is shaken by the memory of certain lives it bore witness to, day in and day out, without being particularly friendly, actually not friendly at all, merely in a proximity. About so many of these one feels as William James did of the memory of a poor epileptic in an asylum: ". . . a black-haired youth with greenish skin, entirely idiotic. . . . He sat there like a sort of sculptured Egyptian cat or Peruvian mummy, moving nothing but his black eyes and looking absolutely non-human. This image and my fear entered into a species of combination with each other. *That shape am I*, I felt, potentially. Nothing that I possess can defend me from that fate, if the hour for it should strike for me as it struck for him."

A neighborhood girl, later a woman, for whom we all felt an intense pity and wonder and a mystical and mutual shunning. The fall of man, the loss of grace; in youth certain pathetic and benighted souls seem to represent the fallen state too vividly and openly to be endured. Without economic necessity, this girl became a prostitute, and spent her nights in the most sordid and degrading dumps and rooming houses, wandering around raw saloons near the old wholesale houses. She was the much-loved daughter of a railroad worker, a responsible hardworking mother, and a tall, fair, old grandmother who smoked a corncob pipe. Juanita! When she was still in high school, before her "career" began, she stood around the yard a lot, with her fat, sausage curls nestling near the collar of her freshly ironed dress. She was very tall, and while perhaps not designed for perpetual good luck, also not born for this desolating misery. I am far from sure that she took money, and I know that she drank but was not a drunkard. Still she suffered terribly from her dissipations and was most lovingly nursed through her tears and pains by her family. Late at night, you could hear the car door slam on the street behind us and down the narrow, dark, moonlit lane came Juanita, her heels clicking on the pavement. Or sometimes she arrived by the street in front of our houses, by taxicab or by car. The yellow lights shone out in the darkness, all still and sleeping. The screen door of Juanita's house slammed gently. You could imagine the bodies of her parents turning, with relief, in their beds. Home at last was this tall, curly-haired, curious voluptuary, asleep once more was the by now swollen and coarsened pleasure seeker. It all had to be paid for. She cried a lot, in pain, perhaps from hangovers, and later from venereal disease. Patience and devotion and sympathy whispered to her at home. "Juanita is not feeling well today," her rawboned old mother, large and neat in her long, full housedress, would say. "Maybe she's catching a little cold." And not too many years later Juanita fearfully died, of prodigious pains and sores, expiring with unbelievable suffering.

When I looked at the awful record of Victorian lechery, recorded in the appallingly cold-hearted and obsessive *My Secret Life*, every hideous fornication of that Victorian gentleman and his wretched street girls, nearly all of them harassed by poverty and born into misery, made me think of poor Juanita and her foul existence. But due to what?

November, walking around the decayed streets where I had lived for so long, everything was sad, empty in the midmorning, broken down. But how unbelievably long the frailest shack stands, unloved, but defiant, much stronger than we are. All of them still alive!

Poor neighborhoods are vulnerable to winter. Gray sky and bare lawns, stripped trees reveal every weakness, every sagging seam and rotting board. Muddy yards and dusty porches furnished with last summer's reclining deck chairs, soggy vinyl cushions, left to the storms. Walnut Street, never much, is a wreck; Duncan Park is a bomb site. (Here my oldest sister and her husband met, with whistles around their necks, as "playground directors.") In Duncan Park we learned to play volleyball and tennis and listened to band concerts on Thursday night, Mama and Papa and all of us, with the young ones parading in Hollywood bobs and hand-me-downs, giggling above the breathless wrong notes of the French horns and the slippery scales of the cornet. I cannot remember a single melody played in the bandstand at Duncan Park during these elated evenings. And this is odd, since my whole life in Kentucky is punctuated by the memory of light classics and popular music of all kinds. The sixth grade and Miss Fox, our music teacher: off we went to the state Music Memory Contest in Louisville, the first step I ever took out of Fayette County. The list of the tunes we were to identify, by a sort of multiple choice I think, are fixed in memory forever: "Poet and Peasant Overture," "Anvil Chorus," "Amaryllis" by Ghis, "Humoresque," etc. In Duncan Park, too, we learned a great deal of dismal wisdom before we wanted to.

Everything now is Negro, black, where Maryanne lived, and Billie Joe suffered, and Hope and Eleanor, and the preacher, and those who went to the Methodist Church and the Baptist Church, and the Crittenden Home for Unwed Mothers, and the house, new, right next to ours, where an abortionist, a woman, strange, sinister as a kidnapper, lived for a short time, and where there was once Old Mrs. This and the Blank Sisters, and those who worked at the front desk of the Lexington Laundry, the saleslady at Purcell's, the man who rode a bicycle, and Mrs. Keating, "a character," and Mrs. Newman, widow of a professor of engineering, her daughter teaching in the Canal Zone.

Red brick interrupted by the blankest of windowpanes, through which could be seen patches of black flickering like dark birds on the edge of the sea. This was our junior high school and memories of it descended on my brain like chloroform. I, a visitor now, skeptically at the door, facing the worn hallway, felt like a wife at the penitentiary on a Sunday. It is not without reason that all these places are called institutions. Young Negroes, heirs to my beaten-down junior high school, seemed to be studying what we had studied, nothing much. And there, flying high above, lost in some smoky cloud, were white teachers, like our teachers—Miss Owsley, Miss Skinner, Miss Wallace, Miss Denney. Surely all that was a thousand years ago, on some green sward, in a smoky, broken hut. A horrible sameness, nothingness mixed in the air: these poor black people had moved up to the nothing we had vacated—the textbooks, the lesson plans, the teachers, struggling through humid summer school in education courses at the University of Kentucky. The merest glimpse of the white teachers and they, not the children, looked like prison inmates, stuck with a sentence. Was there one, carrying like a burdensome tumor some inspiration, some love or devotion? Humor? Life? The principal of the school, a Negro, was going out for an appointment. He told me that the remaining white people in our neighborhood, most of them, had simply within the last year fled the scene, abandoned the turf. Chalk shrieked across the blackboard, restless bodies moved in the seats, the office typist struck the keys. Across the way, the old tumble-down grocery store, foul with pickles and a half a century of artificial flavors, waited impatiently for the afternoon pennies. Trucks braked down Fourth Street. The locked cars of the staff snoozed in the driveway.

Did we learn anything at Lexington Junior High? I have only one blazing North Star that steers me back to the seventh grade. Our class went by bus to Peewee Valley, Kentucky, to visit the house "immortalized" by Annie Fellows Johnston, the author of *The Little Colonel* books. Art and life came together then, in the dappled sunshine, and the house was made of white dreams. A long, maple-lined driveway, gracefully, slowly curved up to the great plantation mansion, laid out as peacefully and romantically as words on a page. Precious little mistress, sweet and gentle Little Colonel: was she there, we wondered, almost sick with pleasure, was she there in the farthest strawberry patch? This does not seem very advanced for the seventh grade and its loss is scarcely a deprivation. The bells rang out, the black students, and a few white ones, filled the halls, and the teachers, convicted, exhaled, breathing hard into the gloomy air. Torpor, nothingness, like an orphanage.

Transylvania College. Constantine Rafinesque, "one of the strangest and most brilliant figures of the middle frontier." Botany, shells, flora, stalking the wilderness, bearded, wearing a cape, looking like a Jew peddler, and perhaps he was, although he claimed Turkey and France and Germany. Too many roots arouse suspicion. My sister Annette was crowned Miss Transylvania on the steps of Morrison Chapel on a June morning. "Dusty" Booth was Mr. Pioneer. Annette was wearing an off-white evening dress, the skirt in layers of ruffles, short in front, and going down in the back. Thus she symbolized the conquest of the wilderness, the hacking of the Indians, the capture of the fields, and the massacre at the spring, at Bryan Station.

High, nasal, "Thank you, ma'ams" in the shops, play-acting domineering fantasies of women clerking in Better Dresses. I keep thinking of the deerlike shyness of country people, making the rounds on a Saturday morning, with their eggs and chickens and sometimes a quilt. I suppose they stand in the place of something else, as the figure in a dream is really filling in for someone more important. These faces, hardly real, and the dingy nylon curtains, the groaning air-conditioners, the empty Coke machines of a downtown hotel seem to unite, to represent the past. At the hotel desk, listening to the courtesies of the elderly clerks, your dreams are made of the pink lampshades in the Bluegrass Room, memories from a hundred towns. The electric organ in the Shenandoah Bar, plastic rhododendron in the Claridge Lounge, green and blue waves on the wallpaper of the South Pacific Club, floors like those of a sour shower stall in the Tahiti Grill: the downtowns from Atlanta to Bangor are the nostalgic remains of America.

Is not Kentucky truly "the dark and bloody ground"? Was there a mysterious race of Mound Builders here before the Indians? White (yes indeed) and of high culture (yes), greatly superior to the Indian tribes who came down from the North, like some Danish barbaric tribesmen sighting Rome? If that is not enough, think of Big Bone Lick in Boone County as the graveyard of extinct animals, prehistoric elephant and mammoth. Tusks eight feet long, thigh bones four or five feet long, and enormous teeth weighing eight or nine pounds! I got all of this from a small blue school book of the 1930s (introduction by Irvin S. Cobb)... Nothing is to be gained by reality, but much is lost in illusion.

The mirror gives back a blur. They'll go to the woods no more, that we know. A bizarre new life, ears tuned above the noise. The pathos of little businesses, their night lights flickering in the dark, their stocks and displays, their expansions and contractions and family lines. Established, 1917, in blood and mud, a little shoe store, fifty years of cash and credit, deaths, disappointments, summer weddings, old report cards. The years chronicled in the A&P ads in the Lexington *Herald-Leader*.

Mary Todd Lincoln is nothing to be happy about. Neurotic, self-loving, in debt at the White House, a bad wife, a rotten mother. Isn't there a story of them in a carriage on the way to meet Grant in Virginia and Mary Todd meanly rapping the whole way, berating him who was no-account? A Lexington girl. Perhaps he was not sorry to go, after all. He had backed off from her once, but then, losing his nerve, returned.

Up the same old streets again, and suddenly, after a broken fence the devastating whiteness, undimmed by the slate-gray November lawn, of the manor house, too grand, at Third Street. Beautiful long windows, clear, calling to the light. On the east, the north, the south, and the west sides: the same old downward path.

"Who speaks of victory? Survival is all."

1969

PURITANICAL PLEASURES

THE FORSYTHIA has already died and blown away in Central Park and the clusters of bloom on the lilac bushes in the suburbs are soon to be a drooping fade. But when you go up to Maine in May the first flowerings are reluctant, not quite ready, not to be hurried. The trees are not yet leafy, not at all. Houses never seen in the summer shadow of tree branches are visible just back from the road even in late spring.

The splendor of the region always retains a pristine frugality in its messages, a puritanical remnant in its pleasures. Like the blossoms, you are reminded that you can wait—and also you can do without. A lonesome pine, country music drift in the air, long-lost sentiments. He'll never return from the sea (the Merchant Marine) and the blue-eyed girl has gone to the office desks of Connecticut, never to look back.

Maine took me by surprise from the first and still, after three decades of summers, it takes me by surprise. I never expected to have knowledge of this most northeasterly part of our country. Perhaps the true Maine persons, those families on the soil for over a hundred years, will dispute the claims to special acquaintance made by a mere summer resident, even if such turns up year after year. Throughout New England there is a good deal of harmless intensity about length of tenure.

When I look out my window in the little Maine coastal village of Castine, what I see is altogether different from the landscape of my youth and my growing up. I was born in Lexington, Kentucky, a beautiful town, proud to be the center of "the bluegrass country." It is rolling land, gentle and moderate, and yet suitable to the production of rather extreme luxuries or vices: horses, bourbon whiskey, and tobacco. Lexington was, or so we believed, the most hospitable and refined setting the state had to offer.

By those steps one takes, the paths that mysteriously open up to become life history or biography, I became bound to New York and parts of Massachusetts and then, quite without preparation or planning, on to Maine, or up to Maine, or even down to Maine, as they might express it.

It is a summer long ago and there you are on a visit to a relation, this one a Washington, D.C., lady who had for many decades made her way from the humid national shrines to the breezes and fogs of Maine. She accomplished this with great stateliness and purposefulness, this passage to the "summer place," in no way as noticeably "summery" as the rest of the country. She came early on by way of the coastal steamers and when they, so to speak, sank like some lumbering victim of practical disrespect, she traveled by Pullman car from Washington to the city of Bangor, a mere stopping place since summer people are on their way to sea and bay and lake—to water.

Water: that is the Maine essence. The dock, the pier, the tides, the coves, the picnic islands within sight. Having grown up inland, I had felt no cause to lament either shore or mountaintop. Often I think the addition of these spectacles is a spiritual gain and also a burden, since "on the water" can become an obsession.

I speak of Maine in the summer and perhaps that is not out of line since the "Pine Tree State" also bears "Vacationland" on its license plates. This may seem a great peculiarity to those accustomed to sandy beaches, deep suntans, and g-string bathing costumes. And I speak mostly of "summer people" as a courtesy earned by those who know the Maine winters. Many summer people have come to Maine as an inheritance. Their grandparents built or bought a large shingle "cottage" somewhere near the water and the generations continued decade after decade since up to Maine is where they have gone and where they go once again. Maine ordinarily is not chosen by oneself in adult life, as one would choose to take a house on Long Island, in Connecticut, or on the islands of Massachusetts. That is, choose to go where others like oneself may be found, perhaps those you meet quite often all year long. For me too, Maine came in a cross-stitch route by inheritance.

The strangeness of Maine is that it is not near anything, unless it can be thought reasonably near Boston, some hundreds of miles to the south. Difficulty inhabits Maine like the great spruce trees. It is a quality in itself, promising and delivering a sort of fetishistic determination upon the management of isolation, cold water, long journeys, boat maintenance, hauls by ferry or scow if the decorative, the fashionable, the useful, and the comfortable are felt to be necessary.

For the rich with a puritanical inclination it was the habit long ago to buy a Maine island or, later, to trek to an island and there to make a prodigious effort, with a nod to the Northeast plainness of accommodation, to establish a version of the grand style. Thus the large cottages at Dark Harbor and North Haven, many of them attached to the names of great American fortunes. There one can see, in a willful translation, the chintzes spread about in the style of the reigning New York decorators. In the driveways and gardens, large tubs of agapanthus, ruffled lilies of a salmon hue quite putting in the shade the yellow clumps of the local, hardy day lily—at least the fuchsia, lusher and plumper than usual in their baskets, seem happy in the mist so freely offered. Where you can take little for granted beyond the gorgeousness of the storm-tossed landscape, efforts of the will perhaps give the summer people a pleasant recollection of the old frontier virtues.

"This world is more beautiful than convenient," Thoreau wrote about New England. In Maine the weather is not convenient, the water is not convenient, the isolation is not convenient. Indeed the state stands at the utmost end of inconvenience. It was covered by the continental glacier during the Ice Age and its hardscrabble soil, its 1,600 lakes, its "embayed" coastline remain as souvenirs. And a certain arctic forecasting seems often to mingle with the breeze-laden heat of summer. In the great spruces the memory of winters past and the promise of winters to come hang like dark birds in the branches.

As the wind prompts the sailboats in the bay, it is not a masochistic shudder to wonder if the house will in January be swept away by the winter tides or uprooted by the winds or simply frozen to death and eaten to sustain the crows and gulls.

As a people we appear to be ready to decline even a gentle descent of the winter season. You might say the entire country has just about *had it* with storm windows, the shovel and the snow plow, the laboriously or expensively gained stack of wood logs. These impositions of nature are a grievous strain on the American soul, now pulsing with a sort of heated-up genetic strain. The tropical and the semitropical, or better a moderate, evanescent changing of the seasons, have become a demand dictated by our sense of suitability and natural right. Drafty houses bring to mind nothing except the sane example of migrating birds resolute in their escape from winter.

Maine, of course, cannot escape winter and so the conversation in the summer solstice often turns to wrapped pipes, thrifty stoves, and the dreamy victories of insulation. Sometimes you can imagine the glare of snow in the sunshine, imagine the pool on the back shore impatient for the scars of ice skates, the hill ready for the child's sled. The eternal return, the relentless course of sun are part of "vacationland"—along with the high tide and low tide, gale warnings, deer crossings. Weather is the protagonist of the drama.

Maine is humbling to ambition and therefore hospitable to thrift and endurance. It is a poor state with a great number of roadside houses and worn-out farms hopelessly decorated with for-sale signs. The woods, the forest, the wilderness. True they are not neighbors to the coast and yet, looking across the bay in a mist, water and tree come together in a large, black shadow telling of things ancient and careless of man. The patient, meditating heron outside the window at dawn, the shivering birch—no, one never becomes cozily familiar with this world. Depending upon the light, each glance about you is a discovery and what you are pleased to call home has a peculiar visual unsteadiness. An interesting melancholy, quite pleasing, drifts in the air. Unexplored acres, vast tracts, live in the memory, even amidst an unfortunately purchased plastic flamingo stalking the yards here and there. And always the stillness astonishes as you drive over the back roads on the way to Route 1 or Route 95. The crab and the lobster, stalk-eyed, decapod crustaceans—what are they except the watery kin of the tough caribou and moose?

The Maine people, the Maine character, or characters? It is prudent to practice resistance here since the Maine person enters published descriptions in the gross, so to speak. He and she come out of a box labeled THE MAINE NATIVE. Literary folk collect the stories, search for the orthographic equivalent of the accent—and so on. He is, the Maine person in that now frozen mold, the friend of the amateur writer, just as the tilting, scrappy sheds on the dock, the cove with its lonely sailboat, the plain white houses, and distant church steeple are the friends of the amateur painter. The human and natural scenery, expressing some kind of genuine difference, long ago took on a difference altogether predictable. What a chore it must have been for the imagination of Robert Frost and John Marin to rescue from cliché their hired hands and light little boats tossing in the waves.

Still, one observes the often-observed crankiness and balky independence that confirm the legend. A certain colonial aspect prevails between the summer people and the year-round native; a late colonialism, perhaps, filled with uncertain advances and quick retreats. The beloved carpenter and the agreeably puzzled plumber will not quite spring to the demand, that hailstorm of demand in the summer months. Or so it seems. And in the end the colonials rail at bills that would occasion relief in the city.

No matter, there is something boldly impractical in the Maine economy, in the measured pace, as well as in the confident and elegant persevering skills of so many. In this economy, useful things abruptly, almost arrogantly, disappear from the village. Gone in the last two years are two garages with mechanics. One went and then the other, more or less except for gasoline; and as for the hole left, well, you might scratch your head like an old Russian peasant and ponder the whim of history.

The Northeast with its old battlefields has a pride of the drowsiest kind, like the nodding head of the antiquarian in the library. Fife and drum, pilgrim dress, the sweetest little straggle down Main Street on the Fourth of July.

My little village of Castine on the Penobscot Bay has a history worthy of the Polish Corridor. It has been held by five nations: the French, the English, the Dutch, the Indians, and ourselves. Gray wooden markers, lettered in blue, point out the old forts and the canal built by the British. During the Bicentennial, the entire nation was made aware that the Revolutionary expedition under the command of Commodore Saltonstall and General Lovell shamefully dozed over their cups while in the harbor and were ignominiously surprised by the British rolling down from Fort George. It was all over there, next to the golf club.

The town takes its name from the French occupation and from the Baron de Castin, a freewheeling character who may or may not have been worthy of memory. This ambitious explorer found life on the Penobscot Bay to his liking. He took as his bride the daughter of an Indian chief and thus there remains a little lane with the name of Madockawando. Everywhere in the state of Maine the crossing signs tell of far-flung voyages: China and South China, Sorrento, Corea (sic), Poland Spring, and Smyrna. Perhaps a kind of internationalism lies buried in the rocks up by the old lighthouse, but on the Castine streets, in the graveyards, on the mailboxes around the county the persistence of local names such as Perkins, Bowden, and Wardwell assures the Anglo-Saxon primacy of tenure. For the state as a whole, the resonance of Indian times outshines all interlopers: Passamaquoddy, the Allagash and Musquash Lakes, Mount Katahdin, Pemaquid, Orono, Abenaki, Kennebec.

Maine is designated a New England state and so it is when you smoothly pass over the New Hampshire line into the splendid, reassuring city of Portland. Southern Maine seems to belong to its sister states, but as you go north or inland you begin to feel you are in a region quite solitary, one that is a part of New England only by convenience.

Rock-bed America it is, yes, yes. And such an abundance of flags about, large ones swaying on their staff and small ones from the dime store in the windows or over the doors of the skinniest little shack, the dwelling place of so many. When you imagine Maine, apart from the southern section, as in some inchoate way a separate country, an old one, it does not appear old as Rome is old with its buried layers of civilization. It comes upon you old as the forest, uncharted, just being there.

Even the forest itself is peculiar, as Thoreau noted. He was not reminded in his travels to the Maine woods of "our" Massachusetts, where "the wilderness you are threading is, after all, some villager's wood-lot, some widow's thirds, from which her ancestors have sledded fuel for generations, minutely described in some old deed...." The Maine forest was just the forest, not tilled and spaced-out, handed-down acres, claimed by some weed-choked bounding marker.

There are fine houses everywhere in Maine. Every town thoroughfare has a number of them and the fields are dominated here and there by large, square structures painted white, topped by their chimneys, often four of them, and even in decay promising spacious rooms. And there are inhabited homes of such smallness and lack you might be in another country, the sparsely peopled Scandinavia perhaps. The poverty stands fronting the road or placed down a ragged path. Hardship, the Depression, a reminder of deprivation and also of modesty and patience, and a sort of huddling domestic chill. Poor soil, short growing season, not much to work with. These conditions create in the spirit a thoughtful contradiction between lassitude and extraordinary exertion in the management of a profound absence of accommodation.

The brutal toil of the fisherman, the zest of the hunter, each a fierce adaptation to the forest and the sea. And then the nights, the darkness. Darkness comes down early in the winter, as if by fatigue. The arrival of the morning sun or merely the morning light itself is the joy of every season. If one would treasure Maine, it is well to forget about the evening except for the full moon shining on a high tide or the theatrical surprise of the yellow, red, and violet northern lights in August. For the rest, near the shore the stars are sketchy, shy, and fleeting. A deep green, a startling green, is the sensation of Maine and for that one needs the first and last light of day.

Thinking of modesty, patience, and rural poverty does not prepare the mind for Mount Desert Island, with its dramatic Mount Cadillac, its coves, ponds, its thundering spots with waves rising to forty feet. And certainly it does not prepare for the spectacular settlements of wealth, the presence of Rockefeller, Ford, and Astor in Northeast Harbor and Seal Harbor.

But Maine is Maine and even Mount Desert is not quite a northerly Newport. There are "palpable piles," as Henry James called the outsize and, to him, vulgar mansions of Newport; yet the Maine landscape casts upon a like ambition a sort of pleasant fog of discretion that reduces the grandeur, if not in intention, at least in function. There is little of the fast, the thrilling, and the glamorously outgoing. Too great a chill in the air for practical ostentation. The sailing vessels at the piers are splendid, but they do not give forth the hope of a riotous excursion. The puritanical tides have their way.

Last summer I saw a fine mansion outside the fashionable town of Camden on the Penobscot Bay, a bit to the south of Castine. The mansion provoked thought, if not for itself alone, but for many others one has seen on islands and towns in the "rich" pockets of Maine summer life. A mansion with a determined bravado that would not be scorned in Palm Beach, possibly constructed by an owner bearing the name of a renowned American invention or a surviving strike in faraway lucky fields. Sometimes the name recalls the flash of interesting divorces in the city tabloids, the flare of deviations, the auctions of loot long dusty in the stone palaces on Fifth Avenue.

Some bygone wish had created the Maine summer castles with

their fine long windows coming down to the imaginatively divided spaces of the terrace. Delicate exterior decorations, Art Nouveau iron garden furniture, curling and swirling in a pattern. One I remember sat high on its site and looking out to the bay with a fond, now haunted, serenity.

In my memory I see the long stone wall at the shore giving way, the planks of the pier rotting here and there, the tricycle of the caretaker's daughter overturned in front of the timbered garage. A place with the sharp, abandoned charm of the grand in a wistful neglect. To me the message reads: *They* don't come up anymore. They? The generational promise unhonored. And one can imagine the bewilderment of new mates without memories and most definitely with ideas for a reasonable substitution of the South of France or perhaps Martha's Vineyard or Southampton. How easy to hear the ring of the pertinent and unanswerable question about the old family estate in Maine: What do you do once you're up there?

Summer in Maine. The gull and the cormorant, the sudden vision of the skull of a seal coming up for air, the unforeseen treachery of the afternoon's sail, the osprey's nest. The tracks of the gray wolf last seen in Blue Hill in 1930, the unpredictable views from the bay, sometimes Japanese in the outlines of the islands and the opposite shore, the fading red of the boathouse at the end of the field of a saltwater farm.

Main Street in Castine gently slides down past the fine clapboard houses, past the post office and the inns and the unaggressive shops, slides down to the water, the public dock, the harbor restaurant. A handsome place this is, the natives say. Yes, it is an endowment of nature and on a human scale altogether reticent, benign, and courteous. Perhaps it is not to everyone's taste. And, true, there is nothing much happening hereabouts, although the first vision casts upon many a powerful longing for some bit of the beguiling landscape. And then the car moves on, leaving behind the old settlement on its point, with its odd locationary divisions, such as "off the neck" and "up at the head."

Yet, the shore village remains, static no doubt, but a gift of immaculate retrospection. The reflections of its tones, long outlasting the summer months, are a strange, even mystifying, baggage for the mind packing up for a return to the city.

1986

THE ÉMIGRÉ

OUR COUNTRY, from the first a vast transcendental diaspora under the celestial protection of two oceans, in the thirties fell heir to, by way of unprecedented disasters, a radiance of genius. The émigrés were of such lofty achievement and possibility that the mere listing of the names is a sort of embarrassment because it seems to reduce the irreducible. Or it seems to try by order and condensation to contain the disorderly solitary eminence of the bearers of the names. Émigrés, exiles, refugees from Germany and Austria, Hungary, Russia, Spain, Poland, Italy—and elsewhere, elsewhere. The density of the arts and sciences and the very luggage of civilization these persons carried with them surpass understanding. In the last fifty years they were among us in such multiplication it seemed as if they were some natural transcontinental cargo rather than an astonishment delivered by tragic history. The national psyche accommodated the savants, when it knew of them, with extraordinary and respectful generosity —and some amused and puzzled wonder. In any case, it was clear that there wasn't enough laurel in the Rockies to adorn this large, polyglot pantheon of the uprooted and the overrun. Some arrived with their Nobel Prizes and more gained them while here. Some appear in encyclopedias as Americans: American theoretical physicist, b. Ulm, Germany. Albert Einstein.

In 1904, Henry James wrote of the "effect of the infusion," the infusion being the swarm of foreign-born persons he found buzzing about and sometimes stinging his sensibilities when he returned to New York after a gap of twenty-one years. It appeared to him the Italians on the Lower East Side were not Italians at all. They seemed to have rid themselves, in a moment, as it were, of the peasantlike hierarchical courtesies, the attractive ancient colorations that made them so agreeable when they were tending the vines of Italy. They were not discourteous; they were simply a transplant transmogrified— a new, mysterious being. Wandering in the downtown ghetto, the New Jerusalem, he wondered, "Who can ever tell, moreover, in any conditions and in presence of any apparent anomaly, what the genius of Israel may, or may not, really be 'up to'?"

To wonder what the later elite Jewish intelligentsia of Europe was "up to" could scarcely enter our minds in a colloquial phrase since it would require not a lovely, drifting social imagination of the kind James shows in *The American Scene* but, instead, immense imagination and information in the higher reaches of mathematics, physics, biology, art history, music, and on and on.

The émigrés from Nazism and fascism and also Russian communism were survivors of every sort and every condition. The Jews were united in their pain and grief, something not transferable to the American scene except perhaps to their fellow Jews of no matter how long a local citizenship. However, for the extraordinary talents simple assimilation into American culture for practical reasons was not a demand, since it was their fate to be exceptions without boundaries, even though they had suffered from the boundaries of their circumstance in a time of catastrophe.

Our institutions and a wide, if sometimes imperfect, hospitality asked of these gifted émigrés only that they continue to be themselves or continue to complete the self achieved with such spectacular promise in the past. This was a benign and unusual condition, something the earlier groups fleeing from pogroms or gross poverty could not have understood. The unusual welcoming was in many cases chilled by difficulties in language and by what might be called "medium" or obscure previous celebrity. And so there were learned art historians, critics, essayists, political theorists, wandering about New York with the merely respectable anonymity of some NYU doctorate.

Nabokov spoke of his European Humbert Humbert, that outrageous disturbance in *Lolita* who swept in his libidinous travels across the continent like a dust storm, as a "salad" of mixed genes. That is, he was French, Austrian, English, with a "dash of the Danube." And to some extent the "salad" defines most of the distinguished exiles. They were German or Hungarian or Russian, but they were also very much European and had moved about from country to country for education and inspiration. Einstein himself lived as a youth in Munich and Milan and was graduated from the Polytechnic Academy in Zurich, where he became a Swiss citizen. He was a professor also in Prague, and when his fame was established he accepted the directorship of the Kaiser Wilhelm Institute in Berlin. Had he not then resumed his German citizenship he could not, as a Jew, have been deprived of it and his property in 1933.

As we know, this European arrived at the Institute for Advanced Study in Princeton and became for America the iconographical "genius," the abstruse incarnate, and also the liberal and tormented spirit about nuclear weapons and civic affairs.

Nabokov, Stravinsky, and Balanchine, Europeans from St. Petersburg by way of the Russian Revolution, do not quite create in our minds the sense of some tremendous and unique burden borne through life. They were not Jewish—Nabokov's wife was Jewish—and they maintained their "Russianness," which had about it an ineffable charm not often granted to "Germanness." Of course, the Russians' memories were of loss of countryside, of language, and like all refugees, they came from a cemetery.

The Firebird was performed in Paris in 1910 and Stravinsky came to America later as a supreme example and influence in world music. Nabokov, who had continued to write in Russian in Germany and France, began here to write in English and to put Humbert Humbert and Professor Pnin into a fantastical American landscape. Where there is an overwhelming invention of style and conception, as with Schoenberg in California, citizenship and placement are simply existence honored and not matters of creative additions. With Balanchine a perfect reciprocity was accomplished—the wedding of imperial Russian technique with American dancers and, when he wished it, the complicated tonalities of a kind of American aura.

Henry Kissinger, so extraordinarily visible and palpable, has never quite disengaged his Germanness, his boyhood in Fürth, but that is surely merely his inextinguishable accent and little else. This curious émigré, or rather this most curious one among the émigrés, has an innate American flair. He alone, among the figures who come to mind, seems to express the old will to exploit the continent, build the railroads, get the copper out of the ground. Still, a Continental sophistication and a Mitteleuropa skill at diplomatic maneuver somehow inform his American endeavors. His "image" announces that he is both the Old World and *us* in a high-flown, canny admixture.

If for Kissinger the United States was still the frontier, the country acted in a custodial mode for many of the others. At the Institute in Princeton the custodial gesture was elaborate, courtly, and rather daunting. Gödel and Von Neumann and Einstein under the trees and spires at the end of the ride through the industrial wasteland of New Jersey. And Panofsky and Auerbach and Thomas Mann and Hermann Broch: one does not like to line them up like a very large cast in *Playbill*.

The New School for Social Research was, by comparison, a modest practicality, utilitarian and saving for many contentious thinkers, among them the philosophers Hannah Arendt and Leo Strauss, and the political historians Hans Kohn and Hans Morgenthau. Nevertheless, no institution in America was a convent, a retreat. Instead, the refugee world was a battlefield—they fought among themselves, about ideas, and often they struggled with the new country itself. They were ambitious, often arrogant, often rivalrous. The quarrels and differences among them are very interestingly described in Anthony Heilbut's *Exiled in Paradise*.

And they came into the postwar world of the H-bomb, McCarthyism, and the Cold War. Thomas Mann returned to Europe in disillusionment. Edward Teller, Hans Bethe, Einstein, and Leo Szilard, preeminent figures of the nuclear age, disagreed painfully and in ways that were important for themselves and for the country. Hannah Arendt's *Eichmann in Jerusalem* aroused ferocious controversy.

Many of the émigrés became teachers, and perhaps it is not amiss to think of them as exercising a certain imperial, if uncoercive, role among our young artists and thinkers. The Bauhaus architects dominated the skyline and the professional schools in an almost military fashion. They left a vast and often beautiful permanency of steel and concrete even the most aggressive postmodernism cannot undo, for such is the nature of buildings. Tom Wolfe expressed his native's chagrin at the imposition of "foreign forms," but his advocacy of a sort of containment of idea in architecture, and painting as well, implies that the America the refugee professionals entered was a sort of Maginot Line, self-important but easily outflanked. And of course this was not true. As a part of the civilized community we were already knowledgeable about theorems, physics, the unconscious, atonalism, Cubism, European fiction and poetry, and the general ideas in circulation. No one ever knows just why certain notions prevail in historical periods except that they serve the creative impulses at large.

Still, there was a need for buildings and there was the money to build them with, and the triumph of the Bauhaus group was indeed noticeable. Psychiatry also seemed to find here a peculiar local demand, as if it were some happy interest-bearing note. "So. Now vee may perhaps to begin," Philip Roth's Dr. Spielvogel says. Bruno Bettelheim, Erik Erikson, Karen Horney, and the manic futurist Wilhelm Reich—in combination a fantastical therapeutic spread—achieved what one might call a reinforced definition. And not to speak of those emblematic practitioners in their intense occupation of New York's Central Park West and Park Avenue.

"Stone by stone we shall remove the Alhambra, the Kremlin and the Louvre and build them anew on the banks of the Hudson."—Benjamin de Casseres, 1925. De Casseres spoke of "things," treasures of antiquity and every period following, bought and displayed and *owned*. He could not know that the Hudson Valley was to be the collector and connoisseur of the actual bodies of creative Europe. France and England and Switzerland had been the custodians for centuries—Herzen and Turgenev, Marx.

Between the enormous fluted Ionic columns
There seeps from heavily jowled or hawk-like foreign faces
The guttural sorrow of the refugees.
—LOUIS MACNEICE, "The British Museum Reading Room"

New York, Manhattan—a fanatical urbanism, a spectacle, a metaphorical landing place. So if you are banished from Frankfurt, Berlin, St. Petersburg, or Warsaw, there is left no possibility except the twentieth-century capital. The city of the future, peculiar, uncomfortable, an orphan brilliant indeed, and no matter the lack of a family album of monuments, cathedrals, old squares, and palaces. Manhattan itself, with those early pictorial towers that seem to end in a medicating hypodermic needle, is one of the "characters" of the last fifty years. Its purpose is to be exploited, whereas the purpose of the Old World cities is to exist as a slowly accreting density and storehouse of the national history. New Amsterdam: Mondrian's *Broadway Boogie Woogie* and the austere Dutchman himself in his studio on the East Side.

"What Piranesi invented the ornamental rites of your Roxy Theatre? And what Gustave Moreau apoplectic with Prometheus lighted the venomous colors that flutter at the summit of the Chrysler Building?"—Dalí in New York. (This quotation and the preceding one from de Casseres are found in a work of almost frenzied brilliance and originality: *Delirious New York*, 1978, by the young Dutch architect Rem Koolhaas.)

In America we are not a Folk in the manner of the Germans, French, English, and even the Russians. We are too self-created, vagrant, of too random and unpredictable congruence for that. The claim to insist upon a folk by the negation "unAmerican" is a bullying and unhistorical folly. The elite émigrés met here not only the great wealth of the country and the Bill of Rights but a rich and porous ground. For the general dissemination of ideas a physical presence is not necessary. The exception is the A-bomb and the H-bomb, the most spectacular achievements of émigré science and perhaps of any science in that the terms of everything were altered forever. In this case the American presence of Fermi and Leo Szilard at Columbia, Hans Bethe and Edward Teller at Los Alamos was of an overwhelming significance, spanning the limits of science, politics, the direction—still unknown—of human history.

The aggressiveness of American mass culture was a challenge many of the refugees seemed unprepared for, even if they were not dilatory in abstracting principles from it. Their complicated intrusions and failures in Hollywood have their own formidably detailed history. Nothing could soften the final fact that this elite was unlike any other. They had been the objects of the worst and most powerfully organized evil intentions the world had ever known. Whatever Weimar or Viennese café-pride they exhibited was only a manner, a style. It was painful to learn to write in English, or to remain, like Isaac Bashevis Singer, a writer in Yiddish slowly finding his audience in the fiercely competitive glut of American fiction.

Surely the only happy exile is based upon caprice and personal taste—French food, sunlight all the year, cheap villas, servants, old cultures, and sometimes merely the escape from a too dear and watchful family and village. Finding Oxford and Cambridge too "down-home" seemed to have spurred the transition of Auden, Isherwood, and Huxley. In the end the most striking thing about the exiles' great influence on our times is that it was marked by a certain equity. What we offered to them and what we received in return was accomplished with rare historical and human balance.

1983

BALANCHINE

"O body swayed to music..."

—W. B. Yeats

I OFTEN used to see Balanchine here on 67th Street where we both lived. The great ballet choreographer was small, neat, wearing, in his late years at least, unremarkable, practical clothes. He was, you might say, not noticeable, not even noticeable for appearing unfriendly or abstracted. A few people recognized him, but I never saw, in what was perhaps intimidating daylight, any fan stop to speak of his admiration. Instead, seeing him there on the street, in the drugstore and sometimes in the wine store, people would step back with a start and, or so it seemed to me, make a slight, nodding bow.

The artist was not a street star in the New York sense and neither are the members of his company as they go about the Lincoln Center neighborhood. Inside the New York State Theater, it was something else. He and the dancers were overwhelming presences, removed, on the stage, in the wings—presences real and not quite real also, for such is the mysteriousness of ballet landscape.

When George Balanchine died at the end of April of this year, a golden age of many kinds seemed to come to an end—his choreography, his supreme example of tradition and innovation, his inexhaustible inspiration. Of course, the ballets survive; the dancers bear his message, his art, and are even tonight fulfilling the dedication. And there will be a fall season, *The Nutcracker* for Christmas—on and on.

Still, the presence of Balanchine was of such a completeness and complexity that he himself was the sum of the parts, the sole possessor, one sometimes felt, of his secret, even though the secret was to be revealed in performance—that is, by others. Since it was dance, the work could not be private, arcane brilliance; all was designed for embodiment, realization, transference. But with him, there was more to it than that.

He was not, after his youth, often a performer, not, like Isadora Duncan, Martha Graham, and Merce Cunningham, the measure in his own body of the vision of his brain. New ballets every year of his creative life, revisions of previous work in a spirit of unquenchable fertility and inspiration—in that he did not differ from the great performer-choreographers who composed for their companies and for themselves. The difference at last was that, being himself disembodied on the stage of performance, he knew no limitations beyond those of others, the dancers, and these limitations he set himself against insofar as it was possible and desirable. He was a fearful challenge, or so I imagine. The aim of it all was to produce the impossible art, ballet, and to reach by its discipline profoundly human depths of feeling—human feeling usually abstracted beyond documentation and narrative, but feeling nevertheless of an ineradicable ancientness. Pure movement, pure dance, music in movement, always—but the work never seemed, as one sat in the dark of the theater, estranged by the purity of the art from the humble universals of experience.

Balanchine was born in Russia in 1904. He studied music, entered the Soviet State School of Ballet as a boy. So there it was—music and dance, the marriage of his gifts, enlightened by extraordinary intelligence and a dedication incorruptible. At the age of twenty, he left Russia and went to Paris. Indeed it was the historical moment, the electrifying time of Diaghilev, Picasso, Stravinsky, the transformation of the heights of the inherited tradition (Picasso could draw like Ingres, it was said), into the accents and rhythms, the restlessness, the ambivalence that were the challenge of the twentieth century.

And it was a fateful moment for us, for America, when this unpredictable European genius, still in his twenties, came here in 1933. It is always possible that he might have remained in Paris; but given the fifty years of his residence here it is difficult to imagine it otherwise, and who has the heart to linger on the idea. The New York City

Ballet, The School of American Ballet, these unexpected institutions, fiercely unparochial or even nationalistic, are nevertheless American. It was the marriage of the New World and the Old, the union of Balanchine's unshakable tradition and imperial integrity with the fluid and open American possibility, something of the American tonality. In this extraordinary combining, the great learning, taste, and dedication of Lincoln Kirstein was at hand, as if by some benevolent design of history.

In the classical ballet of Russia and Europe with its implacable and somewhat alien discipline, the discipline of the impossible, young American men and women became the instruments of interpretation for Balanchine's genius. Girls from Cincinnati (Suzanne Farrell), from Saint Paul (Merrill Ashley), from California (Heather Watts and others), and young men from Massachusetts (Jacques D'Amboise), from Harrisburg, Pennsylvania (Sean Lavery), from Ogden, Utah (Bart Cook) are in the present company, following all those memorable others from Oklahoma and, you might say, wherever. Of course the company of the revered St. Petersburg master or benign despot is international and catches in its net the talents of Copenhagen, Iceland, and Soviet Russia itself.

We have in America our precocious revolutionaries of modern dance, a tradition of distinctive eminence and a kind of evangelical force. When Balanchine was born in 1904, Isadora Duncan was already touring Europe with spectacular zeal and confidence. In the 1940s, Martha Graham created *Letter to the World*, *Deaths and Entrances*, and *Appalachian Spring*. These works, austere and eloquent, seemed to arise out of the national inheritance in matter and technique. The body and the mind, the movement itself were mirrors of the large, democratic vistas of puritanism, frontier hope, and a very contemporary tension. This high, reflective art, on the one hand, and the endlessly beguiling inventions of the popular idiom, on the other hand, are our classics. New choreographers spring forth in each generation and the sheer amount of dance just now is staggering. Sometimes the exuberance overwhelms other theatrical elements and they seem to be running behind, clumsy, hesitant, and unprepared.

Thus, the tradition of ballet is invariably challenged and it, itself, challenges. Owing to Balanchine, no aspect of dance is the same, and his inventions flow effortlessly into the most routine Broadway musical and the elevated insights of modern dance flow back into his work. And if at last nothing is interdicted or superceded, the example of ballet, the classical rigor of it, has been absorbed as an immediacy, released from a mandarin exclusiveness. This is the way of art and if there is education in it, training as there must be for the performers and the audience, it is not scholastic but the very command of our time.

As a genius of the dance theater, Balanchine is able to enhance every demand. *Ballet comique* with its pertness, teasing, and dazzling speed is not now, nor has it ever been, a plebeian intrusion in the repertory. There is a little tart in every ballerina and an Apache in each *danseur noble*. But for me, an ignorant member of the audience, the address to the deepest sensibilities lies in the adagio duets, in the consuming silence, in the presence of something fatalistic and borne with passionate reserve and stoicism. This is perhaps true, if it is, of all such moments in ballet. Still, in Balanchine, the effect upon the emotions is almost archaic, of something hidden in human history, very old and outside of time. Some of it is the chastity of ballet itself, the black and whites or palest pastels, the wordless superiority, the unfathomable subtlety, the refinement and lack of insistence. If all we were aware of was the element of impossibility, the purity of movement, the musicality, the ethereal discipline, we could not be so deeply moved by *Agon*, *Serenade*, and *Davidsbündlertänze*, so different indeed from the gorgeous *tristesse* of *Swan Lake* and *Giselle*.

So you come out into the night of New York City, unable to express or to persevere in this ineffable revelation that is not the story of your life or the rhythm of it either. The golden age is a memory of promise, of suitability of response to the conditions of life, of some lost glory that remains in longings and in endurance. It is the memory of a greater and more complete simplicity, a lament perhaps. This is what Balanchine's "modern" classical arrangements of space and movement accomplish for the spirit.

Here in the city, in this country, he received the means necessary for the elegant, costly performance of ballet. And above all the support to train generations, to establish standards and a pure style. The School of American Ballet, the New York City Ballet, became a fixed point in the dreams of young dancers, a daunting discipline and hope. In providing the means, we may be said to have honored him, Balanchine, as a small repayment of the incomparable honor he bestowed upon us.

1983

FAYE DUNAWAY

"What I always thought the finest thing in the theater, ever
since childhood and even now, is the *chandelier....*"
                                                —Baudelaire

A FILM star is not a character in a book, not a writer with his text
to be thought about, not a personage in history fixed by the glue of
biography, not one of Byron's mistresses who wrote and received letters. A living film star is someone of great visual interest who fills the
space on the screen with a certainty of placement and look. With
women stars, the *face* is content, symbol. It reveals and conceals; and,
it seems to me, once imprinted upon the mind in a vivid way, it refuses
to change its meaning.

A star has played roles, tinting them all with her name, a name
chained to the face. A strength of impression makes one a star and
there is a certain inflexibility connected with film stars. The hardened,
fixed image, so difficult to come by, is a sort of finality and the image
goes through its life, its roles, now here at home and now a princess
in Russia, poor for this moment and wearing jewels and furs in the
next turn. But it is the star cast in stone we go to see again and again
—all quite different from the stage with its distances that blur and
mean that the actor must with each entrance recreate himself.

In *Network*, Faye Dunaway played a woman of villainous ambition.
She was extraordinarily *high* on power—and very, very thin. In the
author's conception, a pomade of old character ideas flattened the
skull of the film. The female television executive, Faye Dunaway, slid
back and forth on the oil like a watchful, greedy cormorant. The
relentless forage will not leave the dark, industrious bird much time

and thus it cannot be associated with habits of love or reciprocity. That was the sentiment. The punitive results of ambition are not creditable to reason or to experience, but if a woman were to be a fierce television executive, the choice of this star in no way violates our idea, our film idea, of Faye Dunaway.

In *Chinatown*, the star was thrown into hermetic immobility by being charged to bear, as if in a permanent mourning, the worst of secrets—a rape by her father that results in the birth of a daughter. The antiquity of the idea did not instruct somehow and the victim, keeper of the secret, naturally did not have much to say. Many silences and black hats.

In *Bonnie and Clyde*, handsome long skirts and beret, silk blouses with fagoting, the Depression, and a superb cinema death. The bandits were history, homely and rickety and appalling in life, brought to the films, under the *chandelier*, as it were. It would not do to make too much of Bonnie's strength, her equality in crime. The bandits are a couple, a love story, with comedy and pity drifting about them. They are accompanied in their travel to the screen by very engaging friends. They are deprived and violently set upon definition, as much as on survival. The pathology of the criminals is bathed in the yearning pathos of the trapped. Bonnie is a role of great importance to a film star and Faye Dunaway seized it with passion and talent. Sympathy, strangely, seemed to seize the viewers. But Bonnie lives only once and Faye Dunaway is anti-romantic on the screen.

The star. Insofar as real life is concerned, the star seems to be either posing or fleeing, hiding or widely smiling. Naive, obsessive fans wait in the cold streets or the hot, wait to draw near, to see, sustained by an agitated patience, restrained and excluded by guards. And the shrouded, protected objects of their patience vanish in their large, dark chariots with such a swiftness. The fans go off into the night, back to the highway towns, to the old subway and bus suburbs, re-turning with all their questions unanswered. They are real questions of a sort, about appearance and reality, flesh and spirit. They learn something: that many handsome male stars are very short. ("Why make that little fellow a Captain?" people exclaimed as Admiral Nelson approached his ship.) And, perhaps, they receive another answer. "Oh, beautiful star, can you love me?" No.

Faye Dunaway was born in Northern Florida and went to Leon High School in Tallahassee. She did not have an easy life in her youth. Perhaps there is a little Florida in Bonnie, but the place, the rural, hard scene has been transcended—if that is the proper word. Marilyn Monroe changed for us when we were allowed to discover her biography of foster homes, rapes, lost father, deranged mother. Russian heroines of mixed natures—Grushenka in *The Brothers Karamazov* for one—began to invade the creamy image. Every image finally looks to rouge or blood.

Poverty, beauty, and ambition are the history for its genealogy. With film stars, we never know whether we are looking at literature of the actress. In Colette, the music-hall singers, the players always traveling about, "the vagabonds"—without poverty, their special actress character could not assume such a touching and complete form. They are creatures with memories. Some will fall. In Balzac and others, the trusting actress-waif is embezzled by men and she will sink; her little oval face and black curls cannot save her as she gives away her last sou or watches the final trinket turn into the scorned capital of the pawnbroker. There are hard ones, too. Balzac's Josepha, very canny about apartment furnishings, clothes, and carriages to be extracted from the beleaguered funds of lecherous men. And there are great artists, too: Berma, in Proust. But something of the vagabond, with her makeup, her costume, her acts, and friends in the business, remain like rocks in the flowing image of the actress.

In the films, it has always been otherwise. When we think of female film stars, we think of power and money. What was not so long ago a girl back home is now a millionairess.

Power and money and hired persons, managers and hairdressers, abandoned lovers and a superfluity of husbands. This is not new. The films have always turned women stars into men—at least in possibilities to impose the anarchic will. No doubt this sense of the will—

and what is celebrity gossip except our participation in the details of the impudent will?—enchants the dreaming teenager. Beauty and dancing lessons turned into striking performance that will return love and power by way of dollars. But in the movies, the frenzy of appearance, in all its assaulting shapes, can deform and disillusion and many tell us the ice-cream cone is filled with ashes. No surprise considering a like discovery by the rest of us.

On the screen, there is something in Faye Dunaway that creates unease, a dislocation of feeling. The puzzle is contemporary, *modern*, rather unsettling. She arrests the attention by many negations, by what she is not. The face almost flat, with a peculiar flat smoothness. She does not possess a large mouth or round, floating eyes to be insisted upon as the identification that announces presence.

Coolness, indeed. This fatality for actresses, one they fear, is the source of her interest, for me at least. She does not slyly intrude the irresistible innocence or ignorance, hints from the psyche outmoded by history. Narcissism also, the flat, harmonious face unchanging, reflecting upon itself, but classless and not especially American. She might be European, international.

The cool narcissism is combined, in her roles and in what she *seems to be* on the screen, with an unexpected circumstance hard to name. Capability, perhaps. In her typical appearances, she *does* something; she has a profession or a job of a striking sort. She has been a television executive, an insurance adjuster (*The Thomas Crown Affair*), and in her last film, *Eyes of Laura Mars*, she was a successful fashion photographer. She does not strike one as, first of all, a lover or a mistress, a wife or a daughter, although, of course, she will have to appear to be at least a lover in the service of plot. A peculiar presence, suitable to the seventies in many ways.

Female film stars: I am interested in the deterioration of their affability, their reasonableness, as a condition often increasing with their power. The art of the film is divided among so many that those on the outside find it hard to credit so much perversity, recalcitrance, waste, *uncooperativeness*. Perhaps, a woman can practice such reversals only at the bottom or the top. At the bottom, miserable oppressors of children and family cast their black lights from an inner gloom and represent the manipulations of dependency. The dominant-dependent woman ruling by disguises and distortions, always on the alert to restrain the freedom of others, to create guilt—this is a sad fact of energy and sense of self shackled by circumstance, custom, or the defeating caprices of character. It was so often the rule in the home, the revenge of wives.

The trouble-making independent woman is another matter. It is, perhaps, the independence itself saying: what can you do about it? A question most of us have heard more than once, but directed to us rather than from us. The star system gives license. To meet a flatterer tells you a good deal about where you stand in the world. Faye Dunaway is thirty-eight, childless, has been married only once and that once not so long ago. She is said to be difficult, temperamental. All reigns are autocratic.

Money and the attendance that follows it separate a film star from other women, even others of outstanding success. In the films, everything is extreme, in multiplication, and what is left that might be called ordinary becomes eccentric by its mere existence. We read in the newspapers that stars are not happy people always. Choice allows one to make mistakes and privilege allows you to make a lot of them.

To play the old stories in the seventies pushes the imagination into a retrograde state, even if the players are, so to speak, in modern dress. Faye Dunaway does not have the expressive contemporaneity of attitude found in Jane Fonda or Vanessa Redgrave, the glow of opinion and action that comes to some degree from their life outside the films. She is not polemical, but she is dominating as a woman. She seems to be expressing a solitariness that is unusual, anti-romantic. In the romantic aura, there is a leaning on, an openness to desperation and to the hurt of misplaced trust. The modernity of her film image seems to rest upon a removal and distance that suggests that, at last, you have only yourself.

Perhaps that is not what she means or admires or what she is in life. She is not reassuring. The sense of equality, not to mention domination, may be a bit chilling to the conventional, particularly to the conventional man. But, to the thoughtful, the electricity of the negative qualities gives her an extraordinary interest.

1979

KNOWING SONTAG

SUSAN SONTAG: I remember when she first *appeared*, appearance signifying in this case not a mere social presence but the offering of intense literary work in an arresting combination with the person, the one writing. Of course, it was immediately clear that she was a romantic. Not a romantic prisoner of love or private history, but a romantic of the intellectual life. She brought to mind as a dramatic entrance the young Mary McCarthy, whom she does not resemble in thought or temperament—and naturally enough, since romantics and intellectuals are personal and have qualities seldom free of disturbance and jarring particularity.

Here was a young woman of special gifts and high style: opinionated, even intransigent, and yet unmarked by dank truculence, indolent fixity. She was liberated from provincialism and the narrowing vanities that leave one standing where one began. But not free of vanity, if that may mean a certain airy certainty of self requisite for difficult undertakings. So she was then, in her twenties.

Now, Susan Sontag lives half the year in New York and the other half in Paris. Not so long ago, she was in Venice for a conference on the art of dissidents; she was in California lecturing on photography. Her mother lives in Honolulu and she visits there. She went to Hanoi during the Vietnam War; she has made a trip to China, to India, to Israel. Nevertheless, because she is a writer, she has spent most of her time alone in her room, slowly enduring the struggle to create serious work.

A list of the titles of her writings would leave the page black with capital letters, but it must be recorded that she has published two novels, two books of literary and cultural criticism. A brilliant work, *On Photography*, came out last year; this month will bring the publication of *Illness as Metaphor*; a collection of short stories will be published in the fall. She has written and directed two full-length films, shot in Sweden, and a complex documentary on Israel. She is in her mid-forties.

So there it is—and there she is—beads on a string that cannot, in the listing, offer the shine of quality and oddity glistening in the works. Here, in America, our reverence is most often stirred by a creative exclusiveness: the poet, the musician, the painter, the scientist, the great performers. We seem to feel most secure with genius in a singular concentration and with the kind of artist who "has a mind so fine no idea can violate it," as T. S. Eliot said not quite seriously of Henry James.

Susan Sontag is all *ideas*. Her essays, of course, and even her films and short stories show the habit of mind of one trained as a philosopher, as she was. Philosophical and theoretical speculation is a natural turn of her mind, and yet the world of the university and the academy is not congenial to her way of thinking or to her writing. She was a prodigy, entering the University of Chicago at fifteen and going on to Harvard for graduate study. Beyond that, the "crisis of identity" led to her most important creative discovery: French bohemian intellectual life, an insistent avant-garde mode, an obsessive concern with form—form as an idea and a practice, a fascination with the extreme, with the theatrical gesture, with outlandish, anarchic styles. ("Notes on 'Camp,'" for instance.)

With the free, independent, unpredictable reach of her interests, the rich grounding in high culture, Susan Sontag became, *is*, an original observer of popular culture, bizarre creatures, pornography, happenings—and always politics, opera, ballet, and literature. Scarcely anyone is more alive to the *interesting*, more willing to contemplate its aesthetic shape, more willing to experience the flow of styles and assumptions. She is very shrewd and witty in defining the sounds of the crash of contemporary life.

In her sensibility, the movies are everywhere: not just in the many essays she has written on Godard, Bergman, and others, and not only in her films. Film art and even film anti-art cast their lights on the pages of her novels and stories. Ellipses, obscurities, innovations reveal this cinematic saturation, always in a singular blending with avant-garde European writing. It is not for nothing that Susan spent her youth in California, flew off to the University of Chicago and then on to Paris.

She is a feminist very much in the way certain persons are known to be cradle Catholics. Thus she is not burdened as a thinker with the pieties and reductions that sometimes attend conversion. She married very young, was divorced, raised her son, made her own living, created herself. That creation is the most interesting American woman of her generation.

1978

KATHERINE ANNE

SHE WAS spoken of simply as "Katherine Anne," whether one was actually acquainted with her or not. But this should not be seen to indicate any folksiness in her image. Quite the contrary was true of this fastidious writer. From the time of the appearance of her very first stories, she occupied a high place in our literature. Everyone who cared about writing knew and admired her work. In the years before paperback publishing, I can remember searching the secondhand stalls for *Flowering Judas*, her first collection, and seeing it as a prize equal to a copy of *Doctor Martino and Other Stories* by Faulkner and *In Our Time* by Hemingway.

She was first and last a short story writer and even in that form not one to flood the market with this and that. Short stories, as a practical matter, are, along with poetry, a small business, and as such they are the object of a certain sentimental honor—a little like the honor a big and prosperous dress designer may accord the coat-lining and button manufacturers who hold on in the back streets of the enterprise. It is not felt one can really survive this way. And, in addition, most of Katherine Anne Porter's stories appeared in small literary magazines, among them *Hound & Horn*, *The Virginia Quarterly Review*, and *The Southern Review*. Indeed, *The Southern Review* was the main publisher of her work, right up through the stories in her third collection, *The Leaning Tower*.

Faulkner and Fitzgerald could put their financial, if not their artistic, hopes in the possibility of acceptance by a mass magazine such as *The Saturday Evening Post*. Of course, a lot of aggressive tinkering went on in those offices, and there the serious writer had to face a most puzzling question: Who reads the story after it's finally in print? Everyone who counted read *The Southern Review*, and if at the height of her fame and for her longest story, "The Leaning Tower," Miss Porter came out with $300—well, that was her career.

During these years her publishers, Harcourt, Brace, helped her along because it was decided she should write a novel. That was it. And this became a sort of comedy, a comedy with a very long run. The novel, *Ship of Fools*, was published when its author was seventy-two years old, and by that time Mr. Harcourt and Mr. Brace had gone on to their reward and a subsequent publisher had had some years of worry about his investment. But in the end, Katherine Anne got hers—a million dollars. Late, no doubt about that, but quite a lot of fun nevertheless.

Katherine Anne Porter was born in 1890 and lived until 1980—that is, she lived to be ninety years old. The attainment of this great age still does not seem quite suitable to this beautiful, blown-about woman who was unsettled the whole time, not hardy and not self-preserving in the matter of health. She smoked for as long as her breath held out, drank when she felt like it, and when she could afford it planned to live, as they say in Texas, "high on the hog." She practiced all her life the many diversions thought of as feminine: clothes, cooking, spend-thrift sprees, pretty houses, four marriages, more lovers, and certain airs of the flirt.

All of this was a sort of improvisation. She did not have the lucky, sedentary fortitude of Colette or, on the other hand, the cascading nervous energy of Virginia Woolf. Yet she was an *artist*, a word I remember her using often. I think it meant a kind of waiting, not properly, or at least not always, to be understood in her case as pro-crastination. The perfection of her stories, the extraordinary simplic-ity and freshness, was hard work, but I am not sure she had the idea of summoning them by hard work. They were, for the most part, begun, put aside; and when they were taken up again, I imagine she felt a surprise that there was something already there, and so in a rush of inspiration each was finished.

For the rest, for the day-to-day, there was the charm of her blue-gray eyes and her striking white hair. There was her somewhat overdressed fluffiness and the almost hallucinated attraction she felt for the *expensive*. It was like a gambler's compulsion. I remember 1952 in Paris, at the conferences and performances arranged by the Congress for Cultural Freedom. In her hotel room she showed me a purse—or rather a "pocketbook," as both of us spoke of it—that had cost hundreds of dollars, hundreds of the old dollars. She said: Would you like it if it were cheaper? And I said yes. Then she said: But you see I wouldn't. Then I'd have to think twice.

Also at that time we sat together for a performance in a concert hall. Just across from us was a very old lady, a well-known American expatriate, who was a fright to behold. Katherine Anne looked at her and said: If I looked like that, I'd kill myself. She herself was then past sixty, and I did not feel she meant any soulless contempt for the unsightly old woman. Horribly, I believed she was stating a plain truth.

None of this struck me as unworthy of the greatly gifted writer, no more unworthy than jogging or playing squash to keep in trim. It was her idea of the preservation of the flesh. And little could be held against her since nothing worked: not the husbands, not the lovers, not the often disappointing houses. I cannot think of anyone more truly independent. If there was egotism involved, independence is no less real for being something you're left with after you've sloughed off every protection.

There was never anyone except herself. When husbands got in the way, she ran off, ran off literally. Her life, for all her passion for the Vermont marble dining table and at last the greatly longed-for emerald ring itself, by way of the success of *Ship of Fools*, was one risk after another. Always on the frontier; always, it seemed to me, very American, an American traveler with a wide range of experience. Not one of her stories is provincial. She was from the first unaccountably sophisticated. The hardscrabble hill of her youth did not leave its mark on the line, on the paragraph, or on the purity and fineness of intention.

She was born in Indian Creek, Texas, on a failing farm and into a family disrupted by the death of her mother when Katherine Anne was not yet two years old. The house on the farm was a two-room log cabin, and while this is a historic frontier structure—bringing to mind another gifted prose stylist, Abraham Lincoln—its challenging presence in Joan Givner's recent biography acts as a stick of dynamite on Miss Porter's later substitution of a more promising setting for herself and family. For instance, she created as her childhood and past the idea of plantation beginnings, all ravaged of course by the Civil War, but filled with precious memories and the persistence of style, the style of the old agricultural aristocracy.

Her father was a feckless and apparently troubled man, but far from being a backcountry illiterate. It appears that he was not quite rural enough by temperament to hold on to his land, and he seems if anything a failed cavalier. The children were raised by their grand mother, and when the old lady died, Katherine Anne was sent to live with an aunt in Buda, Texas.

Buda, Texas, was dull and dispiriting, but the experience of life on a poor farm was greatly useful to her work and served her in the Mexican stories as well as in others. In her first published story, "María Concepción," the living fowl slung over a young girl's shoulder "wriggled their benumbed and swollen legs against her neck, they twisted their stupefied eyes and peered into her face inquiringly."

In "Noon Wine," the brilliance of the conception is enhanced by imagery of a perfect assurance. "The churn rumbled and swished like the belly of a trotting horse." She knows that "slopping hogs" was a hired man's work, killing hogs was a job for the boss, and "woman's proper work was dressing meat, smoking, pickling, and making lard and sausage."

The human landscape of Texas, before the discovery of oil, was a rather unstable social mixture that gave it a special complexity and richness. There was a Southernness in the dying cotton farms and a westernness in the ranches. Protestants and Catholics, Germans and Mexicans, tough, hard-drinking men, and a bourgeoisie wondering about a suitable presentation of its daughters. Katherine Anne's father, if not a prosperous or even a sensible guide, somehow sent her and her sister to be day students at a sort of finishing school in San Antonio. Here they were given singing lessons, practice in dramatic readings, among them Shakespeare recitations, and instructed in some of the lighter refinements of deportment.

But at sixteen Katherine Anne was on her own, entirely responsible for herself, and we see her setting out with the marginal, genteel hope of making a living by giving lessons in elocution and the like. There is a special sadness in this since the frills were meant to decorate a daddy's girl from the ranches and not a young woman in real poverty and desperation. And the pitiful superfluity of the training for Katherine Anne, who was not a cow-eyed shuffling girl of the earth but, for better or worse, a belle from the cradle. Of that one is certain.

So she married right away and into a large German-American ranching family. This was unsuitable, the most unsuitable part of it being the "perfectly nice" young husband, John Koontz. She stayed seven years, the longest she ever managed and the length certainly to be laid at the door of her youth. Then she fled, penniless. And her real life began. And hard, uncertain it was.

She went to Chicago and hoped to get into the movies and had only the smallest success. After that there are wanderings back to Dallas, work as a reporter on the *Fort Worth Critic*, then on to Denver and the *Rocky Mountain News* and near death in the influenza epidemic of 1918, a pestilence that claimed both of Mary McCarthy's young parents. This death threat is the source of her extraordinarily moving "Pale Horse, Pale Rider." Ultimately she came to New York, went to Paris and Germany, knew all the writers of her time: the typical frame of a between-the-wars American author.

"Hacienda" came out of a sixteen months' stay in Mexico, although it was not completed until after she had set sail by way of Veracruz for Germany with the man who was to be her third husband, later divorced. The journey became the setting for her novel, *Ship of Fools*, written much later. The gap between experience and creative use was typical of her life, but that is not unusual even if there is something unsettling about being in Europe while catching up with Mexico and, for that matter, Colorado; she took up "Pale Horse, Pale Rider" once more because Switzerland brought the scene back to her. One of the distresses of a writer's life is that he or she is always behind—overdrawn at the bank, you might say.

"Hacienda" is the most ambitious of her Mexican stories. It is a daring conception, perfectly realized. Mexico after the revolution, the landowners, the peons, actresses, songwriters, middlemen, the cameraman, the director, based on Eisenstein (offstage with a sore throat most of the time), are captured in an atmosphere at once feudal, backward, and sleazily modern. It is a film set, not constructed but found waiting in a broken-down estate where the horrendous liquor pulque, the drink of the Mexican poor, is made. The sickening smell, the peons at dawn loading the casks on the backs of their donkeys, the boredom of waiting for the light or for the actors, the complaints, the slow, sluggish life the revolution has failed to enliven, the guns and horses, the crowded railway train: all of this descends like a poisonous vapor on the tragic landscape. It is a large story with a large cast and unfolds without hesitation.

Reading over the Mexican stories, I see in them the old impulse to find oneself and one's country by being an American someplace else—the South Seas, Italy, England, Spain. "Flowering Judas" and "Hacienda" and "That Tree" are, I notice, also in some manner impersonal. The author is not a heroine in search of herself, in search of love, or in flight from love. Instead she is in Mexico, and sometimes in Mexico with other Americans, looking on with a calm, unhurried eye, observing and abstracting from the flow in a masterly way.

Braggioni in "Flowering Judas" is seen as a corrupt, florid revolutionary a bit past his prime as a leader and as a man. He strums his guitar, scatters coins in the streets, puts on his ammunition belt, tries to seduce; and then he turns native, Mexican, a local, not a foreigner. That is, he goes home occasionally to fall asleep beside his wife. He is a small-time figure of radical upsurge, a spot in the history of the moment, and still recognizable fifty years later.

A young woman, Miranda, appears in a number of the American stories. The pages have the accent and rhythm of the autobiographical, of the remembered, and we feel Miranda is an "I"—no less so in spite of the transformations of fiction. Since the author's family circumstances were uncertain and troubling in a manner not quite that of the southern "old order," we see that the fictions draw upon a more traditional, romantic atmosphere than the facts, the autobiographical facts, would warrant. But what is truthful and saving in the southern scene is the modern sensibility that determines Miranda's resolutions: the need for flight, the recognition of the decline into shabbiness of the once dashing Uncle Gabriel, the pervasive sense that family memories are themselves by nature idealized and that by the passage of time the unacceptable is dramatically shaped and softened or heightened into the acceptable. Funerals and photographs, graves and anecdotes transform, and common memory is itself a form of fictional creation. The stories end on a dying fall. "Let them tell their stories to each other. Let them go on explaining how things happened. I don't care."

"The Leaning Tower" is a *pension* tale, the setting of travelers. The time is 1931, Berlin. Katherine Anne Porter was in Berlin that year, staying on alone in what her biography shows to have been a setting very much like that of the story. The major transformation of experience is that she has made the central character a young man, Charles, a painter from Texas. This is in no sense a creative strain. The brilliant, powerful "Noon Wine" is the story of three men as harsh, tormented, and driven as we can imagine. A hard knowledge of the world in extreme, masculine dilemmas was part of the knowledge she brought to fiction. So it was her good luck after all not to be quite as she would have wished—a southern lady. Instead she was a homeless wanderer, bereft in spite of the satin pillows she thought suitable for the resting of her head. She had a bitter, strong understanding of desperate happenings.

The style throughout her writing is truly a triumph. She seemed from the beginning to be in possession of a magical assurance of tone and image. She is clear and exact; fresh, never mechanical. Nothing is insisted upon, nothing is jarringly decorative, and yet nothing is journalistic. Her fluency is always there to be called upon: that is the way the pages read. Language, landscape, and sudden image fall into place. The psychology is acute, undogmatic, and enduring and under the protection of an aesthetic intelligence unusually discreet and wise.

So, after the stories upon which her splendid claim was founded, she published her long novel, *Ship of Fools*. It was a success—or was it, really? The book sold enormously, was bought for the films, the first reviews were serious and extremely favorable, and the novel is ambitious, extraordinarily well written and interesting. It is 1931 again, and the scene is a ship going from Veracruz to Bremerhaven and, of course, moving toward all that we know from history was to be the Germany of Hitler. A ship is a structure designed to hold human variety for the fixed time of its passage. The fixed scene is both felicitous and threatening to the passage of novel-time, and so there is something claustrophobic in the conception of characters who cannot, unless they fall overboard, do much more than repeat their gestures. On a ship there will, of course, be a long list of characters who will need to be varied enough to daunt the most experienced novelist. This "ship of fools" is no exception. It floats on with a large cast, among them a lone Jew, a charmless person who does not command our sympathy. He is vulgar and, worse, he makes his living selling Christian religious objects, such as rosaries.

Criticism followed the initial enthusiastic reception. It was felt that the book was not up to the historical challenge it posed. The portrait of the Jew was naturally resented—the ship was, after all, making its way to horrors ahead. Thus, by the appearance of a number of vehement objections, the pleasure the success brought her was quite seriously flawed.

Katherine Anne's great age, achieved as it was after a youth of tuberculosis and a life of bronchial troubles, astonished all of us. But live on she did and live to find time for follies, indiscretions, and misbegotten chatterings. Her first two marriages seemed to have gone by like the wind, but she did not suggest that the winds had been useful and it is hard to believe they were. She brushed them away, a bit of ruffling on her coat sleeve. Allen Tate used to say: "Who knows, there might have been yet another husband dropped off somewhere." And this was a kind of admiration, and certainly fascination.

Still, still she never lost her inclination to romance or showed hesitation about fanciful enthusiasms for younger writers, assistants, and companions. In this she brings to mind an ancient *belle époque* figure who, when asked at what age a woman was finished with love, replied, "Ask someone older than I am."

As I look back over the late attachments I knew about from gossip or otherwise, I see in them a conscious and careful make-believe. And certainly a rich and confusing mixture of intentions. Katherine Anne knew the impossible when she met it; and if she was a rather beseeching nest builder, it would have been a naive, foolhardy person, imagining himself at an advantage by age or other perquisites, who thought she was ready in fact to offer a snug accommodation. Thus there was a noticeable resilience after an amorous failure, if failure is the proper word. Someone always turned up.

Her stories are not large in number, but there are quite enough of them to honor her just reputation. A confidence of structure, an unpretentious, unstrained gift for language combined in her talent with a worldly eye for the shape of things rural, native, and foreign. As a fiction writer she gained from going here and there and never quite wanting to stay. Her superb stories are the happy legacy of a hard life that spanned almost the whole of the century.

1984

THINGS

FICTION has from time to time concerned itself with one of the worldly ruling passions, that is, the love of *things*, those specially treasured objects large and small, collected, and polished, to be arranged in a pleasing design or merely to be assembled as items of property. As part of an imagined setting, the things will have movement as they fall under the same drifting shadows and illuminations that accompany the drama of love between human beings.

The objects perform; they take their place on the stage and are subject to action and counteraction, to the aesthetics of fictional structure dominated by character, by surprise, reversal, and ambiguous resolution. It will usually turn out that passionate possessiveness is singular, even if the possessors are a family. It is not psychologically transferable since the objectified passion has itself become character, a summation of wishes, commands, and regrets. The possessor must at last come to an end while the things live on in the mute, appealing obduracy of the inanimate. The decline of one and the endurance of the other is plot.

It is one of the advantages of life over the construction of art that things may come and go in the heart, be surrendered, reduced by subsequent passions, or passed on without too painful a clinging. When things are the definition of being, they will have in fiction a moral aspect, often of some murkiness but nevertheless of a moral dimension in that lessons of behavior, appropriateness, solicitude, and fidelity are profoundly involved.

The treasuring of chosen things is quite different from greed, which is by its nature profligate in its wide absorptions. The collector, the creator by assembly of a sort of landscape of images corresponding to a vision, experiences willingly the penury of selectiveness, of exclusions and renunciations ordained by the unconscious as well as by a certain amount of knowledge, experience, by historical and even by "household" scholarship.

In all of this there is the expectation of the melancholy interlude—the melancholy and defeat that arrive when the things encounter helplessly the eye of others who are not in love or who commend the amorous display in a manner of impugning relaxation that is dangerous to the integrity of the single-minded.

Henry James's *The Spoils of Poynton* is a peculiar drama of windswept objects buffeted about by a storm of desire, fear, exigency; by calculations that grow into a frenzy of manipulation exercised without irony. The author and the reader will feel a measure of sympathy, or at least not a withholding of sympathy, for the treasures endangered, the purchases and placements and the creative will of the one who has collected. It might be said the collector has breathed life into the things by a sort of naming, as Adam in being given the power of naming the creatures of the earth has thereby asserted his dominance over them.

Mrs. Gereth, the mistress of Poynton and of the possessions that she has with careful and studious passion assembled there, is alerted to the despoiling future by the sudden importance of one coming from the domain of the tasteless. Taste is nearly always comparative and identifies its presence by the vast absences surrounding it. Mrs. Gereth has seen an estate called Waterbath, a dreadful and assertive place that is the home of the young girl her only son is attracted to and will probably marry. Her heart is appalled and the future of Poynton is vigorously menaced.

"What was dreadful now was the horrible, the intimate ugliness of Waterbath," Mrs. Gereth had said with a sob. This collector is, of course, a fierce environmentalist and believes her future daughter-in-law cannot escape the almost genetic taint of the "trumpery ornament and scrapbook art, and strange excrescences and bunchy draperies" that are the girl's familial style. Mrs. Gereth will try, with a good deal of heavy maneuver, to lead her son's affections to a clever negative, that is, to a plain young woman who has no possessions, no background, and is therefore a conveniently empty vessel into which the instruction offered by the reigning things can be poured without effort.

But what are the things, the spoils, so ardently brought to Poynton by the palpitating acceptances and rejections of Mrs. Gereth? Here, a descriptive difficulty is likely to inhibit the novelist. In his plot, cabinets, rugs, boxes, and tables are instruments. Their actual shape and hue can be a rather tedious challenge. Charm, workmanship, and a reasonable sort of rarity are asserted. The plot is concrete, but the things themselves are generalized, seen in the gross, as it were.

When we first enter Poynton, Mrs. Gereth addresses the girl who is free to develop "natural taste" because large lacks have saved her from bad taste, by saying with emotion, "Now do you know how I feel?" The line, spoken in the entrance hall as the door is flung open, is the utterance of the perfectionist, the patient and prudent artist of the household. The eye is directed to the discrete vision prepared for it and in this instance there will be no fear of inattention, of the wounds of the hurried, dreaded "formulas of admiration," as James calls them.

But, again, what precisely are the things? As you turn the pages in pursuit you find a Spanish altar cloth, a Venetian lamp that lights up "an admirable tapestry." There is "the great Italian cabinet" and a "sofa dressed in old velvet brocade." And at the end, the supreme *find*, a Maltese cross, "a small but marvelous crucifix, of ivory, a masterpiece of delicacy, of expression and of the great Spanish period."

The crippled execution of the objects does not diminish our belief that the things are fine, handsome, difficult to come by, and assembled with strong emotion. The hesitant description is part of the experience gained in the writing of prose fiction, an experience that understands the forlorn inexactitude of adjectives and rhythms trying to stand for themselves alone, separated from the psychological rope that attaches them to feelings and actions of human beings.

Mrs. Gereth is a morally ambiguous person in the novel because the possessions have made of her an analyst too complicated and angular for ease. They have told her that she can leave nothing to chance and that, if one would perpetuate a setting, a far-reaching control over recalcitrant persons must be attempted with all the beady-eyed attention to detail that formerly operated only in old antiques shops. But she is not despicable in her desperate attentiveness. She is right, in terms of the novel, to see the "dreadful" house of the approaching daughter-in-law as the emblem of a corrupt sensibility. Her own "beautiful things" suggest a Platonic, if flawed, connection to Beauty. She may be monstrous on behalf of the ideal, but there is pathos in her inevitable defeat. The things will without fail attach themselves to the indifferent daughter-in-law who will want them, insist upon them, if only because they are "hers" by way of the will of the elder Mr. Gereth. The spoils are transferred, left to be watched over by negligent, newly hired caretakers, and the house burns down. So, what you have at last is not a tragedy, but rather a bitterness of experience.

D. H. Lawrence wrote a brief story called "Things," which is about a young couple from New England, "with a little money," who go at the end of World War I to live in France and then Italy. They want to be free among beautiful surroundings and to make of themselves a sort of creation. They begin to buy things, a way as they see it to absorb the essence of Europe. Their Florentine apartment is carefully done and charming, and their acquisitions seem for a time a renovation of themselves, erasing their American roots.

Again the "things" are of a generalized value and attractiveness. "Curtains of queer ancient material that looked like finely knitted silk, most beautifully faded down to a sheer soft glow." They have a Venetian bookcase, a Bologna cupboard; they have bronzes, fine tables and chairs "picked up in Paris." But at last they grow bored with their setting, with Europe, and they return to America, where their income will not allow a place large enough for the things, which must then go into storage. The husband is forced to go to work and the couple ends up in "their up-to-date little house on the campus of Cleveland University and that woebegone debris of Europe, Bologna cupboard,

Venice bookcase, Ravenna bishop's chair, Louis Quinze side tables, all were arrayed, and all looked perfectly out of keeping, and therefore very impressive."

Lawrence is hard on his New England couple with their dreamy "idealism," their superficial culture, their proneness to disappointment in the rock-hard, ancient European character that will not long correspond to their picturesque sentiments. In this story, the "things" are not the object of tragic obsession as they are with the mistress of Poynton. Still, in the descriptive generality one might note that the young couple's objects are similar and that the listing of them will furnish the mind with only the shadow of materiality. Chests and curtains are visual, and only some extraordinary attribution to which we, the reader, attach value can confer substantially on the page.

Balzac's Cousin Pons is a collector of a different degree. He is an innocent, harmless assembler of genuine masterpieces, and the collection will turn him into a humble, suffering victim of the greed and predatory fury of others. Pons is an ugly, aged, impoverished man, a failed composer, with some good, but not very forthcoming, family connections. Pons has only one vice and that is the love of good food, which he cannot provide himself and must seek at the usually unfriendly table of relatives and former friends.

His passion for collecting had begun long ago with a *Prix de Rome* that did not make him a famous composer. Still, Rome itself turned him into a collector, a shrewd and passionate one of small means and certain scrupulosities, one of which was that "the finest object in the world had no existence, so far as he was concerned, if its price was 300 francs." By persevering for forty years, Pons has assembled over 1,700 specimens. At first we hear of credible bibelots, miniatures, and snuffboxes. And we accept the delicate little fan, painted by Watteau, and offered to a scornful, ignorant relation in the hope that she will continue to let him dine at her house. The plot is set by the Watteau fan.

If other novelists may be thought of as embarrassed in the face of reputed treasures and therefore remote and vague about their shape and ornamentation, Balzac is very much the opposite. On the wages of his appalling industry as a writer, he had pursued "curiosities" himself with a rather haphazard elation.

As the story of Cousin Pons proceeds we find that he is the owner of sixty-eight pictures, fourteen statues, large buffets holding bric-a-brac, sideboards covered with the "choicest treasures of human toil—ivories, bronzes, carvings, enamels, jewelry, porcelains," and on and on. It is when we come to the masterpieces that we feel there has been a laying on because their names promote visions and values in no need of description.

Among the pictures are a Chardin, a Hobbema, a Fra Bartolommeo, a Dürer, a Knight of Malta portrait by Sebastian del Piomba. Later we learn there is a Greuze, a Breughel, a Claude Lorrain, and a Metsu. And so poor Pons, a man of perfect, almost feckless innocence and loneliness, has indeed been a sort of Catherine the Great with his 100-franc deals. We may question the author's wisdom or see it perhaps as unedited enthusiasm.

The old bachelor's inner life is not ruled by his collection to the detriment of other sentiments. His passion does not appear to be directed toward the world; he is not making a perfect country house or a thrilling Florentine apartment. The things are treasured for themselves—and even that is not quite accurate. We do not know why Pons, doomed to be the leader of a small theater orchestra and accepting the fate with modesty, should have in his youth been so greatly alert. He is not to be thought of as the weaver Silas Marner, with his little hoard of secret gold coins to brighten his lonely evenings.

The quality of the collection of Pons we have to accept as in some sense accidental in spite of his shrewdness and endurance. Perhaps the accumulation is to be connected with his *gourmandise*, that need which lets him sits unwanted at tables weighted with the excess wines, fowl, desserts, and liquors of the Empire. Balzac says that "his small means and his passion for bric-a-brac condemned him to an ascetic diet abhorrent to his hankering appetite."

The fate of the 1,700 specimens will have nothing to do with the wishes of Pons. Instead he is almost murdered by the collection and can see death only as a relief from the torments it has brought to his bedside in the person of a criminal concierge, a malicious lawyer, and a crafty dealer, and, of course, his unworthy relations, who finally secure it and use it as a tribute to themselves as if it had been they who were the origin of it.

Treasures do not fare well in fiction. There is something of a dangerous hidden hoard about them and they leave behind them at best an ironical twist and at the worst the triumph of the wicked over the good.

Taste, of course, is the element that gives the "bric-a-brac" its dramatic power. And taste is not a characteristic with the firmness of courage, loyalty, or honesty. Its arena of consequence is limited. In Swann, Proust created a man of taste, knowledge, and refinement who touches our deepest feelings when he deviates from his own standards under the domination of carnal passion. For Odette, his ignorant, shallow, and beautiful love, he cannot alter the pure contents of his mind, but he can, by way of the devices of the connoisseur, grow into an almost pleasurable acceptance of Odette and "that bad taste which she displayed on every possible occasion."

Odette sees the interesting and complicated aristocrat, the Marquise de Villeparisis, in the street wearing a black woolen dress and a bonnet with strings. She cries out, "But she looks like a lavatory attendant.... You'd have to pay me money before you'd get me to go around Paris rigged out like that." Swann will need to bow to that, with, of course, a pained smile.

In fiction, the pretentious and the ambitious are usually denied an understanding of genuine simplicity and they are inclined to make outstanding mistakes of "placement" when confronted with it. In the same way, the carefully ordered "things" at Poynton and the Watteau fan, "a little trifle," offered by Pons, live in the world with all the vulnerability to bruise and rejection of living creatures. They are actors in a morality play. And yet the acquisitions of Lawrence's young couple and the spoils of Poynton are at last only objects. Pons's snuffboxes and miniatures, among which his not entirely believable masterpieces reside, are also objects. The morality is ambiguous. The pain of the denouement, the final distribution, you might call it, arises from the way in which the human contract has been strained and things and persons confused as in a troubled dream.

1983

PIETY AND POLITICS

ELECTIONS

THE LANDSCAPE of America seems often like one of those endangered kingdoms in old sagas. Nightly, Grendel steals upon the knights sleeping in the hall and slays the fairest and the weakest alike. The siege, chronic, of change is one that we live with—and so we are never quite sure what has come upon us. Are we in the midst of destruction or renewal? Have we been blessed with something better: or have we, instead, merely a replacement?

The mind cannot hold the memory of the old corner before the supermarket came about, cannot remember the seemingly eternal mortar and brick that stood upon the bare land that is now a parking lot, the space that is waiting, as if under the dominion of a lawsuit in chancery, waiting with its automobiles in rows for some final disposition of the property, some lucky mortgage of partnership. What was once a cotton field has become the pasture for a new appetite, or perhaps the flattened strip of an airplane landing.

Sometimes, dreaming, in the country when it is very quiet, in imagination the Indians return to the northern regions and you meet them, melancholy and still as the woods. But the unconscious is shrinking, and those who thought it triumphant did not see the sudden, unalterable obliteration of the past. We had thought—wrongly—that the past slowly, imperceptibly receded, leaving always its traces clearly visible in the new.

We hear and read that we, at this moment, "want" something, we—"the American people." We are also assured that there is a great deal we don't want: indeed, much we "won't stand for any longer."

All through the spring and early summer of this year, small towns and large cities saw the Candidates making their intense visits. They went in and out of television studios, arrived in a rush at motel or hotel for dinners held not so much in their honor as on their behalf. They appeared at the time of day, late morning or early evening, when the citizens are likely to be drinking and eating and hospitality may fall like Grace on the just and the unjust Candidate alike. They went in and out of private houses and apartment buildings, smiling on the like-minded and favorable, soliciting the unfavorable, looking for dollars and cents and names for letterheads and petitions. These persons, flying without cease in and out of states and towns, wish to be President. The Candidate is always saying to us: I wish to be your servant, but first I must, in some degree, be your master.

"Benevolent wishes," as Kant observed, "may be unlimited, for they do not imply doing anything." The mythology of our lives is murky just now; and one sometimes feels that to look inside is to gaze at a screen that is not perfectly adjusted, a mirror that gives up its images in a vertical or horizontal distortion. And what an effort it takes, what patience, to "get the picture."

The new, itself, is never safe from the Usurper, encroaching, with his brighter, more arresting, more puzzling promise. "What is the use of a newborn baby?" Benjamin Franklin asked. The wild question, pragmatism rampant, not quite serious, of course, was part of the old beginnings in the 1770s. Franklin's notebooks with the ruled categories for the thirteen virtues—Temperance, Silence, Order, *et al.*— nowadays would provide the maxims of a failure. Frugality is suitable to the Chinese, not to the American. Yet, a certain element of revisionism in the current air seems to lead back to a suspicion of spending and to the thought of dignified resignation and reduction. But we remember that surrender to circumstance is for others: amelioration and good luck and grand expectations are for ourselves.

What is he *for*? What is he *for*? This year, election year, if we could know what he is for, we could know whom to be *for*. No man thinks of himself as having a bad character; and so, in voting, we are voting for ourselves, for those hints from the Candidate that he somehow represents our own yes and no. Hazlitt wrote about William Pitt,

"With few talents, and fewer virtues, he acquired and preserved, in one of the most trying situations, and in spite of all opposition, the highest reputation for the possession of every moral excellence."

Americans have all become philosophers in politics. They have had to take in thoroughly the difference between appearance and reality, shadow and substance.

Sincerity and the gold of its eloquence: this virtue, limited in politics, is a sort of official philosophy at this time. Our sincerities are strongly attached to our prejudices. That we have observed. The virtue is real and profound, however, and it means something, even if one cannot always be sure just where it is to be applied.

The New World, the New World and its recurrences: When does the New World become the Old? Perhaps we are now the Old World, but in a new way. The long streaking highways, the grasses and flowering shrubs in the falling sun. The struggle for what we are newly to become, through our political leaders and through ourselves, brings to my mind the last race at the end of a day at the track. It is then that the stress of racing, the pain and pleasure of the enormous effort are finally consecrated. In the last minutes we feel the apotheosis of the sacrificial power of the horse and its Faustian contract with the jockey. The end comes suddenly. And soon a *tristesse* falls down upon the scene. The horses are led away to their rest—those creatures whose feelings about the race they have run are unknown to us. And so it is, in the political race for our love.

1976

MR. AMERICA

"When Congress met at the beginning of December the country was in a condition of utter disorganization. A new question
had been sprung upon it before men had had time to discover
where they stood or what the danger really was, or indeed
whether any real danger in fact existed.... And as one passed
southward, there could be no longer any doubt that the danger
was real. The whole country was frantic in its coarse and drunken
way with what it called its wrongs...."
—*The Great Secession Winter of 1860–61* by Henry Adams

George Wallace is one of those leaders whose destiny and strength
are not to be larger than life, but small and mediocre, cut to the very
scale of their followers, exceeding them only in shrewdness and energy.
The idea is not to disguise the smallness, the meanness even, but to
make of it instead the very moral and intellectual center of the appeal.
This is what they have in mind when they speak, these Wallace
people, so feelingly of "courage" and honesty. When you see Wallace,
short and plebeian and unvarnished, coming out of his plane or
mounting the platform for The Speech, the limits of his charm and
grace are apparent. Strangely, you do not feel relieved that he should
seem so—so nothing—and you do not feel gratefully superior. Instead
all his lacks are immediately disturbing, threatening. It is unsettling
to see that the usual bribes and corruptions of public life and power
do not interest him. It is the harshness of power Wallace seeks, not
its comforts. Nixon in his Fifth Avenue co-op, his family shopping
at Saks, the slow and steady rise of a young man from hardship to
country club, the apotheosis of a great Wall Street firm: here at least

is a man with an investment to protect. We are all familiar with the coldness, rigidity, and calculation of an acquisitive spirit. But Wallace seems something new: he seems to ask nothing of life except the prospering of his sordid ideas.

First of all, he is not a liverish descendant of Huey Long, nor, as he likes sometimes to suggest, a sort of Television Andrew Jackson. Huey Long in his pajamas, with his ready supply of bourbon, his costly new Louisiana state house, his passion for the football team, the glory of LSU, his share-the-wealth and every-man-a-king: these diversions are quite unthinkable for Wallace and we cannot imagine him breathing under any sort of popular, comical designation such as "the Kingfish." Wallace has chosen, or is doomed to express, in his own being and style, in his notions, the quintessential anger and misery of certain of the working people of our country. He has no ideas, no programs, that would alleviate misery; instead his aim is simply to give *expression* to grievance and to bring pain to his enemies. Private property, free enterprise—he believes in these, without especially caring for their rewards. And this is puzzling.

Wallace might easily have gone in for the kind of "self-improvement" —accumulation of advantages—we allow, even expect, from a successful politician, but neither he nor Lurleen ever stepped aside from an undeviating lower-middle-class glumness, discomfort, a faithful consumption of catsup and the more shoddy offerings of Main Street. Wallace in his plastic-like, ill-cut suits, his graying drip-dry shirts, with his sour, dark, unprepossessing look, carrying the scent of hurry and hair oil: if he were not a figure, a star, he would be indistinguishable from the lowest of his crowd. In Jersey City and Newark recently what struck me was this country boy's natural, easy union with the blighted industrial scene.

We learn from Marshall Frady's excellent book, *Wallace*, that when the new governor and his wife went to the mansion in Montgomery they brought nothing with them except their clothes. Frady first thought of his book as a novel, and in its present form a great deal of the original intention remains, giving the work an unusually imaginative quality. There is a palpable Faulknerian mood to the reporting.

The remembered—or taperecorded—dialogue has the sharp pleasure and truthfulness of fiction. Every upward, questioning "heunh?" of the candidate, every remembered joke of observers is put down by Frady in a fascinating swirl of outraged adjectives and disturbed adverbs. He says that Wallace is "curiously substanceless"; he is a "political Snopes," with a "dauntless, limitless, and almost innocent rapacity..."

Wallace's political career began in the vein of the more or less liberal Alabama politician, Big Jim Folsom. When, however, Wallace was defeated by a segregationist, he got the point—and he moved immediately beyond the local application of this new wisdom. He quickly understood race as the foundation of his political claim in Alabama and "the politics of the country." Wallace in Alabama is only the first act and it is the least interesting because of the widespread political devastation in the South. Georgia, a profoundly interesting state, is after all guided by Lester Maddox, a feeble seg, mincing about the beautiful Atlanta state mansion, suspiciously peering, with his fixed and yet frightened little eyes, into the maze of doctrine and possibility. Maddox, nerve pulsing up in him from the example of Wallace, made a national try at the Democratic Convention in Chicago and was quickly seen to be too great a fool, too embarrassing a national peculiarity, to survive in even the Chicago circus.

Wallace is not regional and is instead, if we can believe what we are told in the press and the polls, a serious "white trash" candidate. The term is not used here contemptuously; in my view, the pity and sorrow and the guilt of the times lies in just this terrible "trashiness" of the lives of our ordinary people. Wallace very fully embodies in his person and in his ideas the misery of the working class, its joyless patriotism, its stunting deprivations which are all the worse for being unknown to those who must endure them. One of Wallace's virtues, to his crowd, must be that political success has not put a distance between him and them. He met his wife, Lurleen, when he was buying a bottle of hair-oil in Kresge's to soothe his ducktail—a style he kept with him a long time, before deciding upon his present, reactionary but still very provincial clip—and there is nothing in the look of him all these years later that shows any desire to shuck off the social husks of the past. His energies have not been drained away by the Southern vice of snobbery, the desire to work up to the legendary genteel, the fantasy aristocracy. When he first tried to reach out and went up to New Hampshire he found the Yankees there "kinda overbred." Wallace's natural home would seem to be a seedy hotel with a lot of people in the lobby, and his relaxation a cheap diner. For all his knowledge of the counties and back roads of Alabama, his "Hi, honey" and his "How yuh doin'?" he is rootless in the extreme. This is his best preparation for his "historical task"—if indeed he is to have one. There is no sign of play-acting in his role; he is one with his natural constituency.

Wallace's unnatural constituents are foolish rightists of means and military idiots like his Vice Presidential candidate, General LeMay. That is, at the present time. If Wallace is to continue he may need to make a more prudent and thoughtful use of these groups. For the moment he is still alone. On the platform, in New Jersey, soon after LeMay had joined the ticket, Wallace hardly seemed to acknowledge that he was there; he referred to his co-candidate with almost rude brevity and pushed him back like some squat Hindenburg into a literal shadow, from whence came only the gloved handclaps and appreciative giggles of Mrs. LeMay. Wallace is perhaps impatient of organization and temperamentally unsuited to coalition. He appears to look upon his mission as a personal triumph and to be suspicious of the dilution of other groups and organizations. Frady quotes an old acquaintance: "He don't have no hobbies. He don't do any honest work. He don't drink. He ain't got but one serious appetite and that's votes."

Wallace's working class supporters are unhappy white people. But they, unlike the blacks, the unemployed of the Depression, the earlier immigrant groups, do not see their wretchedness in terms of some political or economic demand upon society. The prototypical taxi driver Wallace so often addresses as the vessel of popular wisdom is a tired, underpaid, cheerless American. He would like to make more money, yes, but he has no plan to invade the free enterprise system. The Wallace union member rages against his exhaustion, but he sees his unhappiness in moralistic terms. The narrow, difficult life he leads is a mystery to him. Someone's got to answer for the joylessness.

These men in the Wallace crowds work all week, but they do not earn enough money to have tranquility, choice, security, or to answer the constant demands of their families and their world for more money, more goods, more and more of that consumption which alone can confer a sense of inner worth. These whites are as badly educated as the blacks, but amazingly unaware of it. When a poor black welfare mother thinks of education for her children, she hopes for something more alive, original, and creative than the present public school system. The disgruntled whites, the Wallace voters, want to destroy their own schools. They will not share them with the Negro either personally or ideologically. Therefore, even when they have rid themselves of the blacks, they will have to "stomp on"—the kind of term they like—the free and inspired teacher, bottle up the flow of ideas, further degrade the already bad textbooks.

The white man comes home to his payments on the car, the mortgage on his house in the blank development, to his pizzas and cottony bread and hard-cover pork chops, to his stupefying television, his over-heated teenage daughter, his D-in-English, car-wrecking son: all this after working himself to exhaustion. He is sore and miserable and there is never enough money—and yet he is torn by feelings that what he has is of immense value and privilege. Everything tells him the car and the house and the pre-cooked dinner and the narcotic television are the glories of mankind and that he, himself, is the lord of creation, who will not take any lip from the Commies, the French, the UN, the Viet Cong. In an Alabama version, in Frady, of these conundrums of existence, a judge after listening to Wallace says, "Well, goddamn. We at the bottom of everything you can find to be at the bottom of, and yet we gonna save the country. We lead the country in illiteracy and syphilis, and yet we gonna lead the damn country out of the wilderness...."

The white men, the union members, get their strange feeling of value from the certain knowledge that America is the most powerful country in the world. In their inner being they connect with this power—no one more than Wallace—and yet they also connect with their misery and with that discomfort they cannot name, that cheerlessness beer cannot dispel because it comes from the fact that their existence is not satisfying. What good does it do you in your harassment at midnight, or at seven in the morning, to know that America is the most powerful country in the world? Somehow, if things were right, it ought to be more of a consolation. Wallace, in his own person, has the same joyless but angry life, the same energetic and empty existence. It is as if he were a sort of mythical bearer of the meagerness and the power of America.

The message is that the misery in the midst of plenty, the weakness in the land of power, is not a mystery but has its roots in the blacks, from below, and the educated from above. These working men blame their own sad hours at the plant or in traffic not on the unimaginably rich but on the unemployed Negroes roaming the streets and, as they see it, indifferent to many of the dampening claims and responsibilities taken on by the disgruntled white working class. Wallace in The Speech explains it all. The Kerner Report: "Why, it's you people, it's us who are responsible for the breakdown of law and order! It's you folks who got to pay these people to keep them from burning down the country." Wallace attacks the tax exemption of the foundations, but it is not the vast wealth that vexes him but the fact that this wealth is writing the hated "guidelines" that tell a white working man he must open his schools to Negroes, his housing development and his unions.

The union hierarchy has now undertaken a belated educational effort about Wallace's uninspiring labor record as Governor of Alabama. Yet which of the autoworkers needs instruction of this kind?

It is not wages or benefits Wallace brings with him. No, it is respect for the prejudices, resentments, and fears of disappointed whiteys, super-Americans, many of them, in the North, not so long ago Polish and Irish and Italian.

Wallace is a mean man. The only thing he excelled in beyond vote-getting was boxing. His rhetoric is shrewd in understanding resentments, but it promises nothing except the pleasures of winning a gang fight. There is a strange absence of class and political warfare in his call; it is replaced by the peculiar satisfactions of hand-to-hand combat. "Under the jail" with them, "rough 'em up," and "knock heads," and run down and run over and stomp 'em. "All that's got to stop!" he says. All that is nothing less than most of the civil rights of our society.

Neither the Republicans nor the Democratic Party has made a real effort to expose Wallace. The Vietnam war adds to Wallace's power: he's for it and so the Democrats cannot seriously be against him. Humphrey stands on civil rights, but he bows to no one in his hatred of demonstrators and hecklers and draft resisters. If Wallace should actually turn out to be less powerful than he appears it will not be due to the qualities of Nixon or Humphrey, but rather to the limits of Wallace's program as it is now conceived. Hatred of Negroes and their liberal allies—no doubt this is powerful stuff, but it is still a displacement. Something positive will be needed to fill the emptiness, even the relatively empty pocketbooks. For the moment they do not threaten the privileged; the program is only, in the end, concerned with ideas of exclusion. That would not seem to be sufficient forever. The movement will itself go "under the jail" or else take on new life in some unforeseen, wretched, and appropriate transformation.

1968

PIETY AND POLITICS

ALBERT Schweitzer in his marvelous book *The Quest of the Historical Jesus* writes about, or parodies, the rich, poetic manner of Renan's *Life of Jesus*:

> Thus he rode, on His long-eyelashed gentle mule, from village to village, from town to town. The sweet theology of love (*la délicieuse théologie de l'amour*) won Him all hearts. His preaching was gentle and mild (*suave et douce*), full of nature and the fragrance of the country.

The historical Jesus is never discovered. (Noack, a German scholar writing in the 1870s, thought Jesus was prone to ecstasy because he was born out of wedlock. De Jonge [1904] believed he had discovered in the Gospel of John that Jesus was between forty and fifty years old at the time of His first coming forward publicly. He was a widower and had a little son.)

The political rise of Jimmy Carter who, along with his family and members of his staff, asserts that he is "strongly committed to Jesus Christ" leads us, cheerfully, into the murk of the Christian past, into the cacophony of the Holy Spirit. And indeed theirs is a "born again" world—free and blithe and with the milky theology of a newborn baby.

"Its melancholy, long, withdrawing roar" was the only sound left of the great Sea of Faith for Matthew Arnold. Still the evangelical movement with its plainness, obstinacy, and intensity lives on. The "enthusiasm" rises in the summer conversion dramas, the altar acceptances of Christ, the murmuring encouragement of the communicants humming "Almost Persuaded." These practices maintain their hold here and there, with a few shapings and reshapings, with shifts that are not essentially doctrinal since the central belief is that salvation comes from faith in Christ alone. Changes appear as metaphor, and Christ keeps up, now a businessman, now a sort of early astronaut, a neighbor and best friend.

Jimmy Carter set forth on a period of "witnessing"—passing out tracts, preaching, witnessing in humble door-to-door missionary greetings, revealing his own strong commitment to Christ. He went from Georgia to Pennsylvania and Massachusetts, encouraging people "to receive Jesus Christ into their hearts and lives." On a call back home to his wife he said, "I feel as though if I walked across the street no car would even dare to hit me, because the Lord is with me."

The account above is from *The Miracle of Jimmy Carter* by Howard Norton and Bob Slosser. The Carter "literature" begins in such presses as Logos (New Jersey), publishers in Nashville and Waco, Texas, and finally leads up to the sayings of Carter, put out by Ballantine and called "*I'll Never Lie to You.*" These printed works are presumably presented for our scrutiny and yet the reading of them makes one feel a little sly and unworthy. This is especially true in the case of *The Miracle of Jimmy Carter* and the book by Ruth Carter Stapleton called *The Gift of Inner Healing.* True, here, because of the hasty promotion of questionable experiences and the presentation of the experiences and material in the most barbarous language.

The deep pathos and seriousness of the struggle to preserve fundamentalist beliefs in the nineteenth century naturally come to mind when one faces the biographical iconography of Jimmy Carter. Edmund Gosse's *Father and Son* is a perfect work of autobiography, one of the most beautiful and melancholy creations of memory and intellectual analysis. The elder Gosse and his wife were passionately serious members of the Plymouth Brethren sect. They were dignified, denying, studious people, living for their prayer meetings, their exhausting scriptural and historical investigations, their fervent, dourly demanding witnessing, their union in Christ. "My Father was in the habit of saying, in later years, that no small element in his wedded happiness had been the fact that my Mother and he were of one mind in the interpretation of Sacred Prophecy."

The awful element in the personal history of these evangelicals was that Father Gosse was an eminent zoologist, a well-known botanist and authority on small marine creatures. The term "intellectual agony" is exact as description of the painful state into which Gosse's excellent mind was thrown by the publication of papers leading up to Darwin's *Origin of Species*. Father Gosse's heart was broken and in a gray despair and dark scriptural mediation he came up with his own notion which, in his manic hope, he believed would leave the sacred Genesis whole and undamaged.

In answer to geological development, Gosse proposed the idea that God had created the surface of the earth in such a way as to give the structural forms the *appearance* of a slow organic development. The erosions and successions of the ages, the dense evolutionary evidence, had been "put in" by God, as it were, in the act of creation. The earth was like a backdrop drawn for the stage; the old house and new could be seen by the eye as the curtain went up. The press quickly fell upon poor Gosse and decided his theory meant that "God hid the fossils in the rocks in order to tempt geologists into infidelity." Carlyle was unsympathetic to Gosse's effort to heal the wounds of science. He said, "Lying is not permitted in this universe."

Doubt, discrepancy, and denial gave to many evangelicals a repressed and pinched aspect. As they stood on the street, telling the wind of their scriptural angularities, as they solicited pennies for their work, the Bible seemed to offer the ache of chilblains and the pains of rejection. Dreiser's opening paragraphs in *An American Tragedy*, with the little family standing by the portable organ, singing "How Sweet the Balm of Jesus' Love"—Clyde, very early, resents the fruits of a life deliberately narrowed and stripped. Behavior and dress, arbitrary in their signals, were thought to connect the drab exterior with the hidden illuminations of an inner life.

With the Carter family, evangelical faith appears in a much more practical light. Everything is "as natural as breathing" and the studious isolation of doctrinal particularity and Scriptural tangle is clearly absent. Indeed the evangelical value of religion for these people is found in the therapeutic—God makes you feel better. Extreme moments of recommitment are likely to appear as a pill for depression. It was the loss of the Georgia governorship in 1966, followed by a session with his sister Ruth, that set Jimmy Carter back into confidence and winning.

Ruth Carter had sometime before had a religious experience that restored her to mental tranquility after a time of stress. "She had a deep rooted relationship with Jesus that produced an unusual freedom and wholeness." Jimmy and Ruth talked together in a pine forest near Plains, Georgia. From *The Miracle of Jimmy Carter*:

> Dressed casually, even sloppily, he in khaki trousers and work shirt, she in slacks and shirt, they walked slowly and aimlessly, close friends down through the years, both blond, crinkly-eyed, often smiling.... Ruth told him how she had experienced the release of God's Spirit within her own spirit, the liberation of her being that had come, during a crisis point in her life, some years earlier at a nonsectarian Christian camp meeting.... They knelt there in the forest, brother and sister physically as well as spiritually, and they prayed together. They asked the Lord Jesus for the grace to conform more exactly to his will for their lives....

This experience helped Carter to concentrate on his second try for the governorship. He spent four years on it and he won. In his words, spoken out of a Pentacostal mood, he had "a sense of complete dependence on the Holy Spirit."

Ruth Carter Stapleton is a healer of "world-wide fame." Her attention is turned not so much upon the halt and blind as upon the troubled person who has suffered the usual or unusual traumas of family life, love, sex, depression, marital discontent. She sees Jesus Christ as a sort of psychiatrist addressing Himself to the torments of the "inner child who lives on the subconscious level." He walks about, free from history and legend, partakes fully of the Georgian idyll, and speaks in the language of Ruth Carter Stapleton.

Her scenes are small dramas, Christian case histories:

"... Mary Ann, look toward the front door. See it opening. See Jesus walking in."

He walks in and stands by the oil stove. "Let him come over to you and tell you how lovely you look...."

"Now, Mary Ann, let Jesus go over to your father...."

Mrs. Stapleton records counseling sessions with homosexuals, Jody, for one—"Handsome, twenty-two years old, warm, intense, and not at all 'effeminate.'"

Jesus says to Jody, "I don't want you to have problems. I want to take everything upon myself. I want you to see how strong I am. Lean against me."

Piety and successful ambition are the remarkable qualities of Jimmy Carter. By way of therapeutic invasions of the Holy Spirit, he has reached a confidence of a special kind. Confidence is a neutral quality, morally; politically it is the judicious measure, neither *under* nor *over*, that seems to work. "I have never felt that the Lord required me to run for president, or that I am ordained to be president...." Yet, he also feels that "there's no doubt in my mind that my campaign for the presidency is what God wants me to do." His wife says, "He was praying about whether he should run for the president and it came to him that God wants us to use our talents."

Piety and confidence and ambition have been revealed to the

public as qualities of the Carter family as a group. They tell, each of them, the same stories over and over. The effect is of a cool, calm, honest people quite in control of their feelings, people with nothing to fear from reporters or cameras. But piety and confidence and ambition may lean, gently or heavily as the occasion warrants, on the arm of "honest self-deception," a trait of character devastating to less pious colleagues. About Gladstone, Queen Victoria's religious, moralizing prime minister, it was said by the biographer Philip Magnus: "He conquered the hearts of the Oxford Tories by his exquisite courtesy and simplicity, by his childlike delight in their company and by a fascinating combination of complete sincerity and a seemingly unbounded faculty of self-deception."

"The will of God" is one of the ruffles political leaders baste onto their rhetorical garments whenever it can be made seemly to do so. Again Carter is in the intimate, obstinate "God's Will" tradition of the part, of Gladstone that could write: "Why has my health and strength been so peculiarly sustained.... In the great physical and mental effort of speaking, often to large audiences, I have been upheld in an unusual manner....Was not all this for a purpose? And has it not all come in connection with a process to which I have given myself?... appears to me to carry all the marks of the will of God."

The Carters astonish by their sunny intrepidity. Their faces, that of each of them, are wrinkled by the tracks of smiles. It scarcely seems possible that Carter and Wallace have lived in and come to represent the same region. The grievance and glumness of the Wallace people, their pinched, suspicious glances, are at once defensive and provocative. Wallace himself, now and before, has always seemed to be a mind buried in phlegm, swimming about miserably without any of the elation of freedom. It was said in Marshall Frady's book about Wallace that "he ain't got but one serious appetite and that's votes." This he shares with Carter. In the tornado the calm Carter has achieved, both Wallace and the Kennedys have been pulled into the vortex and whirled into fragments.

The Carter story, as it has been given to us, is a drastic condensation. Candidate, mother, wife, and staff call upon a thin store of memory and anecdote. Georgia village, simple people who have not forgotten rural hardship, familiar, easy acquaintance with blacks within the racist boundaries of the period, Admiral Rickover, Jesus Christ, determination to win in politics . . . It rolls on, automatically rewinding—soft, unpretentious, calm.

The family does not appear to see its story as anything more than its own affirmation. Still there are premonitory whisperings that others, enamored, hooked, may find in their goodness an accusation. The Carter folks exist not only for themselves but as a rebuke to the clever, the sophisticated, the celebrated, the worldly, the skeptical, the urban, the uprooted, the restless, the divorced.

Robert Coles, in a piece in *The New Republic*, even finds Atlanta already morally out of bounds, corrupt, decadent on the day after rebirth. "He [Carter] won, an underdog fighting the capital city boys, the big interests, the self-confident and well-to-do and proudly urbane Atlanta businessmen and bureaucrats, with their Brooks Brothers suits and revolving restaurants and exposed elevators, and plastic credit cards and guardedly liberal picties. . . ."

Only a few political families in some way work upon the national imagination as a composition, framed. The families come to represent an idealized possibility—the Roosevelts and the Kennedys were of this sort. The Carters promise to be also, and if they are too strict to inspire emulation, at least they can inspire in us a not very uncomfortable shame. Political persons must be from some place. The Carters are from Plains, Georgia, with a population of 680. The constant repetition of the number gives an idea of the awe in which it is held. This outstanding smallness is a fact of considerable symbolism, a good deal of it from movie sets which the clapboard storefronts of the Main Street in Plains helplessly, ruthlessly recall.

It is well to remember that the Candidate Carters have been

restless in Plains much as others would have been. When Jimmy Carter's father died, the son had been away for eleven years. He returned, set out for power in the state capital, and spent time in the governor's mansion there. His present destination is not a secret.

Nostalgia and sentiment, a nature prone to many sacrifices and yet alert to both small success and the grandest, highest ambitions. The romantic elements in Carter's history are fiercely contained within a profound attachment to things as he has always known them, to the people he grew up with. In his personal life there has been little ambitious experiment and there is a marked clinging to the familiar. Evangelical religion makes, against the example of Christ, family men in the fullest meaning of the term.

Outside of his own small group, the one person for whom Carter seems to have felt an agitated and preoccupying attraction has been Admiral Rickover. "He was unbelievably hard working and competent, and he demanded total dedication from his subordinates. We feared and respected him and strove to please him." Something of the Deity in Carter's Rickover and much that is Rickoverian in Carter himself —the fine-strung, compulsive organizing of things, the tense, tight control of detail.

The genuinely romantic aspect of Carter's character, the one deep claim he can make upon the country's emotions, is his accomplishment of a reconciliation between blacks and whites. Without this, enormous in moral signification and in political and historical possibility, without this he would be a curiosity, clearly narrow in intentions, one who combined in his own ways the humility and arrogance of the missionary spirit. Again, the blacks are recommended to his feeling by their familiarity, their being in a sense part of his family, his lifetime. He extends his loyalty to them, "naturally" as he sees it. If others find them mysterious and unknowable, he asserts just the opposite. Carter refused, under strong pressures also, to join the White Citizens' Council in the sixties, and in that way his attachments were put to the test.

It is interesting that he is free to speak of all this in his own language. The most compelling trait he has to offer has come about by the understanding, the love that issues forth—he claims—from the lived life of the South. That he could make this genuine, on no grounds but his own, is an unimaginable victory for the real. By his loyalty he has erased the ugly obfuscation of the symbolizations of "law and order," "crime in the streets," "welfare cheats," "busing." He has fit black reconciliation into his peculiarly distant, unquestioning, traditional evangelism, which as it appears in his thoughts knows no intellectual debts and certainly no political debts.

Love and the politics of love. In his acceptance speech, Carter said on this subject, "Now, I have spoken a lot of times this year about love. But love must be aggressively translated into simple justice." Love—isn't there something Southern in the word, in the oval shape of it? It is not easy to imagine Reagan or Ford attempting the articulation. In any case they are elocutionists of the negative, ardent in warning, fervent in surgery, secular in their commercial diction. Carter, uniting love and some, actually much, of his opponents' shudders at libertinage, is a mysterious figure, charismatic in his ascent rather than in his person. It is not love he inspires, but hope. And even the hope that attends him cannot yet entirely break free from its rooting in the arid soil of mere comparison.

1976

THE KENNEDY SCANDALS

THE PRICE of public life is the exposure of the follies, or worse, the disgraces of private life. Nothing new here—rumors, palace gossip, scandals whispered by the disaffected and the competitive, each sometimes adding false transgressions to a mountain of genuine turpitude. Macaulay writes of the "libellers" who, not content with a rich, damaging dossier on Napoleon, were in the habit of publishing "how he poisoned a girl with arsenic, when he was in military school—how he hired a grenadier to shoot Dessaix at Marengo—how he filled St. Cloud with all the pollutions of Capri." Still, nothing in previous history equals the powers available today, available and tempting to scandal: the discrediting accusation, the compromising revelation sent out without hesitation to the public—all in the friendliest way clanging and banging reputations like cans in the weekly shopping basket. And to this our times have added the playful hidden camera and the amusing bug on the bedside telephone.

Noting the large number of possibly loquacious deponents the public person is associated with for a long or a short time, one might expect a measure of prudence or caution. Instead these unprotected celebrities, when inclined to indiscretions of one sort or another, act as if they were anonymous citizens out having a good time. "Topless," a recent offering by a member of the British royal family, would not be remarkable if it were among a dour little group of nudists basking on a rock in some forgotten cove. There is a certain charm in imagining that the Duchess and her friend thought they were just two like any other. But, of course, people like others only for purposes of the occasion, since one would not wish to be anonymous for very long. Even the tireless Casanova, noting insufficient respect from one of his multiple partners, might rise up and say: Madame, do not forget to whom you are speaking.

The Kennedys: surely there is a note of tragic kingship in the calamities they have suffered. The death in World War II of the oldest son, the death of a daughter, Kathleen, in an airplane crash, the assassination of John, while President of the United States, and the assassination of Robert, perhaps to be a future president. That was then, long ago it seems; the present historical condition of the family is in many ways dismal indeed, with the males covered by bruises and welts as they are worked over in book after book, in atrocious items marketed as novels and memoirs, and in the jackal-like researches of the celebrity industry. The dead President left his mark on the Bay of Pigs, the Missile Crisis, the Berlin Crisis, Civil Rights, the Peace Corps—capital letter affairs for historians and commentators who have not failed to accept the challenge. For the entertainment of the public, there was the grand new White House style. The hospitality to the arts both sacred and profane, that is to music, the invitations for talented Americans and foreigners, along with attention to clothes and decoration, came from Jacqueline Kennedy, who is supposed to have said someplace that the only music Jack liked was "Hail to the Chief."

In the midst of all this, the *relaxation* that came to the publishing world began after the death of the President to show him as a voluptuary so extreme as to be almost humdrum, which is the way these obsessions may proceed, ever and wherever on to the next bout. With a prodigal intrepidity he attached himself to a possible spy, to gangsters and their molls, as some still call them, to many others here and there. And nightly the surviving family can hear the ghostly rumblings on the battlements as the tomb of Marilyn Monroe "wherein we saw thee quietly inurned, hath op'd his ponderous and marble jaws to cast thee up again." It must be said that some of the Kennedy men have been extraordinarily cooperative in the ruin of the family reputation, falling even into matters of criminal concern.

The Kennedy bibliography would seem to be of a sufficiency in regard to biography, statecraft, and "revelation." About his work *A Thousand Days* (and almost a thousand pages about a thousand days), Arthur Schlesinger writes that his book is a "personal memoir by one who served in the White House during the Kennedy years." He goes on in his preface to imagine someone, "perhaps a very young man," immersing "himself in the flood of papers in the Kennedy Library" and writing a fuller account of the Kennedy administration. There is such a book, newly published, *JFK: Reckless Youth*, the first of three volumes by Nigel Hamilton, an Englishman and author of an admired official biography of Field Marshal Montgomery. Hamilton meets one hope of Arthur Schlesinger's—he has been granted every privilege as the John F. Kennedy Scholar and Visiting Professor at the John W. McCormack Institute at the University of Massachusetts.

Reckless Youth is some eight hundred pages long and with much more to follow. Everything considered, some doubt about the usefulness of the project can be entertained. However, necessity, gap, lack do not always play a part in contemporary biography. Indeed, redundancy is the rule on the celebrated and even for those of a more narrow appeal such as poets, novelists, painters, and composers. Looked upon as a project, as something to do, the writing of a biography is not an unnatural attraction. After the interminable interviews, with sometimes pleasant travels here and there and new acquaintances picked up from the address book of the subject, after the shuffling of old newspaper interviews to which you have been directed by previous commentators, after the weaving of other books into one's own narration—after all that, tedious as it may be, the thing actually can be done. Industry rather than special talent is the clue.

Mr. Hamilton's biography moves through the Fitzgerald and Kennedy "Boston Beginnings," through boarding school, Harvard, service in World War II and the PT boat affair, on to Kennedy's election to Congress in 1946. There is much in these years that casts a blur on the gloss of the young knight and much that arouses sympathy for his suffering in drastic illnesses and his brave, and bravura, efforts to endure.

However, the biographer does a curious thing in his brief prologue. Here, with a somewhat suspicious impatience, he rushes to alert the reader to the belittlements ahead, a sort of coming attractions preview. In a flash-forward to the funeral, he lets drop, as it were, the President's venereal and Addison's disease, at that moment being covered up by the naval doctors at Bethesda. This along with a very arresting aside: the night before Kennedy's funeral Jackie Kennedy "had a call from the wife of the columnist Joe Alsop, in whose house her husband had committed his first adultery as the president of the United States, on the night of his inauguration." It's hard to know how to name a compositional strategy that introduces such a startling fact by an irrelevant phone call made long after. The provenance of the disclosure is a little murky, like so much of the scandal where possibility and actuality meet without a pause. Schlesinger's account of the night in *A Thousand Days* runs: "At a quarter to four in the morning the President-elect returned to his house in Georgetown from a supper given him downtown by his father after the Gala." However...

About the funeral, certain to make a strenuous claim on the biographer's art at the end of his very long enterprise, we have a bit of not so strenuous forewarning. Thus, the widow: "She had never possessed nor shown the meanest [sic] interest in politics, her husband's career, but despite the fact that her new Greek friend—and future husband—was staying as her personal guest in the White House, she now displayed a version of mourning that would have become Electra." The concluding phrase, taken from Eugene O'Neill's play, apparently came easily to hand, if not being a deft classical allusion for the circumstances of this American tragedy. Now, thirty years on, from all we are told by honest research and also by flamboyant exploitation of Kennedy's life, we might want to say that nothing became him so much as his funeral.

The early years, reckless among other things, seem to have had the promise and the defects of the Kennedy who became president when he was forty-three years old. On both sides the family was political from the beginning, political in the Boston-Irish tradition. There was a certain barroom, ward-heeler bonhomie in the group's practice, along with some spectacular diversions by Boston Mayor Curley, but in the end the pols smarted up and conducted themselves in a manner not so different from the Lodges, the Saltonstalls, and the rest. Old John Fitzgerald had served in the state and national legislature and been mayor of Boston. In this career he was sometimes opposed by Patrick Kennedy, the father of Joseph Kennedy, who would become ambassador to England under President Roosevelt and who himself thought of running for the presidency, an ambition forestalled by his egregious errors in the estimation of Hitler and the intentions of the Nazis. Except for the fortune made by Joseph Kennedy, virtually nothing engaged the men of the family apart from politics.

Jack can be thought of as having an ancestral obligation, like Pitt the Elder and Pitt the Younger, if that is not too high-flown a conjunction. For his son's political debut, the father is said to have spent perhaps more than three hundred thousand dollars. He said, "With the money I spent, I could have elected my chauffeur."

JFK: Reckless Youth—what does it add? It certainly adds pages, in an unconscionable number, of trivia, of parsing and repeating, filling in and filling out the accounts, themselves not quite sparse, available before. One thing it generously supplies is a large selection of letters between the young Kennedy and his boarding school friend "Lem" Billings, letters that even a pedant in the library stacks might wish had perished in a dormitory wastebasket. Many of them are "smutty," cold and careless in their obsession with "getting laid." On the other hand they outline a young man's, or a young person's, defiance of suffering in illnesses that arrived with a savage and pitiable monotony. Gonorrhea just after college, with recurrent urinary and prostate distress as a result; from youth extreme lower back pains later requiring at times the use of crutches, spinal operations in Boston and New York; and the cloud above it all, Addison's disease, an adrenal insufficiency finally diagnosed in 1947 after years of painful testing in the Mayo Clinic and the Lahey Clinic in Boston; after diagnosis treated with cortisone and other medication throughout his life. The mere listing cannot give the true measure of the long suffering. Robert Kennedy said about his brother, "At least one half of the days he spent on this earth, were days of intense physical pain."

The family naturally enough tried to avoid public exposure of Jack Kennedy's miserable afflictions. Later, when he was a national figure, spinal pain and evident weakness would be attributed to the stress of the "heroic" PT boat episode in the Solomon Islands. Arthur Schlesinger's summation, written no doubt with his best knowledge, gives the more or less official explanation for Kennedy's infirmities. "The shock of the collision with the Japanese destroyer in the Solomon Islands had torn his back, already weakened by the football injury at Harvard a dozen years before." On the matter of adrenal insufficiency, Schlesinger sees it as a minor form of the disease, "evidently induced by the physical strain of the long night of swimming and the subsequent malaria [PT boat incident], presented no serious problem." Perhaps nothing presented a serious problem to the Kennedys who, as the melancholy scholarship and published insinuations insist, combined a flagrant rapacity with a mastery of concealment and the absolving pretext.

It took a good deal of maneuver and evasion for Kennedy to be accepted by the Navy and to serve in combat in World War II—this success for once in a cause most people would consider worthy. In the Navy he achieved the post of skipper of PT (patrol torpedo) 109 on duty in the South Pacific. In the summer of 1943 the boat was sliced in two by a Japanese destroyer. Two of the men died and one was so badly burned by the explosion of the boat's fuel it was not thought he could be saved. As the vessel sank, Kennedy and the survivors set out to swim to land, with Kennedy pulling along the burned man by making a tow-line with his life jacket. The swim took four hours. A half hour later, seeing that the spot was not useful for signaling a passing rescue boat, Kennedy undertook another long swim, which proved futile, and he was forced to return. John Hersey described the feat in an article in *The New Yorker*, a feat which was seldom mentioned by Kennedy himself, according to Schlesinger.

The number of PT boat pins floating around the White House would cast some doubt on that, but there is no doubt that old Joe was ignited by the heroic account and arranged for a *Reader's Digest* condensation to fall like manna on the public. About the action itself, some thought it a disgrace of poor leadership that the boat should have been in a position to be attacked and sunk. One book claims that General MacArthur thought Kennedy should have been court-martialed, but later thought better of it, of the court-martial if not of the command of the vessel. Yet, hardly anyone denies the courage and endurance of Kennedy under the drastic challenge. "One of the authentic passages of heroism in the war"—Arthur Schlesinger.

Hamilton gives a full accounting of the naval training, service, the surrounding military scene in the Pacific. The gripping PT boat tale emerges; a difficult battlefront narration it is of surprise, panic, death for two, and extraordinary survival of the others. And then we find Jack indeed back home, a hero, if not of Silver Star quality, but with plenty of earned medals, "for the rescue if not for the action," to decorate the Oval Office. And back home we are, unfortunately, in for other feats of endurance.

A letter to his father, and its presentation in the book:

"When I do get out of here you'll find that you have a new permanent fixture around that Florida pool. I'll just move from it to get into my sack."

But the first sack he intended to get into was Inga's.

Setting off "Inga's sack" in a separate paragraph for dramatic effect at the end of a chapter is what might be called sleaze typography. In the case of the Kennedys, the atmosphere is so deeply infected with pollutants issuing from books and scandal sheets, perhaps we cannot expect a more reserved and stately command of locution from a Visiting Professor at the John W. McCormack Institute in Boston. Section headings in bold type of "Hot Screw" and "Tangling Tonsils with Inga"—we suppose they are meant to add a contemporary drollery to the old-fashioned practice of a three-volume biography.

As for Inga, yes, there is a lot of her and her archival place in history, which seems to rest upon the number of letters received and saved, the agitation she inspired in J. Edgar Hoover, and the historical analysis provided by her son. "If he [Kennedy] wanted to make love, you'd make love—now. They'd have fifteen minutes to get to a party, and she'd say she didn't want to. He'd look at his watch and say we've got ten minutes, let's go. There's a certain amount of insensitiveness, an awful lot of self-centeredness." Thus the bonny prince of libertines.

Inga Arvad, a Danish beauty, twice married, first to an Egyptian and later to a Danish film director. As a journalist for a Danish paper, she was sent to Germany and there met Hitler, who invited her to sit in his box during the 1936 Olympics. A photograph of the two turned up during her affair with Kennedy and was passed on to the FBI, who had already been "investigating" her when she was a student at the Columbia School of Journalism. The acquaintance with Kennedy came about from her friendship with Kathleen Kennedy when both were working for the *Times-Herald*, a Washington newspaper. The infatuation flourished rather longer than most owing to the hero's being in naval training and later service in the Pacific. It was a cause for concern on the part of the founding father, as he is known, and in the end Jack sighed, a little, as a lover and obeyed as a son. And that was that.

Hamilton has not yet, in his projected work, reached the astonishing moment, or moments, with Judith Exner Campbell. Her story, or *My Story*, is a most unfortunate one. To pass from Frank Sinatra to

Jack Kennedy to Sam Giancana, the Mafia boss, is to experience an erotic pummeling that would qualify her for recuperative nights in a shelter. Her distinction is to have "served" in the White House, in whatever closet or do-not-disturb room that could be commandeered for the occasion. In this she was not alone, but she was there. It is interesting to speculate about the more or less universal consent nowadays to impugn oneself in order to provide a revelation about another. On the afternoon interview shows you can see a handsome young woman, now married and with children, telling of her rape by her father, who is sitting there calmly, wearing a tweed jacket with leather patches on the elbows.

Judith Exner said that harassment by the FBI led her to tell her story in print. And there is always the spur of a little money to be picked up, since there is seldom any financial equity between the "servant," sexual or otherwise, and the master. On the other hand, self-validation plays a part, an insistence that one has really existed, a confounding of the sudden and complete erasure the powerful voluptuary likes to exercise at will. Her book did not appear until 1977 and thus was not able to surprise the President, who had been able to count on an unwritten contract between the press and the political celebrity not to print scurrility for the fun of it. Perhaps that was a time of greater civility and perhaps not. But it is gone forever.

The living Senator Kennedy, no guardian of his reputation, has just now after Chappaquiddick and the William Kennedy Smith rape trial, and much else, to see the Kennedy headshot that inevitably decorates these books on the cover of something called *The Senator*, written by a "gofer" who became a personal assistant. Indeed, another "shattered Idol" affair, somewhat gratuitous in that respect, but not without its novelty. Girls, girls, girls, three chicks in a hot tub, cocaine, a wearying round of injudicious revelry.

With Jack and Teddy we are not reading of sexual advances, a mere faltering and bumbling hope that can ruin a fellow nowadays, but of an advancing throng of eager females, a gleeful army ever to be the practical and theoretical discomfort of feminists. We seem to have monarchal privilege in a late resuscitation, even if the engagements are on the unremarkable side. Not one of the women has a secure place in palace history, with the exception of Marilyn Monroe, who may be thought of as our "Sweet little Nell Gwynn of Drury Lane," mistress of Charles II.

Here and there, it is claimed that Bobby Kennedy, more or less temperate in the service of the family vice, fell under the sway of the "goddess," only to find that she was also in the imperial mode and not so easy to dispose of. A seditious pest she could be, on the telephone at late hours, thinking of marriage itself to the President or to Bobby, then father of seven. In some accounts of the night of Monroe's death, we are to imagine Bobby rushing through the dark night from San Francisco to Los Angeles, as if on the ship *The Black Pirate*, to find the comatose body, take it off in an ambulance, then back to the house to be laid out nude with the pink, or perhaps white, telephone hanging, to be later discovered. So they say...or, no, perhaps he merely paid a visit to tell her "It was all over" and later in the grip of night the abandoned fairy princess reached for her pills. All in the grave, a three-act tragedy, not quite classical—farce sprouting on the frozen ground.

The elder Kennedy in Hamilton's words: "failed shipyard manager, failed Hollywood producer, failed diplomat, failed politician—but brilliantly successful Wall Street swindler,...without whom John Fitzgerald Kennedy could never have reached the White House." It is not altogether easy for those who have lived through the two past decades in American finance and who know of the previous "robber barons" and their interesting accumulations, to summon the proper moral indignation about Joe's ruthless dealings. At the Boston brokerage he entered soon after college, an early strike itself for an Irishman, he "learned the technique that would, several years later, enable him to save the New York Yellow Cab Company and earn himself a further fortune. Known as stock pooling, it relied on a conspiracy between traders who artificially bidded up a stock and then dumped it once the market had been duped into raising the price."

It is common for citizens to forgive shady fortunes as they more or less settle down into a conversion to houses, servants, motor cars, clothes, travel, and spoiled children who may not make a dime of their own, but who may, if they have a taste for it, enter public life or philanthropy. The elder Kennedy does not appear a pariah by force of acquisition and ambition so much as by extravagant investment in infidelities. His open alliance with Gloria Swanson included a rape, described, yes, with considerable descriptive fluency in *her* autobiography. Swanson visited Hyannis, and sailed for Europe with both Joe and Rose, circumstances that some believe passed on the father's conquering spirit to the sons. Whether there is a little philandering curl on the male gene is not known. Or perhaps it was just the claim of environmental example. Or the exceptional handsomeness of the sons that, like beauty in women, may set a fast pace.

Irish, Roman Catholic, Bostonian, men of Harvard. So peculiar is the Kennedy family configuration that genuine identification with all except Harvard can appear to need inspection. Joe was a graduate of Harvard, as were his sons, and, on the other side, "Honey Fitz" had been admitted to Harvard Medical School before he was required to withdraw on the death of his father. Both came by way of the public Boston Latin School, although the Kennedy sons went to boarding schools, such as Choate in Connecticut. According to Doris Kearns Goodwin's excellent book on the Kennedy and Fitzgerald families, among Joe's classmates at Harvard were Vincent Astor, "heir to the greatest fortune in America"; Herman Schwab, son of the Bethlehem Steel magnate; and Edward Atkins, "whose father was the Atkins of Westinghouse Electric." These young men, along with others of their sort, were "Gold Coasters," that is, members of the top clubs. Joe Kennedy was in the trough along with the great majority of Harvard students, but this did not deter a sense of awe for the club men, mixed with resentment, as is so often the case when awe arises from mere positioning in the scheme of things.

We are led to believe from most accounts that both Joe and Rose Kennedy felt the sting of Boston class snobbery. This was especially vivid and humiliating when they rented a large beach house in Cohasset, a community south of Boston, then "the private preserve of old Boston families." Membership in the Cohasset Country Club was sought, and after a waiting period, denied, even though at least one member of the committee liked Joe's "cut and attitude." The restrained and traditional manners of the Boston aristocracy, after the great minds had left the scene, displayed a structured and repetitive and treasured provinciality that allowed for the host of benign eccentricities for which they were known. A distinguished, rich old gentleman in his eighties, walking of a morning from his house on Beacon Street to the office on State Street—that kind of thing. Social acquaintance with such persons could hardly have been stimulating for Joe, whose eccentricities were of another order.

In some ways, the Kennedys seem to have drunk a glass of bleaching powder. They do not display a talent for colloquialism, turn of phrase, storytelling, imitations, the delights of blarney that enlivened the kitchens of the fine Boston houses, if not the drawing rooms. With the men humor and imagination are replaced by horseplay and boyish joshing. The outhouse brilliance of Lyndon Johnson when he needs a metaphor does not decorate, so far as we can read, the style of the naughty Kennedys. And who can imagine one of them saying, as Clinton did about the hamburgers and fries on the campaign trail: "I'm becoming as fat as a wood tick." With Jack Kennedy the rhetorical annals have to settle for *Ich bin ein Berliner* and "Ask not what your country can do . . ."—suitable prime minister famous quotations and delivered in the eloquent Boston broad-A accent that was part of the effectiveness and charm of the Kennedy sons. Even old "Lev" Saltonstall, not to mention Henry Cabot Lodge, was no match in production of the Boston style.

In 1926 the father moved the family from the small hub of the universe to the large hub, that is from Boston to New York, a move that left scarcely a scratch on the impermeable Boston fingerprints of the tribe, even though at the time Bobby was only one year old and Teddy had not been born. They moved to a house in Riverdale and then on to Bronxville, in Westchester, but twenty years later Jack ran for Congress in Honey Fitz's old Boston and mostly Irish district. He set himself up in the Hotel Bellevue, across from the State House, to face the slogans of the opposition: "Congress seat for sale—*No* experience necessary—Applicant must live in New York or Palm Beach—Only millionaires need apply." He won the office, after canvassing the Holy Name Society, the Gold Star Mothers, and by the strong appeal of his handsome brothers and sisters, by Rose, as a certified Catholic mother, and by the money and the shrewd instincts of the father, who set himself up in the Ritz Hotel, since he was not on the ballot although conspicuous in attendance.

Garry Wills, in *The Kennedy Imprisonment*, a brilliantly reflective and disillusioned, or illusionless, book, views the "Irishness" of the Kennedys as, for them, a handicap from which all their efforts were to escape. He points out that none of them married Irish and discounts the role of the many Irish cronies, as just that, not equals. But to America, the Kennedys are Irish, and if Jack was named the first "Irish Brahmin" that was a description meant to define an elevation, not a loss of their Irish heritage. Doris Kearns Goodwin sees the triumph in the congressional race as a happy appreciation on the part of the Irish poor for the spectacular rise in riches and power of one of their own.

Are Joe Sr. and Jack and Edward Kennedy Roman Catholics? Only a rich imagination can bring them to the confessional, seeking absolution under the command to go and sin no more. Of course these secular blades married within the Church and their political and religious ceremonies partook of the presence and the blessing of Cardinal O'Connell and Cardinal Cushing, dramatic Boston clerics. Certainly Jack ran for the presidency as a perceived Catholic whose religion mattered greatly in all the calculations and anxieties of the race. Anyone who lived outside the large cities at the time had the opportunity to hear the folk express a fear of having to kiss the Pope's ring, a minor curiosity of the faith that had somehow made a major impression. Concern about the candidate's religious fervor proved grandly misplaced. Garry Wills quotes a line from Murray Kempton written in 1961: We have yet again been denied our first Catholic president.

Rose Fitzgerald Kennedy: a mother and indeed a Roman Catholic. Hamilton's biography is briskly denying to the old matriarch. On the one hand she is seen to display an inane and helpless humility in relation to her husband's religious and marital misdemeanors. On the other hand she is fiercely scolded for her own misdemeanors in almost every capacity that brings her name to the page. Her attention to religion is a "vengeful piety" that would have "a crushing effect upon her daughters." Poor Rose made too many trips abroad, seventeen in four years; a lot of her energy was expended on clothes and personal appearance, perhaps understandable since photographs indicate that it is her Fitzgerald handsome head, not Joe's, that provided the family "good looks." "She is a management executive rather than a mother, giving orders to the staff and regimenting the children," and in another flourish: "Anderson's Ice Maiden, concealing her frozen heart beneath an exterior of courage and self-control."

It is common to lay the sons' licentiousness to the hearty paternal example. In Hamilton, the *details* of the practice are believed to issue from the arctic curse of the mother. About Jack Kennedy, a commenting analysis from a friend: "Rose Kennedy was a cold, unmotherly, and distant woman whose main contribution to Jack's character was his strangely split psyche, leaving him emotionally crippled in his relations with women; a young man who disliked people embracing him, who showered compulsively—often five times a day—and yet perpetually craved the most symbolic and intimate of all touching: sexual union." So we are not to settle for the Kennedy men as driven by caprice and will, but as formed by a conjunction of paternal and maternal infirmity—a sort of Mendelian double dose.

Doris Kearns Goodwin's very interesting research on Rose can lead one to believe that it was her fate to have a strong spiritual inclination awkwardly struggling to survive. The year Rose and her sister spent in a very strict convent in Blumenthal, Holland, created in her a wish for practice that went beyond a mere cradle-Catholic adherence. The convent was cold, isolated, and rigorous, with the day beginning at six in the morning, silence at meals, and a required four-day retreat of complete silence. At the convent, Rose elected to compete for the honor of Child of Mary. The goals were "to embrace a commitment for life, a deep personal resolve to attend Mass...every day; to say the Rosary regularly; to make an annual retreat...to renew one's religion daily so that it becomes inseparable from one's life."

Rose was accepted as a Child of Mary and henceforth maintained a strong sense of vocation. In old age she could say:"As I look back now to that long distant experience, I look back with thankfulness to God for having granted me the occasion for shaping a lasting covenant with Him." If Rose is to blame for a large measure of the "emotional blockage" in Jack's life, perhaps we are to view it as a crippling Catholic guilt. But a leavening of guilt, Catholic or otherwise, would surely have been an addition to the interior landscape of the President. Instead his pagan exuberance was undiminished by his high worldly calling and evidence fails to show a strain of moral ruefulness.

The thousand days of Jack Kennedy were also the thousand days of Jacqueline Kennedy. For a politician it is hard to imagine a more felicitous union. The presidential couple appeared as beautiful, dreamlike, and enviable as movie stars—the icons who set the standard for public adulation. The Reagans, actual creatures of Hollywood, achieved a statistical popularity that was almost entirely ideological, a strange curve in the American mind as it wandered down the road of History. Nancy Reagan, working out at the glamour bar like a determined little acrobat, remained in her way a suburban apotheosis of image, a rich suburb of course but not outside the hopes of a considerable part of the public. Jackie Kennedy was, instead, mystery and distance, offering little scope for emulation, a spectacular footnote in the annals of democratic divinity. She is remembered for a sort of quality magnificence, a step beyond Dolly Madison's famed table settings. And she made what is currently called a personal statement by rounding up White House evenings with guests such as Pablo Casals and André Malraux, celebrities with no hint of the frontier.

The marriage leaves the darkest puzzle unanswered: the brusque denial of courtesy on the part of the President to the consort who brought such a useful and perhaps poetical acclaim to the term of office. It is possible he thought he did it all alone.

In spite of scandal there remains affection for the Kennedys. Even the battered Teddy can still appeal to liberal Democrats for his legislative tenacity. For the memory of Robert Kennedy the feeling of loss has increased through the years. He began as a tough and vindictive operator too friendly to the black shadow of J. Edgar Hoover and wire taps on Martin Luther King, too impatient with the civil rights movement when it moved in ways neither he nor the President was prepared to understand as acceptable politics, but as he lived on after Jack's assassination, it is felt that he made a transcending journey, an emotional awakening that went beyond ballot-box strategy, at least in its origin. This transformation attached him to a ragtag, unexpected constituency—the grape pickers of California, blacks in the inner cities, and to many among the raucous and agnostic roving bands that brought down Lyndon Johnson. He too was assassinated and his funeral had a pop, or populist, quality, with Andy Williams singing "The Battle Hymn of the Republic" in St. Patrick's Cathedral and the coffin in a railroad train which made its way through the modern shanty glades of the road from New York to Washington. The two Kennedys died by unconscionable violence. Perhaps there was nothing to it, no clear political scenario. Just two celebrity murders, like that of John Lennon?

1993

THE MENENDEZ SHOW

COURT TV: December 23, 1993. Waiting for the verdicts in the trial of Lyle and Erik Menendez for the shotgun murders of their parents on August 20, 1989, in their Beverly Hills, California, house. A three-million-dollar "mansion" it was, to set the scene. The crime and the trial, as shown on television, have become a national attraction, one of outstanding gruesomeness, with the parents literally "blown away," a phrase sometimes heard in court, as they sat eating ice cream and, like us, watching television on a Sunday evening. The Menendez sons, twenty-one and eighteen years old at the time of the murders, engaged in an interesting span of activities until, some months later in October 1989, the brothers rashly confessed to a psychologist. But the confession was not given to the police until March and they were at last arrested by, in this instance, a sluggish Los Angeles Police Department.

Incarceration followed and gradually the brothers offered a defense of unusual squalor, or perhaps a usual squalor spreading its scrofulous blight over the American landscape. They claimed years of sexual abuse by their father, abuse almost unremitting in the case of the younger brother, Erik. The tear-stained faces of the two sons described the sexual assaults in detail on the witness stand—"massages," oral

---

I am grateful for Dominick Dunne's articles in *Vanity Fair*, for reporting in the *Los Angeles Times*, *The American Lawyer*, and other newspapers and magazines. Also, I have consulted an advance copy of the highly informative and useful *Blood Brothers*, by Ron Soble and John Johnson (Signet Onyx, 1994). The facts in the press do not always agree and for the most part this article is that of a viewer of the trial on Court TV.

ejaculation, and all the rest. Along with that claim, a more opaque motive or justification of the murders was offered. The brothers testified that, after an unpleasant scene, they threatened to reveal the "secret," and the consequence was that they believed their parents were going to kill them. Bursting into the house with the shotguns blasting away was to be seen as a preemptive strike in self-defense. That the mother was included in the slaughter proved a delicate problem, which the defense lawyers met with a sometimes coarse efficiency in disparagement of any sympathy that might come the mother's way.

When the defense laid out its plans for the architecture of the self-defense plea, the judge did not find the peculiar foundations strong enough to sustain a "perfect self-defense" and allowed the indictment of first-degree murder to stand in the death-penalty, gas-chamber state of California. For its vivid attractions of money, worldly position, sex, bizarre details, flamboyant lawyers such as Leslie Abramson defending Erik, and above all for its being shown on television almost moment by moment, the trial became a huge success in arousing a squabbling public interest.

William Roughead's accounts of Victorian women and their careful attentions to the evening broth laced with arsenic, vomited up one night and freshly prepared to be offered the next, tell of "popular" crimes of the period. For us, the poisoners display a slow-acting simplicity of arrangements in their determination to dispose of the troublesome. The American event the Menendez dramaturgy brings to mind is that of Lizzie Borden, who has grown somewhat trite from long acquaintance. However, she was efficient, rapid, and forceful in her use of the available weaponry of the time, in her ax-parricide followed by forty-one whacks for the mother, step-mother in that case. Family murders, observing the classical unities of time, place, and action, are more gripping to the public than random victims, an aesthetic plus, if you will.

After more than five months of trial proceedings, over 20,000 pages of testimony from the defendants, witnesses, lawyers, and "experts"; after comment from the TV anchors, and analysis by legal professionals, and call-ins from the public ("Hi, Carol. Love the show"), the thousands and thousands of viewers attending the progress of the trial are rich in a large number of new and unexpected intimacies about the dead, their families, and plain citizens caught up in the coils of litigation.

An intimacy of body and soul, psyche and spirit, fears and resentments, fierce compulsions and extended mitigations shaped by the insights of "therapists"—all these are proposed by the defense for the "boys," a locution sarcastically employed by the prosecution for males twenty-one and eighteen at the time they struck. Lyle, the older, had had an unsatisfactory year at Princeton University and was on probation for cheating on an exam; Erik, the younger, was planning to enter UCLA. Along with an exculpating portrait of the confessed killers, the defense undertook a sort of telepathic probing of the dark, satanic depths in the characters of the dead, known to us as Jose and Kitty, appellations more blithe than those of Lyle and Erik. The parents, deplorable man and wife, are to be seen as killing themselves—not just in a metaphorical sense, but through the morbidity of provocation.

And good riddance for the extraordinarily successful Jose, age forty-five when he died with few to say a good word for him. As for Kitty, née Mary Louise Anderson, unnatural, "un-available" (a favorite word) mother; natural enough wife in her fury over the philandering with women of the wide-ranging Jose. And a shrug for the philandering with Lyle and Erik, if she was aware of it, and if such there was to the extent claimed. Sore and depressed, Kitty was proposed as a team player in the wishes of her husband. For the rest, negligent, sloppy, self-centered, a bit of a drunk. Thus the maternal victim, forty-seven years old at the time of death, has been sorted out to aid in the defense of her children. It is very imprudent to be killed.

Christmas Eve: The juries, one for Lyle and another for Erik, are off for the holidays; so Terry Moran tells us as he appears outside the courthouse in Van Nuys, California, where the trial is being held. Lyle and Erik Menendez have been in the Los Angeles County jail for more than three and a half years, with this their fourth Christmas. The Los Angeles County jail is a place hideously befouled in all its appointments, as we have learned from an interview with a young woman who investigates prison conditions on behalf of the ACLU. However, Lyle or Erik, or both, said recently that he would rather spend the rest of his life in the LA jail than return to the life with his parents in the house with the swimming pool, tennis courts, and guest house. Having said they killed in overwhelming fear for their own lives, the brothers are denied any measure of ruefulness for the loss of parents, money, freedom, and youth. A condition of extreme moral and emotional deprivation, if part of the escape from punishment, a wish natural to the human condition.

Of course, it need not be true that regret keeps its distance even as they arrive at the court handcuffed and leg-shackled, which causes them to walk in an awkward, loping movement when the irons are removed.

The road from crime to punishment runs from excitement to misery, a long way, and it has been observed that the one on trial is not the same as the one who committed the crime. "This even-handed justice commends the ingredients of our poisoned chalice to our own lips." So it is with the Menendez brothers, whose only plea and hope is that the victims are the guilty ones and they the instruments of a just punishment.

Jose Menendez—his biography will be circulating in the books that are surely written, set in type, ready for the market when the epilogue of the verdicts is announced on Court TV. Jose's ending was calamity followed by calumny, but up until then he was a curious case, inspirational if financial success is the measure. He managed to leave Cuba at the age of sixteen, and to die with a fortune the press claimed to be $14 million. No doubt an exaggeration and now depleted, if not "all gone," as one of the lawyers said. The trial, taxes, unpaid mortgages on two expensive houses, the exuberant spending of the sons as soon as the bodies were put on the trolley and hauled to the morgue? In Cuba, Jose's family was prominent and respected. On the mother's side there had been professors, lawyers, and doctors. The Menendez grandfather had been a professor of medicine and the founder of a bank. In the immediate family there were exceptional gifts in sports, with Jose's father a famous soccer player and his mother, still living, a champion swimmer.

After high school in the United States, Jose received a swimming scholarship to Southern Illinois University. There he met and married, at nineteen, Mary Louise Anderson, a native of Illinois and of modest background. They left Illinois for New York City where Jose took a degree in accounting at Queens College, while working as a waiter at "21." If there is such a thing as a concrete talent for business, this Cuban émigré reflected it to an astonishing degree. He moved along without special luck, useful connections, or a graduate degree from any of the prominent Schools of Business, and without selling drugs, the balloon trip to expendable income.

At the Hertz Corporation, Menendez rose to be an executive in the car-leasing division. The family moved to Princeton, New Jersey, where the sons attended private school. When Hertz was bought out by RCA, he shifted to the record division. Menendez left the company in 1986, when or because he was not elevated to a vice-presidency post. No matter, he was soon a chief executive officer at Live Entertainment, a division of the powerful Carolco Pictures in Los Angeles, distributor of the Rambo films and others.

Dominick Dunne's researches on the case: "Jose Menendez's success at Live Entertainment was dazzling. In 1986 the company lost $20 million; a year later, under Menendez, Live earned $8 million and in 1988 doubled that." The family is now in California, in Calabasas, a suburb of Los Angeles. This suburban residence became uncomfortable when Lyle and Erik had their first burst of criminal behavior in not one but two "high-class" burglaries. More than $100,000 were stolen in cash, jewelry, and other items. Jose came to the rescue in fatherly fashion with most of the loot returned and damages paid. Reports in the press speculate that Erik took the rap because he was underage and there was a wish to protect Lyle's entrance into Princeton, where he distinguished himself negatively. Erik got off with probation and the instruction to receive "counseling." The counsel chosen was Dr. Jerome Oziel, a clinical psychologist who later heard and taped Erik's confession of the murders. This circumstance did great damage to the brothers and more than a little to Dr. Oziel's reputation by the exposure to the public of unfortunate matters in his own life and practice.

The Menendez family moved to the Beverly Hills impressive spread where the parents met their grisly end. At that time, Jose was making a salary of $500,000 a year with bonuses of nearly a million. The person who was making this sum was described at the trial as intimidating, insulting, humiliating to employees, a "control freak" in positions of power, that is, in the office and at home. Business associates found him overbearing and ruthless. Members of his own family and that of his wife spoke of his intense demands on his sons, his strictness, his concentration on their performance at school and on the tennis court. As for Kitty, she was also a nag about performance, that of her sons, if not of her own, a common inclination of parents. She was clever enough to do most of the sons' homework, but she drank too much, was said by some to be secretive and critical. She threatened suicide and tried it once when she learned of Jose's eight-year affair with a former secretary, whom she trailed, denounced on the phone, that sort of thing.

The life of the couple was in many ways provincial. Most of their social life was with other members of the two families. They did not often try to make the entertainment scene, and there we might count, for the film world, the demerit of the autopsy's finding that Kitty, five feet two inches, weighed over 160 pounds at her death. Jose was also far more clever than his sons, and it is said that he often quizzed them at the dinner table about current affairs, hoping at least to achieve an ornamental acquisition. The couple did not pretend an interest in high culture, Hollywood style, and Kitty's efforts at trendiness in home decoration were uncertain and unfinished—lots of boxes around the Beverly Hills rooms confused visitors. We can read of one attendance at a Christmas Eve high mass and several excursions to the Episcopal church, but there was little more than a perfunctory bow to religion. Self-help books took its place, and in that the Menendezes were creatures of their period. Above everything is the glittering success of the young man from Cuba who may have learned something from the detested Castro after all—the pleasures of control.

The New Year has arrived and the juries will be back to "deliberate" the sulphurous pile of deed, intention, motive, character, confession, interpretation. The parents are dead and the sons killed them, nothing to worry about there. The twenty-four people are to judge Why. And to determine the degree of culpability. In the week before the murders, Erik and Lyle purchased shotguns and ammunition. First they got birdshot and subsequently had to round up buckshot, more powerful, for the matter ahead. To buy the arms they went to San Diego, out of town, used a false identification, paid in cash. A few days later, they came into the house at night, and fired, number of shots contested, but quite enough to leave the bodies almost unrecognizable. The father was shot in the back of the head. The mother was shot and tried to get away, but as she lay moaning, Erik went out to get ammunition for reloading and came back and put her out of her misery—or was it Lyle with the final shot in the face? They picked up the shell casings, changed their bloody clothes, disposed of them in a dumpster somehow, hid the guns, and stood in a movie line, or went into a movie theater, for a short spell before returning home to call the police and to say, truthfully, "They shot our parents." It took more than five months before "they" were identified.

The Menendez affair almost immediately took a turn from tragedy to comedy, with Lyle as the master comedian. He bought Rolex watches, one given away and one worn to the memorial service where the parents were honored with the usual compliments. "In lapidary inscriptions a man is not upon oath," as Dr. Johnson observed. Lyle spoke in accents suitable to a bereaved son, tropes and measures never to be heard again from either son as they fought the possibility of the death penalty.

The spending exhilaration of the next months had the antic aspects of "I've got a million" movies. Lyle bought a Porsche, costing either $60,000 or $70,000, condos, high-rise, were leased, and $550,000 was put down for Lyle's entrance into the entrepreneurial world as a restaurateur in Princeton. "Grief shopping," this is named by the all-merciful therapists. There were bodyguards, trips back and forth from the West Coast to the East. So the months passed from the scene of the "perfect murder."

Then Dr. Oziel, the counselor to whom Erik had been sent after the robberies, reentered the scenario, like the gun on the wall that must go off in act three. Erik had not completed the mandated course of treatment, but Oziel, rather offhand about a number of professional matters, let that pass. Still he was alerted by the murders in a family known to his case book. More than two months later, he either called Erik or was called by him to offer help in the hour of need, perhaps the inquisitive therapist's need. At the interview, Erik said: We did it. And perhaps we can imagine the therapist, true in this instance to his calling, saying: Really? And how did you feel about that?

Either on this or a second interview in which Lyle, enraged by the confession, took part, everything was laid out on Dr. Oziel's convenient tape recorder. The buying of the guns, the ammunition, the false identification, the actual description of the moment of the killing. No mention of sexual abuse, a curious lapse since sexual abuse is as pertinent to the therapist as a kidney to the urologist. Also there was no mention of the motive of self-defense. It was the doctor who was put in a position of defense of self, since he claimed Lyle had threatened to kill him because of what he knew about the crime. So seriously was the threat taken that Oziel stored the tapes, made preparations for the security of his family and of himself and his patient-mistress, Judalon Smyth.

Oziel had asked Miss Smyth to be in his waiting room in a position to overhear what went on at the taped interview with the brothers. It was she who at last went to the police four months later and described the crime, told of the tapes, and finally the brothers were arrested. Matters might have been simpler had not the Oziel-Smyth relationship pitched into a wind tunnel from which Smyth emerged in a state of vehement loquacity directed against Dr. Oziel. She changed therapists and learned that she had been "brainwashed" by Oziel and what she had previously claimed to hear in the office had actually been *told* to her by Oziel. Originally a prosecution witness, she came forth for the defense, cast doubt on the validity of the tapes, and gave being in a state of "denial" as the reason for the dramatic change in her account of how the confessions came about.

The confessions stood and the brothers moved from what they had done to the elaborate justification. Just how and when the jailed brothers and their legal counsel arrived at the very useful claims of sexual abuse and self-defense remains murky. The days before the murders, before the decision to buy guns, the state of mind had to be organized or scripted. The inanity of the hairpiece emerged as a precipitating item of goods or something. During a family quarrel, Kitty is said to have reached up and pulled off the hairpiece worn by Lyle, its disguising configuration making him resemble, as many have noted, Michael Milken. Erik announced he was shocked to learn that his brother was wearing the wig or the rug, and that this act of revelation and humiliation led him to his own revelation to his brother about the long sexual molestation by the father—a sudden cataloguing of family facts previously unacknowledged. The confession, Lyle said, led him to confront his father and say: Leave Erik alone. The father is said to have replied: What I do with my son is my own business. Don't throw your life away. Thinking over the exchange, Erik decided: Dad's going to kill us. So runs the case.

Easy to believe the mother snatched off Lyle's hairpiece during a quarrel, but why was Erik sequestered in the torture chamber when

Lyle was inspecting his hair purchase under the gaze of the fiercely overseeing parents or looking like a coquette at his transformation in the mirror, pondering the color, the curls, a bit of trim here or there? Needless to say, several claimed Erik knew about the hairpiece, but the defense was stuck with this trifling step on the path to murder and attacked the bearers of contrary evidence in the manner of a subway cop nabbing a pickpocket.

Experts and therapists: Each came forth with the grave designation of "Doctor" from his PhD in sociology or social work, psychology or family therapy, and one with a medical degree, he a "forensic psychiatrist." In one of the television colloquies with outside lawyers, a cynical if experienced litigator said with a shrug: experts are a dime a dozen. There were nearly a dozen rounded up by the defense and all commanding more than a dime for their hours with the brothers, hours of preparation and hours on the stand.

This free-ranging clerisy for a secular age each proved to be solemn, predictable, and repetitive in language and diagnosis. One who seemed to make an especially good impression was Dr. Ann Burgess, a soft-voiced lady with a grandmotherly aspect to her performance. Dr. Burgess had, in addition to her therapeutic experience, experience in crime-scene evaluation for the FBI. Although the FBI was not called to serve in the Menendez case, the doctor stood firmly on this impressive imprimatur. Her observation was that the crime scene at hand was a mess, as indeed it was. The wildness of the shooting indicated to her that the crime was not planned, but was an outburst of fear and panic inevitably bred in the brothers from a lifetime of sexual and mental abuse. Also Dr. Burgess offered a rather bizarre addendum. She claimed there was "scientific evidence" to show that abused children had changes in their brain chemistry. Perhaps she meant that the brain cells of Lyle and Erik were rattling around in a deviant pattern on the night of the murders, but somehow got back on track as they churned out a story worthy of credibility in every detail by the brain cells of the experts.

The prosecution was scorned and ridiculed by the defense for not calling up its own experts. Is there such a thing as a prosecuting therapist? Could the prosecution send a PhD of this or that to interview Lyle and Erik in their cells and return to say they were callow and cunning young killers showing all the symptoms of those indicted for first-degree murder? Or perhaps to offer as Dick Cavett did when the microphone caught him outside the courthouse: "They're lying in their teeth, if those are their teeth."

January 11. Erik's jury is deadlocked and the judge has asked them to try once more to reach a verdict. The admonition was termed "outrageous" by Leslie Abramson, Erik's defense attorney. If the deadlock holds it will be an extraordinary victory for Erik Menendez, which he will owe to the tactical skill and intensity of Miss Abramson. She is a distinguished opponent of the death penalty, a small woman, with a pretty face and a mop of curly blonde hair that might be called famous so often is it remarked upon. In 1989, she defended a Pakistani gynecologist charged with murdering his eleven-year-old son, cutting up the body, and putting it in a trash barrel. Miss Abramson practices a total preparation for her case and projects a compelling, insistent belief in her client that seems to suggest that not only is the first-degree charge a cruel imposition, but that a reduction to a lesser charge is a defeat of justice. The Pakistani gynecologist case ended in an acquittal.

As she began her intense three-day summation on behalf of Erik Menendez, we were told by Terry Moran, the commentator in Van Nuys, that every eye in the jury box and in the courtroom was fixed upon her. Her description of the sexual abuse by Jose was not squeamish, as it had not been in her opening statement when she claimed there had been a

carefully calculated pattern of grooming the child for his father's sexual gratification. This pattern included repeated acts of forcible oral copulation, sodomy, rape, and the intentional infliction of pain by the use of foreign objects upon Erik's person. Jose Menendez's obvious purpose was to use the child's body to satisfy his lust.

Tennis: the game came to be seen in the trial as a form of mental and physical abuse of both sons by the father's wish to make them stars. They had expensive coaches, along with much interference and instruction from Jose. They competed in tournaments all over the Middle West, and Lyle reached a high ranking one year in the Juniors. When they lost, Jose was said to be furious enough to drive them to tears. This conduct for once is not surprising when one remembers the notoriety of tennis fathers: Steffi Graf's, for instance; Mary Pierce's father denied entrance into the arena of the French Open after appalling interruptions and antics; Jennifer Capriati dropping out after her brilliant start because of what some believe to be troubles with her father.

Miss Abramson described the long, long hours on the court in the hot sun as if they were a cruel term of duty on a galley ship under the lash. But that is tennis and the hours of practice do not recede for Pete Sampras or Jim Courier at the top of their game. Practice itself is not to be compared with the energy required for actual matches of high tension that may last hours in heat of over 100 degrees. One circumstance not mentioned by the defense in proposing, in a vivid and condemning manner, the hardship of Jose's tennis regime as a contribution to the conditions of life that could reasonably lead the sons to murder: in the months after the killings her client Erik had dropped out of UCLA, and was in a tennis tournament in Israel, along with his $50,000-a-year coach, when he was arrested.

Also tennis, a one-on-one sport, makes one strong, fast, agile in mental concentration and skilled in evasive tactics. The results of the autopsy showed Jose to be in better shape than he thought after having had heart pains and continuing to smoke. Nevertheless it is a mystery that an eighteen-year-old man had to submit like a rubber anatomical doll to "rape" by his father even up until the week before he found the protective strength to go after him with a shotgun. Self-defense and loud denunciation might have been more natural than the exhortation to run away, leaving your cars, clothes, gear, and in the case of Lyle, a collection of stuffed animals.

In her summation to the jury, Miss Abramson cast Erik as the vulnerable, less favored, more disappointing child for the ambitious parents. In certain respects she impugned Lyle in her attachment to the younger son and was perhaps free to do so since the juries hear only the testimony relating to their separate cases. Referring to the "grief shopping," she said in a dismissive tone: Erik didn't buy anything . . . a jacket. Further along she argued: Erik didn't kill anyone. That would appear to leave Lyle with the problem of two dead bodies.

The atrocity of the death penalty in California, ordained as a deterrent to violent crime, has shown its contrary aspect in this long, very expensive trial—expensive to the defendants and to the unhappy taxpayers of the state. Leslie Abramson's fee, reported to be near a million dollars, comes from the Menendez estate, as does the considerable cost of Jill Lansing's months of work in behalf of Lyle. On the other hand, taxpayers are responsible for the professional fees of the defendants' second lawyers, Marcia Morrisey and Michael Burt, since co-counsel is required by California law in death-penalty cases. About the resources for the prosecution, one of the lawyers described them as K-mart style.

Important to the unraveling of the family's dour history is the possibility that brothers, sisters, and cousins might not have been so obliging in their belittling memories of the dead were it not that the sons, the last of that Menendez branch, were themselves facing death. It is unlikely there can be much pride, in any case, to adorn the splattered family name. It is also fair to speculate that the death penalty played its part in prodding business associates, in no way central to the matter, to agree to speak about Jose's unfortunate nature.

In the spring of 1992, Robert Harris, the convicted killer of two young boys and himself a child of profoundly abusive parents, who left him on the road at age eleven, never again to be picked up, was executed in the San Quentin gas chamber. KQED, a public television station in San Francisco, had filmed the trial and asked the prison warden for a drastic extension of the coverage: the right to film the actual execution. The warden denied the request for reasons of security, the privacy of prison attendants, and the possible effect upon other prisoners. KQED took the warden to court and after a surprisingly vigorous assembly of arguments, standing on the First and Fourth Amendments and other issues, the court ruled in favor of the warden—in this instance. Robert Harris expired with only the usual selected members of the press to tell the story *first-hand*.*

Court TV—An idea as old as America. So the program announces itself. The right to a public trial has the prestige of age upon it and the exposure of judicial proceedings on television is an idea, perhaps an American idea. The marriage of the cold granite of the village courthouse and the hot fibers of TV transmission, begun in 1991 on this unique, round-the-clock cable station, has become with the Menendez trial a rival to the competing network confessional programs shown five days each week. Talking things over with the millions out there seems to be a therapeutic reward for those maimed by life and often for the "perpetrators" who also shrink from the obscurity of silence.

The judicial proceedings on Court TV are shaped by the rules of law, the counterpoint of defense and prosecution and decisions from the bench. The public does not, from the courtroom, see or hear anything beyond that offered the juries, those with press passes, the families, and the fans who might stand for hours outside the stage door and sometimes find a place within. Indeed, the television coverage is superior to actual courtroom visitation. It is a ringside seat, with announcers, analysis, and, in the more lively contests, call-in viewers, a chatty superfluity most notable for their patience in hanging on the line.

*See Wendy Lesser, *Pictures at an Execution* (Harvard University Press, 1993).

Court TV offers many trials, confrontations serious for the principals locked in the tedium of repetition and delay and sputtering oratory by the lawyers who go through the lessons like a teacher at the blackboard. A day at court. A trial is part of the public record, open to those who seek it—scholars, reporters, journalists, and so on. In the Menendez case there are over 20,000 pages of testimony which the passive television audience is spared the need to study and to assess. Entertainment value is the guide and the privilege; one can, as the Menendez case winds down, choose the "Malicious Wounding" matter in the case of the severed penis and turn off the suit for damages in a skiing accident.

Court TV is a seriously designed and seriously produced public offering. Its text depends entirely upon things citizens will do to each other that can lead to an indictment; or what perfidies, lies, extortions, and broken promises may be alleged and adjudicated. It is not a work of the imagination, but a work of fact, if legal matters are fact. At the least it is a demonstration of legal reality. The ambiguous aspects of filming this reality have to do with witnesses, subpoenaed or volunteer. In a proceeding like that of the Menendez case, witnesses have been accused by the contending lawyers of lying, remembering, or misremembering with malicious, biased, or self-serving intent. Unfortunate matters from the past may be excavated by private detectives to impeach credibility. Speculation by neighbors, memories of friends and former lovers, are entered as relevant, especially in custody and divorce cases. Manner and appearance may be an embarrassment, like a passport photo. At stake are baneful possibilities for families and, for the witness, the risk of being diminished in the public's perception. Employers may find a disadvantage in one who has been subject to the voracious appetite for discreditment typical of a trial.

In the Menendez hearings, certain witnesses were accused of edging their way into the trial merely to be on television. Wide dissemination is the critical concern about the existence of Court TV or any television in the courts. In the Menendez case, a witness had a turn before the camera not once but again and again throughout the weeks. Appearances were repeated when there was no action, "nothing going on in Van Nuys," or to fill the blanks during weekends and holiday recesses. As for the lawyers, they got their As and Bs from the commentaries of the anchors and assorted legal colleagues. For the "experts," some may encounter a diminishment if they fail to "project" effectively in their role. More likely, they will receive free advertising for their next employment in witnessing.

We notice that television cameras are not at the trial of the accused in the World Trade Center bombing, six dead, thousands injured, huge losses in property, and of outstanding importance to the government and to the citizens of a country previously more or less free of international terrorism. A wise decision for federal criminal cases. The cast of characters in the bombing might have cosmetic and linguistic attributes not entirely acceptable to public taste. While we must believe these matters do not inform the verdicts, they could, if shown for months on television, bring about a rise in the national temperature.

Verdicts: The jurors, six men and six women, pronounced themselves deadlocked in the case of Erik Menendez. The judge asked them to try once more, offering a choice of first- or second-degree murder, voluntary or involuntary manslaughter. Again they could not agree, or would not budge, from their clashing opinions. A mistrial was declared and the jurors dismissed. The district attorney said the state would bring a new trial on a first-degree murder charge.

January 18: An earthquake around Los Angeles, a serious disaster with loss of life, fires, highways and bridges damaged, power lines out. The members of Lyle's jury will not convene on this the morning after. Were they soon to come together, they would have to return to the contemplation of malicious intent, premeditation, imminent danger, matters they have long considered without resolution. Deliberations that may seem of greatly diminished importance amidst the tragedies of the earthquake.

Lyle, the first born, made himself heir to the fallen tyrant and gathered his legions around him: limos, sports cars, first-class air travel, credit cards, leased hotel suites, and heavy investments meant to indicate his claim to the corporate throne. What lies ahead is unknown just now, for the prince and for his brother. Perhaps they will receive a greater leniency than many of the damned, perhaps not. But there is nothing agreeable in the future of the Menendez sons. Their forfeiture was larger than any defense strategy or counsel can restore.

There is no equity in life or in judicial decisions. In any case, you can't go to heaven on other people's sins. In Florida, Jeffrey Farina is eighteen years old and on death row, along with his brother, age twenty. They are bad numbers who brutally slaughtered a young woman and a young man in a robbery. The biography of the killers is a record of maimings, torture, and abandonment by their parents— a common index listing under the names of those who end up in what is called the criminal justice system. On death row, Jeffrey, in a tabloid account, is credited with a poetic coda about his situation: Everybody dies some day. It's just a fact of life.

Then there is the pathetic, bathetic Jim Bakker, once mate of Tammy, sentenced for fraud to sixty-four years—and nobody missing.

January 20, 1994

FAMILY VALUES

I.

LYLE AND Erik Menendez, two furtive suburban churls, gunned down their parents in August 1989, almost seven years ago. The brothers were not arrested until six months after the murders; during the gap they had quite a good time spending the impressive bank account of their father, Jose Menendez, a corporate executive, self-made, forty-five years old when he and his wife, Kitty, forty-seven years old, were killed. Jose and Kitty, the parents, Lyle and Erik, the sons. One needs a bit of caution to keep these now familiar couplings from tripping off the tongue as if they were family skits in the old vaudeville days. The brothers' incarceration came about when recordings of a detailed confession made to a psychiatrist were at last turned over to the police. They were brought to trial, each with his own jury, neither of which could agree on a verdict, and so they went back to prison to await a retrial and to find themselves displaced in public interest by the indictment of the former football star O.J. Simpson for the murder by stabbing of his ex-wife and a hapless friend who happened to be at the scene. In any case, the Menendez brothers and O.J. Simpson, by way of the cameras in the courtroom during the trials, became international double-homicide celebrities.

More is known about the accused and the victims in these trials than about many of the public figures whose actions and opinions will have an effect upon the national life. Politicians, facing their shackling positions, past and present, will have to wait for election night to command the dramatic preeminence of the final returns in

the trials of L&E and O. J. This raging intimacy and emotional attentiveness came about from the extraordinary span of the television
coverage. The fanatical hours were not only set aside on Court TV
and CNN, specialized channels, but also on the regular stations. The
purest measure of demand and urgency came when the vast audience,
resting its feet or nodding off a bit in front of the long-established
afternoon soap operas, was interrupted for the California judicial
theater, an offering as slow as the plot clips on *As the World Turns*
are quick and efficient.

"Millions all over the world," a favorite statistic, seemed to wait
for the arrival of O. J. Simpson's mise-en-scène: the "alleged" himself,
the lawyers in a circle around the front table, spectators and family
in the rows behind, heads and hats of interest, and above them Judge
Lance Ito with black hair, black beard, and black robe, all bringing
to mind a drawing by Daumier. Long ago it was Extra, Extra, Read
All About It!, the lad in his woolen cap, the clang of printing presses,
the folded newspapers flipping by—archival memories of a primitive
way to announce the evil folks will do for love, hatred, or money. In
the old sob story, as in classical tragedy, "situational murder," in the
family, was most gripping to the public imagination. The two cases
at hand do not take place in a castle or palace suitable to tragedy, but
they have more than a little contemporary signification as settings.
They are LA "mansion" scripts: swimming pool, tennis court, patio,
guest house, deluxe motor cars, residential emblems giving a certain
cachet almost invariably lacking in criminal justice scenery. For
Simpson it was Rolls-Royce, Bentley, and Ferrari, and the rather lowly
but unfortunately significant white Bronco. For the Menendez family we learn of a reticent Mercedes or two and for Lyle an Alfa Romeo
at the time of his high school graduation.

The Menendez trial was a literal sob story as the brothers famously
sobbed and sniffled on the witness stand, where they and their lawyers
elaborately proposed a family chronicle of such great squalor that
nice boys, as they were said to be, would have no recourse except to

rid themselves of the elders by blowing them to bits. The infamy of the parents was to be the center of the choice of a punishment that might be death by lethal injection in San Quentin prison, the fate offered as appropriate to the crime by the Los Angeles District Attorney's Office. At the present time there are 438 prisoners on Death Row in San Quentin, rows of cages Senator Robert Dole and his wife, Elizabeth, president of the American Red Cross, strangely chose to visit on the campaign trail in California. There are no votes to be solicited on Death Row, but for the idea of Death Row there are votes throughout the country and an impatience for the amount of time it takes to proceed with the sentence.

Jose Menendez, foully murdered, was an interesting, thoroughly deplorable man. He came from a respected, prosperous Havana family, all of whom settled in the United States after the Castro revolution. Jose came first at the age of sixteen to join his brother-in-law, went to high school, and in college met Kitty Anderson, whom he married and who would bear the parricidal sons, creatures out of the mist of antiquity even though this family line began in a courtship at Southern Illinois University. After classes in accounting at Queens College, the Cuban exile immediately displayed a talent for business. This is an indefinable endowment, a sort of genetic luck perhaps, in which one need not invent anything or even start up a useful enterprise. Intelligence-corporate seems to be similar to intelligence-military, a gift for strategy in serious battle. Menendez quickly held high positions at the Hertz Corporation and after that at Live Entertainment, an agency in Los Angeles where under his reign profits were indeed notable.

Just as notable was the ruthless nature of his executive style, so extreme as to be almost a caricature. Ruthlessness is not embarrassing in the corporate world if it is somehow believed to be a stone in the structure of profit. However, Jose was seriously sadistic to those with whom he worked; he was forever insulting, humiliating, raging— habits that do not render a profit beyond whatever pleasure they may give to the one who feels free to display them. Research indicates that many talented people left Hertz because of his offensive behavior, and when his murder was made known the joke went around that everyone who had ever worked with him would need a good alibi.*

It must not be imagined that the sons were anything but deeply proud of their father's titles and compensation. They gave no indication of a sort of youthful socialist contempt for the cruel practices of capitalism as they had viewed it at home, none of the questioning of the reputed terms of our beginning and end sometimes noted in the preacher's son. In fact Lyle and Erik have no ideas at all that one can discover, although they certainly practice the poet's call for "no ideas but in things." They had things, cars, and clothes, and they lived expensively, went to private schools, took tennis lessons, had girlfriends. The trouble was that their parents somehow got the notion they should or could become superior in all things, in sports, in school, in ambition, in avoiding trouble—which they didn't. When first in California they lived in a suburb of Los Angeles and broke into two houses, stole a lot of valuable things, and had to be bailed out by their father.

Lyle was accepted at Princeton for his talents in swimming and tennis, thus achieving the sort of prestige his father violently desired. However he was soon on probation for failing grades and after that expelled for cheating. The rage of the father is easily imagined, even if for these delinquencies most parents would be given to strong expressions of disappointment and disapproval. Lyle and Erik played around the country in junior tennis tournaments with some success but never enough for Jose, who was hysterically eager for them to win, an embarrassment in the stands, and fearful at home with his punishing rage at their weakness and failure. What the parents raised were spoiled, indulged sons forcefully denounced for their insufficiencies. A controlling, relentless father and an unhappy, unsupportive mother.

Constant dread of criticism or punishment can create an addiction

*See *Blood Brothers*, by Ron Soble and John Johnson, reporters for the *Los Angeles Times* (Signet Onyx, 1994).

to lying in the hope of covering mistakes, lacks, and wrongdoing. Those experienced in lying will often tell several lies when one would suffice. To cancel a previous engagement: I've got a terrible cold and . . . er . . . my dog died. Lying or not lying was critical to the way the brothers' defense would be evaluated. In the first trial half the jurors believed them and half did not. In the second trial they were not believed and thus were convicted of first-degree murder and doomed to spend the rest of their lives in prison, although they escaped the death penalty. The case turned on their assertion of extraordinary sexual abuse by the father, the memory of which caused the sobbing on the stand.

Erik was the principal victim, claiming forced fellatio, sodomy, and "massages" from the age of six until eighteen, that is, up to the very moment they decided to kill their parents. Lyle too was the alleged object of abuse from the age of six to eight, and since he was two years older, that tidily gets the father off him and onto Erik, to speak in the spirit of the exchanges brought out by the doleful, patient questions of the defense attorneys. The mother, also murdered, must, to round things out, show an inappropriate attention to her children's bodies, and so we hear of considerable interest in bath times even when they were in their teens.

Many peculiarities in the plot skillfully performed for the audience. Lyle hadn't been aware of Erik's twelve years of servitude to his father's wishes; Erik didn't know his brother had bought and was wearing a hairpiece, Hollywood style. The discoveries somehow brought a confrontation that led to a death threat by the father and so in fear of their lives the sons attacked first. It was necessary to reload and shoot the mother twice before she expired, and killing her even once was a troublesome decision when the father's murder might alone have achieved the change desired. They added to their indictment that their mother had known about the sexual abuse all the many years, an assertion meant to assist due cause.

The relation between the husband and wife seems to have been a good deal more banal. Kitty Menendez was in a bad way owing to the "other woman" problem, a longtime mistress she feared her husband might want to marry, and for that dilemma and heartache she drank, threatened suicide, went to psychiatrists, and so on. A canny and calculating Jose Menendez knew that divorce was not a bottomline plus in his personal account books, and also as a shrewd operator he was not likely to think he could kill two grown sons and get away with it. As for the brothers, had they immediately confessed and told their gruesome story they might have been freed. The blur in this picture is that perhaps they didn't have the story until they had spent some months reflecting in prison.

So, home was a cave of misery, but hidden within the dark recesses was a horde of gold which one could reach if only the ogre, or ogres, guarding the entrance were somehow overcome. The ecstatic, embarrassing, and deeply foolish profligacy of the sons as soon as their parents were in the ground gives little reason to dismiss money as somehow implicated in the decision to murder. In a remorseless rush of giddy expenditures, such as a $64,000 Porsche for Lyle, greed would naturally form the basis of the prosecutor's interpretation.

In the second trial, Lyle did not testify, a cause of wonder to those who remembered his talented performance in the original trial, a trial he and his brother had managed to make for some a judgment not of themselves but of their parents. In the first trial a former girlfriend testified that Lyle had wanted her to falsely accuse Jose of sexual advances, but she had refused. That could be seen as hearsay, but more damaging was the new discovery by the state of an actual letter, written by Lyle to a friend, proposing false testimony. It would not have been advantageous for Lyle to submit to questioning in this matter and so he like O. J. Simpson sat as a sort of silent spectator in the dock.

The verdict of murder in the first degree was an expression of a disbelief, or at least an imperfect belief, in the credibility of the defendants and their proposed justifications. The jurors were called back to decide between life and death—the "penalty phase" of their duties. Suddenly there was a disturbance having to do with Erik's lawyer, Leslie Abramson, the only "personality" in this case to make the big time in the manner of the legal team assembled by O. J. Simpson. Leslie Abramson was well known in California as an opponent of the death penalty who defended with striking success some of the most loathsome of the accused. Her advocacy for Erik Menendez was properly belligerent and vivid in every detail; in addition she seemed to feel a genuine, not a merely practical affection for her client. After the first trial ended in a hung jury, she entertained the jurors on "her side," arranged for some of them to appear on television shows. She flayed the parents mercilessly and even in one exhibit showed a picture of Erik's genitals into which she stuck pins. This act was attributed to Jose Menendez and since she could not have witnessed it the accusation must have come from the brothers' tendency to dramatic overkill.

During the presentation of the arguments in the penalty phase the prosecutor was questioning one Dr. Vicary, a forensic psychiatrist employed by Erik's defense. The prosecution found that the notes Dr. Vicary was consulting did not always correspond to the notes from Dr. Vicary's sessions with Erik given by the defense, as required by law, to the prosecution in the first trial. Dr. Vicary then said the discrepancy between his first notes and his later ones came about because Miss Abramson had asked him to delete observations and statements prejudicial to Erik. He had done so out of fear of being dismissed from the case. The statements from Erik to be deleted: (1) A week before the killings he hated his parents and wanted to kill them; (2) Said he was sexually molested at the age of five by a male babysitter; (3) Claimed Lyle's sexual relation with his mother was only "in his head"; (4) Said that a homosexual lover of his father had visited the house and told the sons their father was going to kill them. Later admitted that this was a lie.

2.

The Menendez brothers did not display suitable symptoms of mourning after the atrocious death of their parents. With no one about to advise them, they acted according to their dismal natures and this moral nakedness unwittingly created skepticism about their large claims for mitigation. In O. J. Simpson's case, extenuating circumstances were not to be argued since there was no confession, no eyewitness, no murder weapon recovered, and the plea was a total denial of responsibility. Innocence, with the addition of a resounding 100 percent. Simpson did not offer himself for cross-examination and instead his many predatory advocates spent the many months cross-examining the prosecution, a civic agency Marcia Clark usually referred to as "the people," an acceptable designation of the courtroom-appointed representatives of the taxpayers even if it cannot represent a totality since the people, that is the jurors, ignored the earnest hopes of their legal representatives and declared O. J. Simpson not guilty of any of the charges. Relief, joy, for himself, his family, his lawyers and friends. Once more back into a white Bronco, down the LA freeways to the place known in the trial as the "Rockingham Location." A celebration on the handsome lawns with the inevitable news and TV cameras on the ground or above recording in helicopters with a long lens.

Fastidious sensibilities could question the propriety of anything other than a quiet, private gathering, question the subsequent golfing trips, girlfriend along, the unwise calls to talk shows, interviews requested and subsequently canceled when it was remembered that an interview is a questioning, or at least it would be in this case.

The long years of celebrity seemed to be a deterrent to Simpson's understanding of what had happened to him. The thousands and thousands of cocktail napkins with his autograph scrawled on them have betrayed his hold on reality. Of course, his impervious celebrity was fairly earned; athletes since antiquity have been honored by the state, the crowd, the mob. The grace, speed, strength, and physical discipline of the stars form a mysterious coming together of the powers and possibilities of the body. We can say about O. J. Simpson that he ran and he won and on his walls and tables rest the trophies and medals, our honors, like the odes and marble statues of the ancients. In his middle age, a long, long trial for murder and then the beautiful redemption from punishment, freedom; and yet an irreparable diminishment in public esteem. A large number of his fellow citizens believe he brutally stabbed to death two young people and there are those who think otherwise, that some other person or persons committed the deed and vanished into the night. The violence in the marriage cannot be doubted, even if many can remember demerits of their own scored at the hearthside. No matter, squandering on such a scale leaves destitution everywhere.

Destitution: not for those brought into the light by the trial, spear carriers at the opera, minor parts, and *heldentenors* and divas, major litigants. Simpson himself came forth early with the idea of a book as a quick source of income. He "wrote" with the help of an experienced book-helper, Lawrence Schiller, a sort of soulful tract entitled *I Want to Tell You*. He tells us that he has received 300,000 letters, and this while the trial was still in progress. (Lyle Menendez had received over 100,000 and Erik probably as many.) A few are from hostile correspondents, calling him a "scumbag and coward," but most are inspirational and lead the answers and the commentaries very much in that direction. "I want to state unequivocally that I did not commit those horrible crimes." He speaks of prayer, of people like his girlfriend, Paula Barbieri, being "very spiritual." He laments the "lies" and careless exploitation by the press. He offers a rash projection: "I'm going to come out of this with my dignity intact. I've been saying from the very beginning: Let me get in front of the jury. Let everybody say what they're going to say, then I'll get up there and say my piece—and let them judge." But he did not testify, claiming that his appearance would lengthen the trial and add to the burden of the jurors who had been so painfully sequestered. Not a strongly cogent bit of human sympathy, but take it as you will.

To be brushed by a first-class scandal can be a bit of luck, even if one is merely a well-placed doorman whistling for a cab on a rainy night. Hungry television and tabloid agents thunder across the Great Plains in search of copy and if it has to be a neighbor or an old high-school teacher they will settle for that and settle with you in exchange for a chat on what is called a "segment." More respectable and more profitable, if it works well, is the production of a book, or what passes by that name. The book may be written with or without assistance and the gestation period need not be long and arduous, nor should it be. Speed of publication is very useful. The public may appear to be insatiable, but within a pause staleness can be a worry and the novelty of a new case is always a threat. The hacks who filled the *Police Gazette* and *True Detective* had to work, pad around the neighborhood, get the jailhouse information, and then write the story. Now the celebrity books are apt to be a communal effort, like a victory garden.

The Simpson trial has produced three lawyer books thus far and more are said to be in process. Alan Dershowitz and Robert Shapiro from the defense and Christopher Darden for the prosecution are already in print. Mr. Darden's book, *In Contempt*, has been No. 1 on the bestseller list and Mr. Shapiro's book only a few notches behind. Alan Dershowitz has the distinction of having written his own book, *Reasonable Doubts*, without assistance, and has published a number of other books "in his own write." Each of the advocates wishes to assure us early on of his personal integrity in his professional life and in his decision to participate in the Simpson case. The high publicity, the large fees, and the large questioning of the verdict are matters perhaps of occasional twinges of discomfort for the defense. For Christopher Darden, a prosecutor, his distress and need for vindication lay in his being a black man trying to send a charismatic fellow African American to prison for life without the possibility of parole.

It is not easy to imagine Lawyer Dershowitz in discomfort about his life decisions although he does tread carefully in this text. He informs us that he is a tenured professor at the Harvard Law School and works very hard there and is in no need of employment elsewhere. "I agreed to join the O. J. Simpson defense team, in large part, because I knew that this case—for better or worse—would be an education for America, and indeed for the world, about the realities of our criminal justice system." Dershowitz's book is clearly and interestingly written, informative about the law, rich in legal anecdotes, and has the virtue of an index and notes citing sources.

The books by Christopher Darden and Robert Shapiro are personal accounts of their lives during the trial and in Darden's case of his life as a whole, his biography as a young black man growing up in Richmond, California, in the San Francisco Bay area. His personal and family history is interspersed with the account of his service in the prosecution of the Simpson case. The conclusion of the trial brings him to grief and outrage and the title of his book, *In Contempt*, does not so much refer to the legal term as to the fact he has written in contempt of O. J. Simpson, whom he despises. He expresses his contempt by a long passage, in the first pages, written in the style of hard-boiled fiction.

> *Through the window, you watched Nicole put away the dishes, didn't you?* ... You believed she was yours on that first date, when you tore at her pants to get at her more easily, when she seemed to like that. ... You came out of the shadows so quickly, so smoothly, you must've surprised yourself a little. You hit her with your fist and with the knife handle, right on the crown of her head. Then you grabbed her by the arm and drove the knife deep into her neck, four times.

Poor Ron Goldman appears and is slaughtered ... "*You couldn't find your hat and glove, but I'll bet you stared at her for a moment. ...* It was her fault, wasn't it? You owned her now. Completely. Forever."

Darden goes through the trial, the death of his brother from AIDS, his decision, regretted, to let O. J. try on the glove, his relation to Marcia Clark, the Goldman and Brown families, to Johnnie Cochran. From this book and from Shapiro's we see that lawyers are prone to rage with their colleagues, on their own side as well as on that of the opponents. Shapiro has some animadversions about Cochran and will not shake F. Lee Bailey's hand henceforth.

Darden believes the evidence against Simpson is overwhelming and he leaves the courtroom after the acquittal in a stricken state. Robert Shapiro goes through the matters that rightly, in his view, constitute reasonable doubt as it is defined in law, although it is clear we are not necessarily concerned with innocence here. About the client in the last line of the book: "We never had a personal relationship before, and we won't have one in the future."

The case for reasonable doubt is best made by Dershowitz, who was not often in court but who has the case in all its detail in hand and asks all the questions of an advocate as well as those of an opponent, that is a doubter not swayed by "reasonable." He lists the treacherous items more or less as follows:

1. The blood on the glove found at Simpson's estate, said to be a match for Simpson and Brown.

2. Blood on the back gate at the crime scene. Said to be a DNA match for Simpson.

3. Bloodstained socks found on Simpson's bedroom floor. DNA match for Simpson and Brown claimed.

4. Blood on the door of the Bronco and on the floor and console. Match claimed for Simpson, Brown, and Goldman.

5. Blood near the victims at the crime scene. DNA match for Simpson.

6. Hair and clothing fibers found at crime scene, proposed as a match for Simpson.

7. Bloody shoe prints. Simpson's shoe size.

8. Simpson's blood at his own estate.

9. Spousal abuse history.

10. Time: "window of opportunity" for Simpson to have committed crimes and return home, meet the limousine driver.

The defense: Contamination at the crime scene; bodies dragged around before fibers and hair samples obtained; failure of the police to notify the coroner until hours later; failure of police to obtain a search warrant for entry into Simpson's estate and misstatement of intention of visit by Detective Vanatter, who, in addition, carried about for three hours the blood taken from Simpson on his return from Chicago before booking it; criminalists failing to find blood on back gate in the original investigation and in the first photographs taken of Simpson's bedroom there were no socks at all to be seen on the floor; negligent handling of blood samples in police laboratory.

Sloppy police work, missing blood, if it was missing, from the vial taken from Simpson, insufficient protection of the Bronco when impounded; the six or so minutes Simpson would have had to leave the scene, return home, change his bloody clothes, and get into the waiting limousine to take him to the airport. This was the dossier offered by the defense and from which apparently the jurors, deliberating less than four hours, returned a unanimous verdict of not guilty. For Dershowitz, the case was won by "work done by our experts, which cast grave doubts on the police investigation and by the legal strategy that locked the prosecution into its initial mistakes at a public preliminary hearing."

Dershowitz makes a deft presentation of his conviction that the verdict properly rested upon reasonable doubt about aspects of the impugning evidence. Some of the jurors did a good deal of chatting on *Primetime Live, Dateline NBC, Today,* and other television programs; the transcripts have been consulted and references duly noted. They remark on the original lie, if such it was, that the invading detectives did not consider Simpson a suspect when they went over the wall but were concerned only to notify him of the murders and the presence of his children at the police station. In the annals of doubtful police testimony, nicely known as "framing the guilty," this instance can be seen as a mere smudge. The jurors speak not of a wide police conspiracy but of a "conspiracy with some." The presence of EDTA on the dilatory examination of the socks and the blood on the back gate was puzzling since EDTA is an anti-coagulant, used in laboratories to prevent clotting of the specimens, and is not found in human blood—suspicious matters indeed. Dershowitz reflects that "had the five detectives been more candid with the jury about the original search, it is certainly possible that the jurors might have discounted all these suspicions as coincidental." On the matter of coincidence, Marcia Clark in her summation is sarcastic about Simpson's good luck in cutting his finger on the night his ex-wife and her friend were stabbed to death. (Simpson spoke of cutting his finger on his cellular phone to account for his blood on the door of the Bronco, on the driveway, and in the foyer of his house.)

Robert Shapiro criticizes his colleague Johnnie Cochran for playing "the race card from the bottom of the deck." Here, the intrusion into the trial and quick extrusion from it by the loquacious LAPD Detective Mark Fuhrman. When on the witness stand under oath and under questioning by defense attorney F. Lee Bailey, he was asked if he had ever used the word "nigger" in the last ten years. Fuhrman coolly said, no, I have not. Owing to the embarrassment of everyone in the court, "nigger" became the N word. It turned out that the defense had discovered tape recordings made with Fuhrman by a hopeful screenwriter roaming around Los Angeles in pursuit of material for a police script. To a stranger, Fuhrman volunteered his vehement detestation of Negroes, interracial couples, and a number of other citizens. He used the N word forty times in the tape and indicated that his aim as a police officer was to club the Ns, stop them in traffic without reason, manufacture evidence against them, and, as another person testified, Fuhrman would like "to take them all out and burn them up." It was Fuhrman who, in the early morning visit to Simpson's house with other detectives, noted the blood on the Bronco door, found the bloody glove at the back of the guest house.

The glove, the glove, the ring of an aria to come and first to be sung by the tenor, Fuhrman, and then by the ill-fated baritone, O. J. Simpson. Since Fuhrman had lied about the N word, it was fortunate for the defense that it was he who, ever alert, wanders alone about Simpson's place, takes in Kato Kaelin's account of the knocking on the wall the previous night, the murder night, grasps the significance of the spot, and supposedly drops the purloined glove there. One glove was recovered from the crime scene; the alleged conspiracy would have Fuhrman finding the second glove, overlooked by the overlooking LAPD criminologists, and putting it in his pocket or somewhere, ready for malicious use. However, had Simpson's blood not been at the crime scene it could not have been on the glove. Nor could the blood have been planted there during the dawn of discovery by a badge villain or villains, since there was no "extra" Simpson blood available until his return from Chicago at mid-morning. After the damning revelation about the N word, Fuhrman did not testify further, retired from the police department, and went on his way to Utah.

In spite of the blurs, confusion, murky demonstrations by the defense of possible errors in shoe prints, and so on, the fact that there was *any* of Simpson's blood to be accounted for was a deeply disturbing circumstance. If there is such a thing as the irrevocable, unchallengeable DNA peculiar to every individual on earth, with the probability of a duplication to be almost unimaginably remote, then bungling, contamination, and deterioration could not lend credibility to a complete dismissal of the blood swatches containing the DNA of O. J. Simpson.

The defense facing this had to *imply*, strongly imply, a deliberate infusion of Simpson's blood on at least some of the relevant items, a sort of blood conspiracy, risky and daring. For this the motivation was again an implication, "the race card" Shapiro condemns Johnnie Cochran for imposing. But what other motivation except racism could accommodate this elaborate fraud? The memory of the almost joyous beating of Rodney King by the LAPD officers lent some credence, we imagine, to a verdict that was essentially a repudiation of police evidence.

Christopher Darden: "Experienced lawyers were amazed at the amount and the level of scientific evidence we had against Simpson.... Never in our legal system has so much blood and DNA been amassed against one defendant."

The curtain came down and the drama was at an end so far as

courtroom television was concerned; but we can still hear from the commentators and "this evening's guests" about the civil suits brought against Simpson by the Brown and Goldman families. There are certain cast additions of interest, notably Simpson's friend, Al Cowlings, who drove the white Bronco through the streets of Los Angeles before a surrender by the accused. And for the addicted there remain the austere and informative trials on Court TV, many of which are for murders. An almost empty courtroom, a few spectators, a relative or two for the dead and the accused, a sparse congregation of lawyers, one or two at most for each side; witnesses having their say with few objections and few sidebars. We cannot judge whether the quiet, almost somnolent afternoons at the bar of justice are equitable: Dershowitz reports there is a likelihood of conviction in approximately 75 to 80 percent of contested criminal cases.

Simpson, wearily facing in some of his old playgrounds an almost leprous isolation, was heard to say: "What do they want me to do? Go to Africa?"

1996

HEAD OVER HEELS

THE SHABBY history of the United States in the last year can be laid at the door of three unsavory citizens. President Clinton: shallow, reckless, a blushing trimmer; Monica Lewinsky, aggressive, rouge-lipped exhibitionist; Judge Kenneth Starr, pale, obsessive Pharisee. There was collusion among back-country elected ayatollahs stoning the adulterers in the public square while intoning the satanic verses of the Constitution. And washed up on the banks of the Potomac, the burrowing otters, Linda Tripp and Lucianne Goldberg.

Humiliation, resonant, aching word, near to the sacred, fell at its worst upon the nation as a whole, as a conception, a nation among nations, enlightened despite the wish of some for a premillennial accounting in the wings. Humiliation has at the first dawn fled from Monica Lewinsky; with Judge Starr, many a stumbling perceived, with many to catch his arm before a fall; Clinton, the president, not a sports announcer or a political "adviser" set up for exposure in a Washington hotel, for him the awful moment, or moments, of surrender; the bad dream, to follow him to the grave, of being nude in the streets. Or to lower the tone in an obscurely derived current idiom: He's toast.

Move on, move on, friends and enemies say. Put the nation in a Santini van, wrap its underwear in brown paper, and, horn honking, move on. That's the word for a country of road hogs, for the proper business of the state, for that woman, Miss Lewinsky, for Judge Starr, who seems to threaten to stand in place, still tapping away.

The sad, sad sin of location. As the reigning Head of State, a celebrity with his Marine band and honor guard, he has certain restrictions based upon his high, none higher, recognition factor. So it cannot be a Rooms-by-the-Day Motel, but the Oval Office of the White House, its bathroom or some private corner, whatever, wherever. The President has his oddities of practice coming forth to us from his partner and other deponents going back through the years. Looking over his *Police Gazette* profile, starting in Arkansas, we can say he is having bad luck due to the Zeitgeist, the historical moment for girls, or women. Previously they were somewhat restrained by self-protection, by not wanting mother, family, children, or job supervisor to know what was going on in the back seat of the car, in the after-hours office. Now there is the book, the lawsuit, the settlement, the chance to join the others on file which gives a jog to old unhealthy memories.

We are told that Monica Lewinsky early on, after her belief that the President had in a crowd cast lustful eye-beams her way, went home to read Gennifer Flowers's memoir called *Sleeping with the President.** Monica's bleak "sensual" engagement to come will in no way match Miss Flowers's hot twelve-year affair, albeit off and on, with the Attorney General of Arkansas and later the Governor of the state. She was much better housed for action, with her own flat in Little Rock, and later her rooms in Fort Worth. "So there I was, head-over-heels in love with the married attorney general of Arkansas. And there he was, head-over-heels in love with me." The author meets the often encountered measly aspect of words when hoping to describe sexual transport, but she makes her own strenuous effort in passage after passage, of which the following is the cleanest, we might say. "We continued to make love for several more hours, as Bill demonstrated more sexual libido than I have ever seen in a man. I'm not sure how many times he came, but he seemed to be inexhaustible. I remember thinking this is the kind of drive a man needs to become president of the United States."

*

Sleeping with the President: My Intimate Years with Bill Clinton (Anonymous Press, 1998).

There were reassuring polls for the President as the dismaying revelations, depositions, false oaths, and actual impeachment by the House of Representatives fell upon his head, brick after brick. No matter, he seemed to get back up as mysteriously as those creatures flattened in a comic strip. Throughout the pummeling his performance as president was approved by the public. This was due, we heard, to the good economy, more jobs than job-seekers, a little bump of a few cents in the minimum wage, the affection of the black population for the sense he gave of at least knowing they were around. *Oh, Captain! My Captain! Rise up and hear the bells.* And then for some, he's kinda cute.*

In addition to the charges of perjury, the prosecutors and the Managers in the House of Representatives seemed to want to rebuke the State of the Marriage Union. (What may have been on Legislator Livingston's plate that led the poor fellow to resign under threat of exposure of violations of his marriage vows, to run into the woods as if there were a posse on his heels—it is altogether pleasant that thus far the public has been spared inside information.)

Weary yawns from the hinterland may partly have arisen from knowledge of Life: Life Science, as the extension courses name it. Philandering husband held in the family pen by the mortgage, the "kids," debts, in-laws, neighbors, affections, familiarities, fatigue. For the working class, there is nothing to be gained by going public, telling your story, giving the real lowdown on him when nobody knows who he is. The truck-stop waitress who has caught the attention of the tired trucker, attention for a time until he doesn't show up again. Well, she can overstep, call his home, serious offense, tell the wife all about it. Shut up, bitch, the wife says, and returns to the patio where he is putting a match to the charcoal. Where is the outrage? A good people should be displaying more outrage about everything, so the prompting Mr. William Bennett insists in mournful cadence.

---

*One wit wrote that perhaps Jews liked Clinton because in high school instead of going out for the football team he signed up for the band. (Philip Weiss, *The New York Observer*, March 15, 1999).

It appears that men are men, DNA. Even the abstemious Prosecutor Starr seemed to have an inkling of this and thus ordained that his desired impeachment of the President should not be about sex. The dread business at hand was lying under oath about sex when summoned to the courts. True, the President's prevaricating affidavit in the Paula Jones case might have passed as an unfortunate deception. Still and yet, addressing the world on television, solemn as a rogue in a Molière comedy, and denying that he had ever had sexual relations with that woman, Monica Lewinsky: that is a haunting bit of dramaturgy.

Lying under oath. In the courtrooms, a ringing Not Guilty plea is not always taken literally. It often says: Prove me guilty if you can and meet my defense attorney here by my side.

Courtroom scene, imaginary:

Did your wife threaten you with a gun?

Yes, Sir, she did.

Did you then in self-defense take the gun from her?

That is correct.

The gun went off and your wife was accidentally shot and killed. Is that your testimony?

Yes, Sir, it is.

Verdict: Murder in the First Degree.

The wanton licentiousness of the questioning of Monica Lewinsky by the Independent Counsel's Office made this a most interesting, vivid presidential scandal to rest in all its skulking, panting eternity in the basement of the Library of Congress. The detail so rich, so concrete, a riveting pornography elicited with a bug-eyed tenacity, a prosecutorial relishing in passing beyond the intention to establish that sex had indeed taken place between the two in the White House. Many, indeed most, of the legislators voiced one after another a concern not only for themselves but for the corruption of our children and grandchildren. The unborn innocents got a lot: nine instances of oral sex, the responses of the performers, extravagant documentation of completions or what appear to be withdrawals; what rewards, if any, for the performing female, and how achieved, the interesting possibilities of the telephone as an instrument of excitation.

Did the President ever use a cigar in a sexual way? Did he touch her on the breast or in the genital area? Was it through her clothes or in direct contact with the skin? Had the President masturbated her when he put his hand down her trousers?

As this speculation dragged on about Monica Lewinsky, the sole witness, it was feared that in the minds of some of the old-fashioned, largely Christian folk waiting in the House of Representatives she might be what their generation called a fast number. A certain sanitizing of her image began in the Independent Counsel chambers. After the voluble and valuable tape recording of her tone and practice by her friend Linda Tripp, it was prudent to shift the accent lest it veer away from the central figure, the President. The predatory groupie of the tapes became the "young intern," a sort of medieval page at court and above all young, which she was and is.

Monica's Story, by Andrew Morton. A vertiginous accounting of bantering baby talk mixed with her extraordinary bordello reminiscences. She it is who proudly wears the bright red A on her bosom but it is he who "will not speak." When at last Clinton is forced, or thinks he is forced, to address the nation and admit that his denial of the sex affair was false and that what he did was "wrong" and "inappropriate," Monica, listening, was, as ever, Niobe, all tears. She had wanted him to say that what he did he did for love and so what was this stuff about wrong and inappropriate? "I was very hurt and angered by his speech. I felt like a piece of trash." He should have acknowledged her worth, her suffering, and that of her family.

Her story has a pleasant beginning. Mr. Morton is chatting with Monica Lewinsky in a "smart apartment building in Beverly Hills." She's free and on the television screen Kenneth Starr is giving his twelve-hour testimony in the impeachment trial of the President. Monica is knitting, worrying "about changing to smaller needles to make her scarf less bulky." Soon he reports that his subject has a "remarkable capacity to remember times, places and dates with precision and accuracy." To the point since this is her story. She is poised, articulate; she is also suffering from low self-esteem. She is demure and polite, "a far cry from the brassy Beverly Hills babe of media mythology."

She has a weight problem. We learn about her family, her high school days, her parents' divorce. At Beverly Hills High School drama department she met up with a big moment, one Andy Bleiler, and then, and then, when she was nineteen she lost her virginity to him who had in the meantime married. He tells her he's moving to Portland, Oregon, and she transfers from Santa Monica College to Lewis and Clark College, in Portland. The affair with Bleiler continued, off and on, for five years, "a time she remembers with a mixture of tenderness, sorrow, anger and bitterness." He's unfaithful to her and to his wife as well. It's a mess.

Her candor, a cataract of expressiveness that got her in trouble on the Linda Tripp tapes, has not abated in her interviews with Morton for purposes of the story to be presented to the public. It's a curiosity.

Things aren't going well with Andy and so she has a "fling" with his younger brother. Here her constant thought of being fat, of looking too fat, of having a closet in Washington of "fat clothes" indicate that she truly was fat, although in good shape now for her appearances. Anyone who has lived in a town or small city can remember that fat girls "put out" when they got a chance, or so the gossip went. In any case, Monica said that the "fling" with her lover's brother was not only done as revenge for Andy's infidelity but because he had told her his brother would "'never like [her] because he only liked tall, skinny women.' Monica felt that she had shown him otherwise."

The story proceeds as it will, and perhaps unfortunately for many. Monica Lewinsky is off to Washington to serve in the White House as an unpaid intern. One day, a public gathering, and there he is, the President himself. It's Hail to the Chief and to the intern who finds that he "exudes a sexual energy." On to another occasion, the President going down the line shaking hands, and her turn in the hand-shaking: "He undressed me with his eyes." Second sight, perhaps: "the capacity to see remote or future objects or events." And yet once more, at a public gathering she throws him a kiss and he laughs. "The following day saw Monica . . . fondly expecting the Secret Service to call her discreetly. . . . Every time the phone rang her nerves jangled. The day passed, however, without the dramatic presidential request for her company." A mind of such wondrous concentration is a cocoon, or like a succulent oyster ever floating in its shell.

As the internship's term elapses, she accepts an offer to stay on as a paid employee in the Office of Internal Affairs (well named), quarters in the White House. Before the new situation could begin there was the government shutdown, but being still an unpaid young courtier she could be useful in filling the gap left by the absent regular staff. The chaotic scene is also useful and there is the President running about and there is Monica saying "Hi!" and soon she decides to "raise the stakes." A famous moment in the imperial history narrated by our Saint-Simon: "She put her hands on her hips and with her thumbs lifted the back of her jacket, allowing him a fleeting glimpse of her thong underwear where it showed above the waistline of her suit's pants." And she is invited to the throne room where the first oral sex takes place while the monarch is on a phone call from a congressman. "We clicked at an incredible level. People have made it seem so demeaning for me but it wasn't; it was exciting and the irony is that I had the first orgasm of the relationship." What can you do with a poised, demure, intelligent, articulate, insecure, witty, vulnerable, low-self-esteem, overweight girl like that?

Meanwhile the halls of the White House have become like a bowling alley with Monica knocking down ninepins—Betty Currie, guards— with every throw. "When clouds are seen, wise men put on their cloaks," a citizen opines during the raucous, disorderly reign of Shakespeare's Richard III. Clinton cannot be named wise and was slow to put on his cloak, but Monica, as importunate as a tornado, was to find him unavailable to her whirling solicitations. The business was to be closed down, for the duration as they said in wartime. At last a wise person appeared on the scene: enter the noble Mrs. Evelyn Lieberman, who, seeing Monica dashing about the halls, requests her pass. Who goes there? When she learns that indeed it's a paid employee with the right tag around her neck, she provides a sharp, swift bit of dialogue: "They hired you?"

The pesky clerk is exiled to the Pentagon and at first this would seem to be a welcome all-clear, noontide whistle for the beleaguered White House. Instead, a missile launching was ahead. In the fortress, Monica is miserable and has nothing on her mind except returning to her former post, about which wish Clinton and others had said they "would try"—a white lie for once. Telephone calls, presents sent, messages delivered by courier, demands to return to the White House. She dashes to the line outside the church the Clintons attend.

She manages to be in New York for the celebration of the President's fiftieth birthday where, "in the crush of people around him, she was able to briefly brush his crotch with her hand as he is greeting well-wishers." At the inaugural ball for the second term she waits "five hours behind the rope line so that she can see him on the stage with the First Lady." She's not always standing in line and so for one whose boast is to be ever "comfortable with her sexuality" she has a three-month "relationship," another favorite word, with an older married man, a colleague at the Pentagon. The relationship led to an abortion.

Even though she no longer had a White House pass, Betty Currie, the President's secretary, could invite her for certain gatherings. This she did for a small occasion, and after it was over Monica was allowed to go alone to the presidential office and this produced a prime exhibition for the courtroom drama. Miss Lewinsky had felt "demeaned" by the habit of the President, who "in the middle of oral sex...pushed her away." She complained and he agreed to go, as it were, all the way, and Monica felt that "at last he truly trusted her." Later, it was found, with Linda Tripp's assistance, that a telltale semen stain had hit the Gap dress, a garment on a coat hanger that would provide a star turn in the impeachment trial. The stain, like a bloody footprint, and *his*.

Filth, squalor, folly, and base inanity—the tale grows wearisome until a speeding diversion. Mrs. Linda Tripp, a Pentagon colleague. An ear for Monica, who is still in the matter of discretion running a big deficit, as nurses name it when describing the victims of a stroke. Mrs. Tripp, forty-five years old when the alliance began, divorced from a soldier, two children, secretarial school, work in the administration of George Bush, said by many to pass boring office hours by gossip and intrigue. Disapproved of the style of the Clinton folk. A weight problem once more. And when facing the cameras, a sort of celebrity, needing a bit of a makeover of hair and wardrobe, like Paula Jones. Things certainly come Linda Tripp's way, a fortuity not unwelcome.

For a time she stayed on in the White House after the Bush defeat, and when Vincent Foster, Deputy White House Counsel, committed suicide she was the last person to see him alive. She testified in Kenneth Starr's investigation of the suicide. She had connections with the lawyers in the Paula Jones suit against the President; she knew Kathleen Willey, who told her about the sexual harassment incident in Clinton's office. Contrary to Mrs. Willey's story, Tripp said Willey came out of the office "disheveled but happy."

Monica, a river of startling words, flowed over Linda Tripp day and night and the receiver found the words refreshing indeed, a dunking most valuable since she was posting a book proposal about the misdeeds of the Clintons. She encouraged the younger woman to continue the pursuit, a superfluity like asking a barking dog to keep at it. And then Linda Tripp began to record the telephone calls, without permission and illegal in Maryland, where she lived. She got out her notebook for a listing of Monica's lovers, tape rolling. Seven or eight if you count a "health-nut boy" whose name she doesn't remember.

It is at this point that Monica takes the view, also expressed by the President, that oral sex isn't truly sex; sex is intercourse. Mrs. Tripp murmurs, "I'm getting an education late in life."*

Why the taping began is somewhat confusing or purposefully muddled even though it doesn't need explanation because Linda Tripp was as loquacious as Monica and liked to tell friends and reporters that she had some hot information about sex at the White House while refusing to name the girl. According to Mrs. Tripp, the suggestion to tape Monica's calls came from the book agent Lucianne Goldberg. The agent is a woman of striking intrepidity, colorful speech, dramatically conservative, a hound on the trail of useful scandal. She had been involved with Tripp on the failed first book project about the Clinton administration's misdeeds, and when the much more inflammatory story of Monica came to her notice she advised Tripp to wake up, get it down, documentation, on tape. Tripp's contention later that she needed documentation for her own protection against threatening enemies and so on was not entirely convincing, to put it in a way that avoids libel. In any case, the show was on the road. Goldberg put Linda in touch with Paula Jones's lawyers and Monica Lewinsky entered the case as indicative of Clinton's "pattern of behavior."†

Nevertheless, Monica Lewinsky is going along in her own dear fashion. If a bomb went off outside her window, she would probably think: Oh, good. He must be calling me. He was calling less often and keeping his vow of celibacy outside marriage. Linda Tripp knew what was ahead for Monica: the tapes, a subpoena, exposure, big trouble. After encouraging the hapless one to hang on, she began to advise her to get out of town, to New York, where her mother was living. A job preference list was sent to the Oval Office and the response was like a splendid, beribboned basket of fruits and flowers

*Communication from the Office of the Independent Counsel, Kenneth W. Starr, pp. 2263–2264.

†The most interesting, densely argued, and reflective examination of the Starr Report appeared in articles written by Renata Adler. See *Vanity Fair*, December 1998, and the *Los Angeles Times Book Review*, March 14, 1999.

delivered express by Vernon Jordan. The United Nations was on the list and by way of the White House staff, not Jordan this time, there was the US ambassador to the United Nations, "Bill" Richardson, on Monica's phone saying, "Hi! I understand you want to come and work for me." And she is off for an interview in his Watergate apartment. After a thirty-minute discussion, he offered her a job in his public affairs office. It turned out the place didn't appeal to her. So it's a "working lunch" with Vernon Jordan in his office and interviews with American Express and Revlon. She met with the top executives at Revlon, where Jordan was a member of the board of directors, and was offered a job paying $40,000 a year.

The interventions for this clerk are indeed a saintly generosity. Busy and kind corporate gentlemen must nevertheless have a reason for choosing one among the many needy that cross their path. Of course, the reason here was pressing: Monica had the goods on *him* and everyone concerned knew it. On the other hand, she, who has no more sense of nuance than a coyote, could well have believed that lawyers, jobs, lunches came her way because she was a friend people would naturally want to help.

The subpoena to appear in the Jones case intervened and Vernon Jordan secured for her the respected lawyer Frank Carter. Not telling him the truth led to her signing an affidavit that she had only met the President several times as an employee, that she had not had sex with him, and that he did not offer her employment or other benefits in exchange for a sexual relationship, and so on.

She was packing to leave for New York when Linda Tripp seduced her into a lunch date where she was met by FBI agents and taken to a room in the Ritz-Carlton Hotel. "For ten hours Monica was alone with as many as nine armed FBI agents and Starr's deputies, hard-boiled characters who normally hunt or prosecute those responsible for the most serious and brutal federal offenses." Linda Tripp, placed in another room, was in touch by phone with the Paula Jones attorneys.

Monica asked to call her lawyer and was strongly encouraged not to do so. A lawyer of their own choosing was proposed. She asked to call her mother and was told that her mother too was not necessary. Starr's lieutenant gave her the choice: twenty-seven years in jail or immediate cooperation. Susan McDougal in handcuffs and leg irons made its point. The detectives themselves suggested that Monica, as a bit of cooperation, wear a wire and she refused. She was told that her false affidavit was a felony, even though it had not yet been filed by her lawyer, Frank Carter. Her mother arrived from New York and it was after one in the morning when they went back to their Watergate apartment.

Mr. Ginsburg, a legal friend of Monica's father, was brought into the case and into the long struggle of refusing to testify unless granted immunity. Ginsburg was found to have too much fun declaiming into the microphones of the press and on talk shows, a bit of harmless celebrity malpractice which accorded with his specialty in law as a malpractice attorney. A new legal team was hired, immunity to prosecution granted, and the degrading, capricious trial, the tapes, the blow jobs were given to history and to the world. A rough time indeed for Monica Lewinsky, but she eased into it and the members of the grand jury entered their opinion into the record. "We wanted to offer you a bouquet of good wishes that includes luck, success, happiness, and blessings." Her interview with Barbara Walters was beamed to the world in spectacular numbers, as if for a declaration of war. *Monica's Story* is crossing the plains and the oceans. She does not underline the gravity of what has occurred, the drastic diminishment of the civil and political life of the nation. But she's sorry and has many worries on her mind, especially the frequently expressed fear that no one would want to marry her now.

For months and months and still remaining, perhaps never to be expunged: a druidical Halloween of rascals with law degrees lighting fires and casting spells. And the biggest, saddest spook of all, President Clinton.

1999

ON BEHALF OF THE UNBORN

AS THE Republican Convention gathers in San Diego, many middle-aged and more than a few elderly fellows are rousing themselves into a passion about a woman's right to abortion. Of course, Pat Buchanan, Rep. Henry Hyde, and the Rev. Pat Robertson have never missed a period and yet they have much in mind for young women who have done so and placed themselves and their future in a distressing state.

The legislating men are of interest because of their inexperience in the matter at hand. They seem to believe girls, as some may still be spoken of, have reached their pregnant condition quite alone, out of reprehensible indulgence or folly or criminal impulse, and so must live with the consequences, that is to give birth. A gun went off, you might say, but the hand that pulled the trigger is of no moral, religious, or legal concern. Can it be that the San Diego gentlemen were themselves free of the raging, insistent testosterone of the male in youth and beyond? Or perhaps they feel that when the testosterone bullet hits the girl the man is acting in a sort of metaphysical self-defense. In any case, he is acquitted and the penalty, if you like, is hers alone.

It would be honorable for the Republican platform to consider the following plank—a heavy piece of wood indeed. In their frequent suggestions for constitutional amendments, as if they were a corner stoplight, they might propose, on behalf of the contested unborn, a command that young men remain celibate until marriage. The Celibacy Amendment deserves the floor.

The nation's sons are a valuable resource, but if our sons willfully break the Celibacy Law and, to use an inspired phrase of ancient coinage, "knock up" our daughters, the fate will be forced marriage and active fatherhood. For many it will mean leaving high school or college or law school, and perhaps pumping gas to buy the crib, the mashed food in little bottles, and the first refrigerator and rearing the slowly maturing human child, once unborn but now born in partnership with whatever pretty, or passable in the dark, face was in the back seat of the car some time ago.

The lawmakers are not likely to know personal hardship from the Celibacy Amendment. Most are married and too busy even to take time out for an hour or so in a motel. They are in a punishing mood and history is on their side. Unmarried women have inflicted terrible tortures on their own bodies, hoping to undo or to conceal. When that failed, as it usually did, society often gave them abandonment, disgrace, and, in some cultures, death.

Men of imagination have understood the appalling dilemma for the woman that may follow a night or two of pastoral young love under a summer sky. It would be a spiritual advancement in San Diego to remember Thomas Hardy's *Tess* and Tolstoy's *Resurrection* with the peasant girl and the prince visiting his estate. There are profound moral reflections therein about the sweetness and naturalness of love and the sometimes awesome consequences for her.

However, a rich political life does not find time for the wisdom of fiction. And so in the mundane interest of equity, the antiabortion zealots would honor their obsession by proposing a sort of balancing of the human budget: a Celibacy Before Marriage Amendment to the US Constitution. Let us see how that goes down.

1996

FEMININE PRINCIPLE

THE AMERICAN WOMAN AS SNOW QUEEN

THE MUDDY waves of American self-reproach beat upon the European shores again. Nothing seems to have happened in thirty years. The postwar generation of young Americans is back in Europe, but it has skipped the last war and everything goes on reassuringly as before, the needle is stuck in a conversation from *The Sun Also Rises*. Comfortable with government funds or savings, there is nevertheless often a shy and wistful glance beneath the crew-cut—these new expatriates seek after all a place in time, the consolations of history. Conservative, like a reluctant old Victorian gentleman they cling to their past, the bad old times, an original stew of the 1920s and '30s. Sighing, they find themselves and their ideas among the dear, remembered deprivations of their parents' lives: starving, disenfranchised workers, the outlawed artist, apple-sellers on the street, fascism just around the corner, the shamefully rich owners of production insisting upon a new war. It is touching—so history is preserved in character.

But there is too much of it and in the historical attitude there are always footnote disagreements. It is easier to take simply one unchallenged notion—our own and the consequent European horror of the American girl, who is also away from home by the thousands, dog-paddling in the European waters, gasping and calling out helplessly, "Me, I'm different. Don't think I'm like the others, please!"

In a French café an alarmed and somewhat shabby French girl accompanies an American "painter" in blue-jean battledress. "She looks after him. She's not spoiled like American women." The other Americans yearningly approve his luck. A Frenchman with a stunning companion arouses envy. No one knows quite what they may be talking about—the depths of this dialogue are not to be plumbed with hotel and restaurant French—but no matter. Who could fail to note that shot of stimulating benzedrine that *must* be in the French woman's conversation, her "active" listening, her artistic prodding here and there, her smile of comprehension and fascination? "What animation!" the American boys say, their eyes popping. And then there is the more earthbound type of young American—oh, the Italian girl's exquisite, rumpled, and plump submission to fate!

"But your women are so cold!" the French say and we nod bleakly. The Italians shudder. "I'm afraid of them, they want so many things all the time. Our girls are not like that." Only the Turks, with their scarecrows in colored rags doing all the work in the fields, seem to feel a disgust with the native product equal to ours; and there it is not so much a comparison with foreign brands that arouses their scorn as the comparison with their male selves snoozing in the cafés.

No one could cast doubt on the obvious and tremendous charms of European women, but the licentious familiarity with the subject of American women that is commonly undertaken, the repetitive exchanges, fill one with gloom, this eternal dining on stale cake. Perhaps verbal liberties are the only conceivable ones, since the woman in reality is held to be so fleshless, bleak, and buried that other intimacies are unthinkable—the violation of a corpse. She appears as a creature of legend, the snow queen—tall, beautiful, appallingly splendid, all cleanliness and whiteness, living in her empty, silent, frigid palace. Her kisses freeze the heart, her wintry smiles hide a depreciation, her glittering, spotless, squeamish magnificence lulls one to the soft slumber that kills. Criticism and horror of her are the cries of the root and bud, the crackling of the frozen earth longing for a Latin sun; nature screams, but she does not listen. Unapproachable, self-isolated, she is nevertheless as restless and rapacious as a terrible cold wind, and, as in the fairy tale, the little boy can only be released from this glacial death by the hot tears of love—a foreign love.

This threatening apparition has the persistence of a folk belief, a native wonder of the world, exported along with the cowboys and gangsters to other countries. The foreign traveler to America is no doubt fascinated. Skyscrapers, energy, wealth, automobiles—these at least can be seen; their weight, undeniability, even their moral content (the obvious is also sometimes true) may reasonably chagrin the stranger who prefers in well-known places to refute common observation, even his own at times, in favor of a fresh judgment. At first glance the American woman he has heard about—and she is our own creation —is not on view. Something fantastically contrary meets the eye: the informal, independent, lively American girl whose manner recalls the old evangelists swinging over the Sunday circuit. Far from realizing the wicked somnambulist, she must seem self-confidently forward and as incurably folksy as a peasant. But her very contrariness to expectation only serves to make the legend more profoundly appealing; it becomes not a mere fact of experience but a serious, subtle observation hidden to superficial knowledge. This naive, friendly surface is a disguise, we are told, a marvelous baroque invention masking a soul shriveled by Puritanism and vanity swollen by leisure and power. Bold and generous in appearance, it was a difficult act of the imagination for the American intellectuals, both men and women, to discover that this ordinary woman was in truth as greedy and anarchic as an infant. It is nearly impossible to think of her as a mother, but even that has been made so painless in her belief that a new conscience-stricken generation takes lessons from the doctor in how to have a baby without modern aids, like a pioneer woman in a lonely cabin.

Mrs. Trollope describes the life of a rich Philadelphia lady in the 1820s. The lady has a handsome house with elegant furnishings, servants, and abundant leisure, but her existence is as cheerless and repetitive as a squaw's. She does her needlework, goes to the missionary society in the afternoon, where she has bare bland conversations with other privileged Philadelphia ladies, and no conversation at all with her Husband, who returns from his work in the evenings, "shakes hands with her, spits, and dines." Mrs. Trollope regrets the lack of social drama in this destiny, yet even this unbroken, dreary life, calm and endless as the prairie, must seem one of excellent serenity to the young American man of the present—at least it spares him the frustrated expectation and consequent peevishness he professes to find in every American woman now.

The contemporary woman supposedly lives in a solar emptiness warmed occasionally by the dim sounds of the soap opera, and of this fearful nothingness she, and not her husband, is the complete master. Bored and idle, she may play bridge in the afternoon, but even the card game is only a pantomime, a wordless ballet simulating sociability, for she has no true friendship or communication with other women. Her evenings are more interesting because they suggest the rudiments of social intercourse, although always an exchange of remarkable hardness and intimidation. Silence often prevails because she cannot discuss business, politics, or art, but the silence is poisonous; it demands, defies, and dominates with the power of some querulous, bitter, festering law of her own spirit. The evenings end with a triumph, which means she has easily found a way to attack her husband's self-esteem before she retires to the twin beds. It would not be believed if it were suggested that this creature, in between barks and bites, does three times as much housework as the European woman of the same class and purse, who gloriously does none at all, enjoying placidly the comforts of a $12-a-week full-time French slave or the $12-a-month nunlike, dawn-to-midnight, devotions of the Italian domestic.

But this is only the *Vogue* model, captured like an Ivory Soap carving as the American Wife. There are other images of the American woman that haunt and belittle the American man and chill the Europeans—one is that absurd busybody knocking at the door of culture, or only killing time in the drowsy afternoon lecture hall, a sour figure with a roll of concert tickets in her over-the-shoulder bag. Even to see her toiling up the steps of foreign museums makes us wince—we have seen her before, so many times, in travel books and English novels, mispronouncing the names, grabbing it all with that overwhelming denseness and energy. Americans laugh shrilly at this yearning mind because of the closeness of the young men, particularly the articulate ones, to the sensibilities of the mother. Dancing lessons, piano exercises, the drawing box, illustrated classics, and children's encyclopedias—these things embarrass us sorely. The effort, the effort! we remember shamefully, seeing it all as rather priggish and unreal; in Europe, however, Americans begin to think learning and art are breathed in, unconsciously, from the atmosphere, and even though the grossly unmoving modern pink and blue Virgin on the most beautiful, ancient altar is a slap in the face, we soon, by a miracle of hospitality, forget it and only our own contemporary bad taste remains.

But what is so much to be scorned after all in this culture-eager woman? Women are always, according to Schopenhauer, the guardians of the spirit; this hunger for art and excitement is a "natural" role, the very opposite of a humiliating compensation for sexual denials. We sympathize with the peasant woman in fiction who saves her egg money so that her son may become a gentleman in the city, or treasures some little book or picture or gift that will stimulate her children to a less laborious and more intellectual life. Yet the moonstruck wife of a prosperous businessman who clings to her pure and "inspiring" friendship with a weak but gifted young man, reads novels, and likes to discuss the theater is condemned as unbalanced. Her eager and, of course, too freely given appreciation of "fine things" in no way preempts the male prerogative, which is still the grand one of the highest creator of art, philosophy, and science. (That this should still be true for women, after the vote, freedom, wider experience, is one of the jokes of history.)

A recent European testimony, Simone de Beauvoir's *L'Amérique au jour le jour*, comes upon the subject of American women with a bald and instructive directness. A busy observer in her own right, this author's impressions are not confined to sight, but modified by her knowledge of prevailing intellectual opinion in America and particularly by American self-criticism. This criticism is a spectacular cultural achievement and to try to disavow it in the formation of one's own mind and opinion is altogether fruitless and stunting. Disagreement with a specific point of the acid verdict is not likely with us to be a wholesale endorsement of the national character so much as a criticism of a criticism, a yearly revision that seldom disturbs the basic text.

Mlle de Beauvoir's firsthand impressions of American women are so cordial that they have, in this way, a kind of originality. She notes the women's clean hair, amazing health, the good humor of the college girls, their spontaneity, courtesy, goodwill, and their conversational freedom without impudence. With more than a hint of irony, de Tocqueville, a century back, declared himself "frequently surprised and almost frightened at the singular address and happy boldness with which young women in America contrive to manage their thoughts and their language amid all the difficulties of free conversation...."

The amiable details in Simone de Beauvoir's picture have considerable weight, but in terms of the whole they are merely flashes of bright color that make an abandoned landscape seem more desolate. It would, perhaps, be impertinent for a stranger to ignore the attitude of the Americans to whom she talked and whom she had read, and so, against the uncertain evidence of the senses, the venerated, hostile opinion asserts itself. She notes the rancorous accent in which American men talk about women and remembers that it is a commonplace for them to say the women are frigid; she talks of the battle of the sexes, the frustration of the women, the absence of purpose in their lives, the fact that American men don't like them. And the most overwhelming statement is this: "The tragedy of those who have discovered passionate love in Europe and can no longer live with their cold husbands or wives is a stereotype."

The buzz of this theme song is certainly very loud among American intellectuals, but, at its best, it is a miserly way of expressing the American character even in its Puritan aspect and omits the fact that the Puritan heritage is complex, varied, culturally expressive. True, to the American, the voluptuary suggests the pathological—with us love is not an "art," nakedness not without its embarrassments, the body often an uneasy and improbable partner of the soul. We do not have the instinct or the habit of the rich and elaborate European flirtation, the gift for relaxed psychosexual drama. The American finds many things outrageously comical that are at the very heart of the European romance. Seeing this, not in *fact*, but in a parody comparable to the parody we present of ourselves for Europe, we cannot quite take comfortably the heavy-lidded coquetry of the middle-aged French couple (one of Europe's advantages being the recognition that ardent feelings do not disappear at twenty-five), the dark wisdom of the experienced matron with her opportune flatteries one moment and her tolerant smiles another, the luxurious, smothering drapery of the rendezvous, the hardworking charm and artifice that perfume the air. The scene seems to us all ludicrous movement, quickness, dramatic posturing, like one of those speedy silent films of the boudoir—heaves and sighs, black-eyed winks, muscular avowals. Our only equivalent is an imaginary and tired comedienne: the Southern belle with her ruffles, sky-blue costumes, flirtatious physiognomy—the decorations of a romantic pose which the "plain man" loathes because it is calculated and therefore, in his view, spotted and unappetizing like an overripe peach. Love can never be an art with us or even exceptionally artful, because we think it real only when it appears without human aid; it is rain from heaven, not the work of a clever imagination.

It is only a slight exaggeration to say that elaborate concern for "holding a man" or making a woman "feel desirable" are attitudes that would seriously wound the pride of Americans and can be, without humiliation, invoked only during a crisis, when a loss is threatened. In spite of the advertisers' effort to stimulate these activities, we are still not able to practice them with enough seriousness or fundamental belief to please the Europeans. Inclination is the only motive acknowledged as honestly relevant to relations between the sexes, and inclination is mysterious. It is not a drama or something earned or deserved; it is a gift, a sort of election. To marry for the most honorable human needs—loneliness, insecurity, desire for a family, *faute de mieux*—these are not quite enough and it may even be said that we feel, superstitiously, that the presence of these needs is hostile to true love. They inject a worldly and universal factor into a personal mystery—and to marry for money or physical comfort is almost a sin and certain to bring misery and repentance! Inclination is of course exclusive in its object, which is why Americans are so sentimental about love and so clumsy in the casual love affair. When a married person finds himself attracted to an outsider he is in agony and must make a choice immediately; without the choice, representing the exclusiveness of love, he cannot be certain he loves either one.

This intensely romantic conception, exclusive, mysterious, self-questioning, unworldly, and impractical, is not a rude and coarse hatred of pleasure, a narrowing of experience out of fear and shame, but *a kind of idealism* which seems to exhilarate and heighten the existence of most Americans. It closes its eyes to man's animal nature, is too pious and extreme, and carries its own doubt and despair with it, but it is just this that makes it the normal expression of a progressive, democratic culture. Love is not pure sensation or need or understanding; like the Bill of Rights, it is a noble possibility that both inspires and constantly accuses. That people are often able to believe they can live by this romantic idealism, contrary to "nature" as it is, reinvigorates it apparently. The picture of the old couple married fifty years gets a prominent spot in the small-town newspapers, and even our high divorce rate, offering the fallen another chance for the ideal, is an expression of it.

Tenderness and the permission of equality between men and women are the surest signs of love in America, but it is just this aim, which is not of course always our practice, that has come to be considered an insidious degradation of both men and women. It is felt that tenderness has degenerated into providing luxuries for the women and that the man who cannot do so suffers intense guilt. There is no doubt that success is highly valued in America, but American women also have a particular fondness for ne'er-do-wells and failures, of which there are always enough to satisfy the demand. I should imagine most European women would think this impossibly crude and unreal. The pride taken by well-brought-up, pampered American girls in the impoverished intellectual—anyone who can put a sentence together, read books, or listen to decent music—frequently amounts to slavishness. To love such a man, without hope of what is ordinarily meant by success, is evidence of having kept faith with the ideal, of having accepted a passion which is simply itself, unalloyed by worldly motive.

There is a dismal sadism and regression in the contempt for American women one finds nowadays in novels and hears in conversation. Their health, outspokenness, and much-exaggerated leisure are scorned; the ravaging labor of a peasant woman is raised to a high moral principle and with fantastic disingenuousness the poor, defeated European prostitute is sometimes believed to be humanly and aesthetically superior. What most startles one in these notions is the absence of a certain kind of painful emotion supposed to be typical of Americans—our feelings that the daughter who becomes a prostitute, the village without doctors, the hours spent beating the laundry on the riverbank, are the very heart of tragedy. We are often accused of triviality in this respect and perhaps we are the only country that wants to send the leukemia victim a present so that he may have his Christmas in November—a gruesome notion of the last pleasures of life, even a child's life. And yet our squeamishness about physical suffering and deprivation are a large part of what is most free and just in our character.

It's hard to know how seriously to take the chronic, soggy indignation about the "freedom" of American women. Strangely enough, only Henry James, an expatriate, considered a snob and an aristocrat, seems to have truly enjoyed the independence, luck, and "un-European" charms of this New World creature. To him her virtues and inadequacies were an invigorating and romantically honorable expression of the American spirit. He would have thought it cruel to expect her to deviate from the moral and psychological inhibitions of the whole culture, unimaginative to despise her aspirations and candor, and inconceivable that American men, born in the same culture, do not really like or understand her—all of which it clearly is.

THE FEMININE PRINCIPLE

THE OLD feminist, the brilliant, self-assertive, daring, reforming woman, is as extinct as a dodo, and the movement called feminism could not fill a small lecture hall. There is not much need for agitation, in the political sense, because legal, social, and economic rights for women are fairly well won. "Don't get me wrong. Of course, I'm not a feminist or anything like that," we say with a shudder.

Nevertheless, "bad" habits do not die so quickly, snuffed out by a reprimand. Teasing refusals and a vast block of irritability proclaim the rock of feminine self-assertion that declines to soften even in our present bland moral climate. Just now, after the exhausting effort of the war and the unexpected continuation of psychological and political strain, we are living through years of slack and fatigue, a kind of mental depression, cushioned by material prosperity. We seek and find an after-dinner repose, the mood of repletion, slumberous satisfaction. The conversation at such times will be anecdotal and suitable to good digestion. We say things we don't really mean in order to be pleasant, to further the national relaxation. A good many people complain that we are suffering from complacency and self-deception.

If this mood is not necessarily wicked—and how can we know the full degree of its errors and carelessness?—if it is not wicked, it is not particularly accurate either in its power to represent our reality. In this period, under the terms of the truce we have signed with our fatigue, theory and practice are blithely separated. When practice disputes our theory or our preference, we feel it is disagreeable to be reminded of it and we become suspicious of those critics who do not like to leave well enough alone.

And so it is with feminism. In this subject the worm of journalism lies curled at the core, waiting for the incautious tooth. Helplessly, the writer falls into a bantering, breezy tone, fit for an elegy on a dead subject; or if one is feeling more alarmed than resigned—hostility often masquerades as alarm—the tone taken toward women may be moralistic and threatening, with talk about gains being actual losses, freedom being slavery, and independence, tyranny. Lightness or lugubriousness—or silence. The quip, the insight, the turn of phrase, the hard-breathing rhetorical effort: what are these in the face of the wide, indeed the *ostentatious* yawn on the subject of woman's place, women's rights, whatever we decide to call them. The yawn is the reality and the indifference is, to some degree at least, realistic.

Not long after the Civil War, Julia Ward Howe wrote that her engagement in the Suffrage Movement brought her relief from a sense of "isolation and eccentricity." If we remember Mrs. Howe at all, we recall the photograph taken in her old age. She is a wrinkled old lady in a white cap and she sits in a great, hooded rattan chair on her veranda in Newport. At the moment, fashion having resurrected yet another group of corpses, our minds reach out greedily for the delicious rattan chair, an old object once more le dernier cri. And that is about all of Mrs. Howe we would seek to have about us. She was not a woman of supreme genius and yet the vigor of her preparation for life seems, by comparison with that of our own time, near the prodigious. "The first writer with whom I made acquaintance after leaving school was Gibbon . . . I have already mentioned my easy familiarity with the French and Italian languages. In these respective literatures I read the works which in those days were usually commended to young women. These were . . . Lamartine's poems and travels . . . Racine's tragedies, Molière's comedies; in Italian, Metastasio, Tasso. . . ." It is humbling to go on with the list—Dante, Goethe, Cicero. And, again, Mrs. Howe was not intellectually or artistically quite of the first order!

Our great women are not much like the gay and worldly, experience-driven great European women. Margaret Fuller remembers it was "on a Sunday" that she first took a volume of Shakespeare in her hand.

She was eight years old. Her "other friends," as she puts it, were Cervantes and Molière. There is a good deal of pathos in Margaret Fuller and also in Mrs. Howe. They were cut out of Puritan cloth and have therefore a sort of cramped and uncertain note in their characters, something pained, earnest, and tireless. Margaret Fuller died too young, at forty, in a shipwreck off Fire Island, yet leaving the hint that she had used herself up in the effort to define herself as a person. And that effort was monstrously hard for a woman of the early nineteenth century in America.

At the present time there is a genuine reluctance to look sharply at our lives. Longings for the past are allowed; indeed they are the only acceptable form of social criticism during a spell of national pride and self-consciousness. Nostalgia is one of the most narcotic and beautiful aspects of a comfortable state of being. Backward yearnings are seldom a radical criticism of society; they represent a wish, a benign and soothing dream of lost pleasures and purities. And thus in a state of lamentation, as brief and light as the cap of a wave, a good deal of money can be made by reprimanding the cookout, the car pool, the TV dinner, the picture window, the Disposall. These are little tidbits, footnotes, subplots; our national vanity permits a chuckle over the very, very new and up-to-date. We are, chuckles and pieties smoothed out in the blender of our prosperity, wildly concerned with our reputation, our popularity, our character, our future. When the words "American woman" appear on the cover of national magazines, there is something overwhelming in the use of "American." The charged, stressed, underlined "American" is the signal for dizzy self-congratulation or for animadversions, light spankings, based upon old yearnings. "Is the American woman really happy?" Whatever the answer, it will represent a discontent that will not hinder our devotion to things as they are.

The postwar period has been marked by early marriages and a consequent rise in birth rate. This has led some commentators to sugary conclusions about the return of the American woman to that

Eden, the American home. We are reputed to be once more discovering the joys of a role fixed by nature and custom and to be, in droves, happily relieving ourselves of the burden of a personal destiny, individually worked out, suffered, and enjoyed. These conclusions are too speedy—they are also too broad and vague and grand to describe the world. Our syrupy "togetherness" is only matched by our sour "apartness"—divorce. The new morality, the new domesticity: one must be as sharp-eyed as a spy or a knight of perfect faith to discover in action these dawn-fresh purities whose existence is primarily literary and journalistic. The high divorce rate, juvenile delinquency, the collapse of family authority, the reported muscular weakness of car-happy young Americans, the inordinate lust for television, the decline of the willingness to study difficult material: these are the depressing conditions of the world in which the American wife and mother lives. Perhaps if we had not decided this was in some desperate fashion healthy, democratic, the hope of the world, we would not be able to bear it. The "new conservatism," the current "back to the home" movement, for women seems to be nothing more than a call for a sweet, devoted girl to share the nest of the solid American man. Such a notion has about as much force as the flight of a butterfly when we remember the real situation of the American family.

The moral conservatism so much talked about is like some great wonder few have seen but all know "by reputation." Those women whose circumstances are such that they cannot help themselves appear to be the most "morally conservative," while those who are in command of their own lives use their opportunity with all the ruthlessness, liberalism, and forwardness they can muster.

Infidelity, allied with beauty or charm or fame, is the great drama of the daily press. A total commitment to the feminine principle, the expression of the self by love, romance, and marriage are explosive, presuming all the possible fireworks of a life devoted to the senses and the sentiments. Is Liz Taylor really in love at last? the headlines inquire. All of us thrill a bit as romantic hope again visits this young woman.

The powers of a movie star are close to the absolute. These actors partake of the magical, the infinite, the perpetual. We are always being told that acting in the films is hard work and perhaps it is. And yet few wish to abdicate; in that respect acting has something in common with politics, where the hope of public office is so beguiling that men will subject themselves, over and over, to the greatest indignities, exhaustion, and fatuity rather than return to private life. The money a film star earns is only a small part of the magic, even if in the case of women it is unusually important because of the lack of other careers in which women can earn huge fortunes. Beyond the money lies the golden treasure of beauty, endless, matchless possibilities. The very name of a movie star, be it past or present, great or small, has prodigious value. You cannot disown these people; the memory refuses to evict them. When they have lost their beauty, their youth, they can go on television, design dresses, marry rich men, manage real estate, nightclubs, or restaurants, sell their life story to the films.

Like some oil-rich sultan, female movie stars need not fear their poor subjects; their image is irresistible, their power is exceptional and peculiarly accidental, like that of a king or queen. *Yet* it is gloriously theirs. The chanciness of a film career, the luck of being discovered at the soda fountain are part of the glow and wonder of the whole thing. It is the more beautiful in that talent is far from necessary. When an ordinary mortal passes a well-known, or just a *known*, actor on the street, the plain citizen smiles involuntarily and the film image passes on, its tight, concentrated features leaving a secular, movie-star benediction behind for a moment.

How do these women with such power behave? They seem to forget they are part of our new era, a statistical item in a huge barrel of names called "the American woman," a citizen living and voting under the dispensations of a religious revival, the new conservatism: these things are at hand for the asking, but our beautiful, lucky American film star might just as well be living in the last days of the Roman Empire for all the use she makes of them. Her morals and her habits are curiously resistant to our current notions of woman as a dependent being and yet we continue to love our star and to need her face on the cover of even the most conservative parts of the popular press. Movie stars go on preferring rights to duties. They are, in their demanding way, genuine feminists and usually utterly subversive to our professed moral standards. Dewy-eyed, in sacramental white, they marry again and again and their marriages are reported in the press with virginal enthusiasm and romantic exaltation. No suggestion is intended here that the movie stars are in need of punishment. Their vast impudence is fantastic and interesting; they are a vivid and brilliant example of the difference between theory and practice. The wish to be irresponsible, to seek pleasure, to escape consequences—these things are largely impossible for most women. They are not only economically but *personally* impossible, and if this were not the case the future of our social institutions would be uncertain indeed. But for those who cannot have freedom, there is the substitute of unlimited gossip about the famous person, the indiscreet and daring woman, the tremendously, insolently unfaithful.

Except where movie stars are involved, our whole society seems to concur in the rebuke given to the career woman who wishes to live outside or beyond strict domesticity. There is an evident distaste for the unusual and superior woman of the sort men of talent and importance formerly sought. Women have the vote and needn't take a chaperon about with them, but they must beware of being too clever. To be interesting is no longer an enviable state—a woman born in this state is often at a distinct disadvantage. It is not possible to be interesting without a good deal of egotism and a tendency to take the spotlight. Clever women want admirers—and above all, auditors. If one is even discouraged in her hope of being a *true woman*, how much more unlikely does it appear that she can be an interesting woman and get by with it.

A great deal of happiness and vivacity died in social life when anatomy ceased to be a sufficient designation of one's sex. The worry about whether one is feminine enough or masculine enough inhibits the free and natural development of the spirit. It weighs down most heavily on the intellectual woman. Under the everlasting scrutiny of a hostile eye weighing one's sexual characteristics, as a salesgirl in a smart shop cannily tries to size up one's real prosperity—under that glance, conversation withers and character dries up. Poor Ninon—was her promiscuity a sign of frigidity? And Madame Récamier's "peculiar impenetrability"—could such a creature be a woman at all? George Sand in her trousers, with her love affairs in which she was like a mother hen cradling her chicks under her feathers, her vast literary productivity, like that of some manufacturer in the early years of the industrial revolution. George Sand's character is an encyclopedia of complication and perversity. Or George Eliot's situation—sexually scandalous, and not because of the fact that her "husband" was already married but rather because of the way he gave in to her, submerged himself in her career. Nowadays, our constant questioning of the sexual nature of everyone has made bachelors embarrassed and maiden ladies tense. Some of the questioning can be laid at the door of psychoanalysis and much can be assigned to social timidity, fear of eccentricity, and the insatiable need to be acceptable. The Baron Charlus would now get married and have a couple of children.

The description of Queen Elizabeth in Green's *History* tells of a woman of such overwhelming diversity that it is exhausting to try to hold her in our minds. We would have to conclude that Elizabeth was not "our kind of gal." Queen Elizabeth, and a great many of the other extraordinary women of the past, were dominating and of very limited domesticity. One cannot easily be an important, able, memorable woman outside the family and local circle by practicing the virtue of humility and by seeking restrictions. (Saint Theresa was a splendid organizer, we understand.) Consistency, modesty, and equanimity are admired—in others. Aggression, discontent, striving, desire to rule are frequent inhabitants of the feminine body.

As our superstitious flaying of our psychic flesh increases with the everlasting question, there is a noticeable relaxation of secondary sexual function. The man helps with the dishes but resents his wife's brilliance. The woman drives the car and repairs the plumbing but there is a mistrustful look in her eye when her husband doesn't dominate the neighborhood scene. Is he too much of this and too little of that? These psychic measurements are far more dismaying than the old bourgeois standards of income and social position: those at least were truly measurable. But who can know his own hidden soul, his balance, his furtive, fascinating, mysterious genes? Repression of individuality, forced return to archaic and unnatural patterns lead only to decay and dryness.

In our new, challenging, retrogressive air, what is offered to women? If they are to give up independence, perhaps it is the power of the muse they are being offered, the source of man's inspiration, the grandeur of the White Goddess who is the source of man's poetry and philosophy. Indeed, women have always taken their abilities as the inspiration of man with great seriousness—often with a seriousness so ferocious and literal that they have claimed more as divine muses than some great men were willing to grant them.

Women are most successful as pure inspiration when their role is unconscious and instinctive. There is something comic and spurious in taking on these divine functions as one would take on the cooking. In his book *Choir of Muses*, Gilson has an instructive tale about Maeterlinck and his mistress, Georgette Leblanc. Georgette confused courtesy and gallantry with fact: when Maeterlinck said that he owed everything to her, all his work, Georgette believed it and wanted her name listed as coauthor on the title page. Maeterlinck drew back, amazed, but in the case of one bit of inspiration Georgette's brother sued, wanting the realistic reward for her to whom so much was owed. As Gilson says: "Dante placed Beatrice in heaven, but he never said that she had written *The Divine Comedy*."

Boredom, fear, constraint, bullying: these lie behind the new attitude toward women. Women are *commanded* to cease their struggling, *directed* to forgo independence—and yet human beings cannot move from a complex to a simple state without turning away from civilization itself. Ease is poisonous and simplicity is decline. From a false simplicity and an assumed dependence only hysteria and breakdown can result. The American woman in her American home with her two and one-half children and her appliance debt—who can plumb the spiritual history of that strange creation of industry and optimism? If she becomes as compliant as her dishwasher, all the music of the human drama will die away and that great gurgling whirr of domestic efficiency will be heard about the house. And nothing else.

1958

WOMEN RE WOMEN

WOMEN? This is not a subject one can approach with confidence. Generalization is unconvincing when it is not worse—absurd. All that one observes and feels is an assertion; the instances contradict and certainty is confounded by the vastness of the world's female population. When we look at our customs and traditions, it is hard to decide, with women, whether custom follows nature or is merely accidental, sanctioned by time and expediency rather than necessity. Exploitation, or a sensible acquiescence?

What follows here are merely notes and suggestions. Two notions from books recently published stir my mind to speculation. First: Bernadette Devlin, the twenty-two-year-old Member of Parliament from Northern Ireland, describes her father in *The Price of My Soul.* "If my mother had been pretty busy during the day, he would cook the supper—and we preferred it when he did, for he served us weird things.... He thought nothing of doing the housework on a Saturday if he wasn't working, and was totally unashamed of hanging washing on the line—a thing most men in Cookstown wouldn't be seen dead doing.... He was quite happy going shopping or pushing the baby's pram or buying clothes for the children."

In Erik Erikson's book on Gandhi, he speaks of that part of Gandhi's nature that loved to nurse and to mother, that made the spinning wheel an emblem of his revolutionary plans for India. Gandhi, the liberator of a whole continent, saw in simple, communal living a chance for salvation; he saw his own loincloth and naked legs as a serious comment upon the follies of society, and practiced, as a way of spiritual truth, "an abandonment of malehood." This was prophetic, "for in a mechanized future the relative devaluation of the martial model of masculinity may well lead to a freer mutual identification of the two sexes."

One of the most interesting things in the current talk about women's "liberation"—the new term for "emancipation"—is that it bases itself upon the possibility of a profound change in the role of men, in the way men see themselves, and in the surrender of the more rough and dominating modes of *machismo*. And thus, Mr. Devlin hanging out the wash is perhaps to be thought of, by some at least, as a heroic man, courageous enough to free himself in the interest of family happiness from the bondage of prerogative and custom, from a useless assertiveness. And Gandhi, bizarre and gifted with a natural flair for symbolic behavior, surrendering privacy and property and adornment in order to discover possible ways to live in the modern world, would seem, among young people, closer to some of their feelings than their own parents, with their acquisitive manliness.

Emancipation, liberation—most women are squeamish about "feminism" and talk of "rights" and are quick to dissociate their ambitions and discontents from anything that hints of the organizational, of planned struggle, of insistence and determination. Even women scarred by bitterness and anger are afraid to be thought insufficiently feminine, as if this were a quality that could be measured like body weight. Of course, one is feminine or masculine by virtue of genes, and all else is human variation and circumstance and temperament.

How difficult it is to speak of the present. It is impossible to be alive without feeling that important changes in behavior and social sanction are going on everywhere. How deep the change will go we do not know. No doubt, when one goes back home, to the mythical "middle America," away from the cities and the universities, one may expect to find that the more ancient and respectable forms of breakdown still hold: divorce, alcoholism, illness, failure, infidelity. Wishes and dreams are still familiar: appliances, cars, yearnings to move yet a little more securely into the social structure of regard and money. How is one to judge the natural persistence of the more usual forms against the meaning of hippie culture, of the flight of groups of young persons to the wood stove and well water, to poverty and plainness, to contempt for accumulation, the demotion of fidelity and the elevation of equality among the sexes, the contempt for jealousy and ambition? Is this merely a little sect or cult or does its message float on the air, subtly changing the atmosphere? Of course, the choice of style here is a privilege. In most of the world, in the world of the struggling, starving, laboring masses, style is a fate.

In the film *Alice's Restaurant* a somewhat older man, very eager to swing with the young, nevertheless cannot help acting out the peculiarities of his own generation. When he feels jealous of his wife, his instinct is to get into a fight with the other man. And, naturally, he is more than a little drunk as he asserts his right to protect his ego with his fists.

Clothes: the masculine turn in women's dress does not offend nearly so much as the feminine aspects of certain young men's fashions. To some, long hair and beads are abhorrent; the cuffed, man-tailored pantsuit for girls is simply disliked when it is not approved. The violent resentment of the long-haired young man is a measure of the greater importance accorded to the behavior of boys, the threat their swerving from the traditional paths poses for all of society. The masculine role is not a preference; upon it almost every institution of society depends: government, business, medicine, law, police, defense, heavy labor, sports. Or so it is still believed by the older generation.

I feel in my bones that the clothes of the young are rich in signification, that long hair is serious, that more is involved than restlessness and spending money. I do not know what is involved. For it is all often like some new medicine whose side effects cannot be measured for a number of years. Will middle age bring these young people "back home"—that is, back to the more or less stable family unit, with all the responsibilities and permanent obligations that has meant in the past? How will they support themselves? What will they want for their children?

Children—here I must return to speculation about women. Children naturally pose the greatest hindrance to drastic changes in the role of women. They instantaneously create that incredibly complex network of circumstance and demand, love and bondage known to us through the conventions of bourgeois life. Equality dies, fidelity is a convenience to keep the household together, work is a necessity, continuity is the measure of love. In this world, as in the world of women generally, the problems are always particular, daily, mundane.

Today, young babies crawl about in the nude, ride papooselike on the backs of mother and father and friend. They are not the occasion for the assumption of the usual burdens, but instead take their part in the free and casual community. Love comes from all; oatmeal may be spooned by a friend, as a delight, not a duty. It is felt that many of the questions I would ask are irrelevant. I do not know what the questions are and how they will be answered by time. They would appear to have to do with continuity and responsibility, and it is on the challenge of these conceptions that so much of the youth revolt rests. The ability to manage the maintenance and rearing of children into adulthood will be the severest test of the new life style among young men and women.

The housework: I have read an article by a brilliant young woman, Ellen Willis,* who tells of her resentment over doing the housework just because she is female. Many girls of advanced opinions take the question of the dishes quite seriously, and, indeed, it is from the humble moments that the great hours of existence are formed. Many young men seem emancipated enough to consider it reasonable to share in the housekeeping, although this work, which is of its nature routine, is more likely to be accepted during a sort of revolutionary elation, lived on the barricades of challenge, than during normal times. But for the moment, the girls do not demand a fatherly, money-making, everlasting commitment from the boys, and they in turn do not expect that she, like a pigeon trained to its route, will gladly find her way to the stove and sink, day after day. In the part of the youth that resists war and conformity, there is also a questioning of the traditional role of women: a reawakening of the dormant "rights"

*Mademoiselle, September 1969.

movement of our grandmothers. Perhaps these young people still live in a world in which home life is not very important, a world still close to that of students, and graduate students, adults more or less without privacy and possessions. Possessions are a threat to the soul and a solace to the senses; doing without them can also be one of those invigorating resolutions, like dieting, that give freedom and purpose. A "commune" in the country or in a slum can impose a backbreaking domesticity because of the absence of accommodations—no heat, no furniture, everything unexpectedly hard and time-consuming. It has in it the aspect of the monastery, and it is a natural part of the religious content of the youth movement—a sort of Reformation, as Paul Goodman sees it.

In the next decades, the right to have children will be seriously questioned by intelligent women. The distinguished and humane biologist Dr. Jean Dubos speaks of the alarming overfecundity of the American suburbs, of the complacency of the well-to-do in re-producing in a bitterly overpopulated world. With smaller families, or often no families, the changes in the day-to-day life of women will be beyond our imagining. Appallingly painful adjustments face us in every aspect of our lives, and even if we practice sensible austerity— a highly unlikely possibility—modern history does not offer much to be hopeful about. Miracles have a way of leading to some new and unexpected liabilities. The constancy of the miracles of technology can only make a sensible person wish to turn them aside for a moment. They do not seem to have been paying off in happiness, leisure, and health. But worst of all, there is something genuinely frightening in beginning to question all those benefits so many generations longed for and so many talents labored to produce. Surprises are always around the corner—they are not the results we were imagining.

Men dressing like girls and girls in bell-bottoms and pea jackets, like sailors—there must be some wish in all of this for a melding on some level, for equality, for release from the foolish traditions of masculinity and the devitalizing absurdities of femininity. However, do they really, the boys and girls, stand together against the older generation? If there is a war between the old and the young, as some believe, where will the girls stand, finally? For mostly this war is against the young men; the older generation considers the girls to be followers, not leaders. And this is true, in the main. Still, mothers, even middle-aged ones, are girls, and where will they stand; where, indeed, do they stand?

The changes that are coming about in the sensibilities and the existence of young girls have to do with the enormous alterations in the minds of the young men. This is not because of the inferiority of girls, but merely that the fantastic and improbable challenges to the young men are of such a fundamental nature that they include automatic changes in the status and customs of women. Work, marriage, war, moneymaking, ambition, education, authority. A young man who challenges the authority of the dean, the master sergeant, the boss, will not expect to be in authority over his wife. For authority is an essence: you give it and you take it.

But there are oddities and curious appendages: women are demanding equal pay in a world in which work itself, as a fact and as almost a sacrament, is losing its authority. So you are demanding equal rights in something that is itself losing ground as a fulfillment. Society does not need the amount of work it once did. That is, according to the critic Leslie Fiedler, the meaning of long hair. It means that you do not fulfill yourself by work. That the young man, beginning in life, is not living and dressing to create an image of himself that will please and reassure some future employer; his foot is not on the first rung of the ladder. He seeks instead authenticity, self-fulfillment, community. In New York, we hear of those young men with long hair, far-out clothes, who work the computers, make their money, go home to live as they please. There is no doubt that somehow, some way, society, authority, will manage to use whatever skills are necessary, and it will swallow its wish to have its machines operated by authority-loving young men in Dacron suits, white shirts, subdued ties, and polished shoes.

What seems to be ahead is that the women will have the new problems created by the new problems men have. Perhaps doing without the sanctity of work will be one of them. Many persons overburdened with work will find this infuriating. Many who have suffered to raise their children and who suffered as children find it hard to give up authority and distressing to know how their children will grow into decent people without curbs on anarchic impulses, without the treasure of experience. These are real questions. We have seen almost every ideal we have worked for tainted in its realization —improved health leading to overpopulation, the sufferings of the aged: the pollution and destruction of nature to give services to mankind, the wars that lay hidden in the last peace, and so on forever. Only the sentimental would not worry about the snakes in the paradise of the young—the tortures of nudity, the emptiness of leisure, the tyranny of the love of youth since all must age.

There is nothing more beautiful than a free spirit. This freedom is always a special gift, like beauty or talent; it falls like grace and seems to combine sweetness or intention with a hard, spontaneous courage. It has never been the aim of any society to produce these beings, although the corrupt are constantly pretending otherwise. A free man or woman is a rare thing. The world does not seem to be getting better or happier or wiser. If the differences between men and women are of less interest than their basic humanity, their nature as people, what can we wish for ourselves? The rising to the surface, in men, of the submerged maternal, or the opening up for the women of the hidden ability to be masterful? One thing seems certain— mastery without care, without the love of nurturing and preserving, is suicide.

1970

THE TIES WOMEN CANNOT
SHAKE, AND HAVE

I HAVE never felt free. I do not speak of the constraints of society but of the peculiar developments of my own nature. All my life I have carried about with me the chains of an exaggerated anxiety and tendency to worry, and an overexcited imagination for disasters ahead, problems foreboding, errors whose consequences could stretch to the end of time. I feel some measure of admiration for women who are carefree, even for the careless; but we work with what we are given, and what I know I have learned from books and from worry.

When I was young, living in Kentucky and later in New York unmarried, I was emancipated in my ideas, even radical; and yet I worried a great deal about "disgrace": about pregnancy, promiscuity, gossip, mistakes. And here I am remembering the fears of a girl in her middle twenties, not those of a teenager. Suppose, I would think with a shudder, Mama and Papa *knew*! Looking back, I believe my watchfulness, in the midst of what the conventional would have called daring, had to do with the fear of losing the greater freedom, something beyond the moment. There did seem to be a happiness and usefulness over the horizon that one wanted to be ready for, worthy of. Life was a minefield, strewn with traps—the wrong man, the wrong marriage, and, because of them, not being able to live where you wanted, to have the friends, the life you wanted.

When my daughter was born, her smiles were, in Sylvia Plath's phrase, "found money." But what an enslavement my feelings were. Not necessity but grave intensity of feeling made me wish to be spared pleasant possibilities for travel, too many opportunities to "lead my own life." It was a joy to sit around with even the most commonplace women, "talking about nothing but their children." The truth was that for a few years my pleasure in my child was greater than any fatigue or restlessness, and it was a misery to be away for any length of time. This fury, fortunately, abated after a while, but not entirely. I well understand the nearly deranged passion that led Madame de Sévigné to write volumes and volumes of letters to her daughter, a girl who, alas, turned out to be greedy and ill-natured.

I have always worked, but I never felt I was working hard enough. Fitfulness of ambition seemed to accompany the general anxiety, and yet *to do something* was an almost puritanical pressure, bearing down like the pain of a boil. This sounds agreeable enough, even with the image of the "boil," but it was not pleasant and soothing in the least. Creative and intellectual work is difficult, hard, and disturbing in the deepest way. You are up against the limits of yourself, your mind, your knowledge, your talent, your courage, your fineness, your energy.

Perhaps a woman needs to have worked not to hold herself above the splendors and miseries of the daily, the domestic. The cloth of memory is made of all those sofas and back stairs, the Sundays in the kitchen, the alleys and avenues. Your parents give you, in your youth, their unique dailiness and this becomes a part of your "I." There is a sovereignty in housekeeping, and housework itself is a matter of honor. Old housewives, left aside, forgotten, cking out their last days on Social Security, are not more to be pitied than retired secretaries and schoolteachers.

The German writer Gottfried Benn tells of a bitter proverb he saw on the face of a sundial, commenting upon the hours: "All of them wound, the last one kills." Loneliness, a hard end, will come to most of us if we live long enough. We must not ask too much of our work. It is not in the nature of work to be always gratifying. Humanity is desperate. A good person need not be ashamed to make the bed or even to turn it down at night if that makes someone else happier. What difference does it make?

We are as good and as useful as men—everyone knows that. Equality is self-evident. We do not want to be slaves or married to slaves—but this is the condition of so much of the suffering world.

When that happens, human beings can only cling together, huddling under the blanket. In his beautiful book *Tristes Tropiques*, the French anthropologist Claude Lévi-Strauss tells of a miserable, angry tribe, the Nambikwara, going to sleep by the fireside at night:

> Always they are haunted by the thought of other groups, as fearful and hostile as they are themselves, and when they lie entwined together, couple by couple, each looks to his mate for support and comfort and finds in the other a bulwark, the only one he knows, against the difficulties of every day and the meditative melancholia which from time to time overwhelms the Nambikwara.

The self always matters, no matter how great the crisis and disruption of the world. If you are allowed to live, your singular, solitary self will be gnawing at you all the time; you never wish to surrender the whole of yourself to the general. We do not want to be engulfed in the universal; but interferences are everywhere, in the nature of things, in the recalcitrance of others, in the world of accident, necessity, circumstance. Our desires war with those of our fellow men.

Dispersion, loneliness, rootlessness—these are carried on the wind like a pestilence. Everywhere one goes there are young or middle-aged women raising their children alone. "You will be aware of an absence, presently, growing beside you, like a tree," the same Sylvia Plath poem said. It is called "For a Fatherless Son," and it does not refer to the downtrodden and orphaned but to the children left by the educated, sophisticated man when he has changed his mind.

Some of these lone mothers are sad, some are managing, but none seems to grow used to the missing person. It was not Women's Liberation that left these women ironically sunk in self-reliance but a slow and steady corrosion of the sense of responsibility to the past, to consequence. We will never get that back; it is one of those things that will not be reversed. The right of the self for renewal, change, another chance is more sacred to us than gratitude or accountability.

The brevity of love must be acknowledged. I look at little girls with wonder and with anxiety. I do not know whether they will be free—the only certainty is that many will be adrift.

1971

IS THE "EQUAL" WOMAN MORE VULNERABLE?

FOR THE past few years I have been corresponding with a friend from Boston who has moved with her husband and children to live in Florence, Italy. "Is the women's liberation movement *serious*?" she asks me. *Serious*? I see, in my mind's eye, their large, bare, beautiful rooms in Florence, the nobly cold stone floors, the balconies warmed by the noonday sun even in January. Yes, I answer, yes. I think it is quite serious. It is not a fad like doing the twist, nor is it exactly a protest like the student movement, flaring up, dying down, changing tactics, growing older.

I send off my thoughts with a feeling of absurdity, of saying something tedious and ideological, something just a little rigid and grim. Even now we find it hard to suppress the romantic conviction that certain old European cultures, such as the French and Italian, have a practical, humane wisdom and worldliness that impugn our own puritanical flirtations with the ideal.

No, it is not so much that I think in this way but that I imagine my friend, living among the olive trees on the hillside, the black and white stripes of marble façades, feels strongly that human patterns are tough, old, tenacious. She wonders whether this should be a cause for despair or for thanksgiving. Doesn't Italy say: Look, we have all been driven from the Garden, man and woman alike. *That* we must understand first.

Why do I feel defensive? The subject of men and women is impossible. It is both brutally large and maddeningly vague. We may ask all the questions we like and we are not guaranteed an answer. History often simply fails us and certain matters of justice and goodness echo forever, never coming to rest. Too many women have lived for too long in history and the contingencies of existence are too pressing and various to allow for generalization. It is, as Chaucer said, "like trying to catch the wind in a net."

Particular women—every crime and virtue have been theirs! Turgenev's mother liked to flog the serfs. In Octavio Paz's *The Labyrinth of Solitude* he tells of a seventeenth-century Mexican nun, Sor Juana, who was born an intellectual as one is born with long legs. She wrote, "Two little girls were playing with a top in my presence, and I had hardly seen the movement and figure when I began to consider, with this insanity of mine, the easy *motu* of spherical forms...."

"Do you remember J—?" my Florentine friend writes. "She used to chuckle and say, 'Well, one thing is sure. Men and women ain't the same.'" For some reason this vexes me. It seems firm if somewhat too common ground and I begin to question it. Not the same? How little we know of the feelings of others. I can never know what it is like to wake up each morning as a man. Perhaps there are fundamental, fascinating, peculiar differences in the sheer perception of things, in the way reality and possibility present themselves. How can we know? We do not even know what it is like to be another of our own sex and in the end much about ourselves bewilders and persists beyond our control.

Here, in America, the days for many men and women are much alike. This is especially true for those men who share most in what we think of as the rewards of life, of success. Love, ambition, fear, power, frustration, money: these preoccupations know no boundaries and there is a likeness to the marks they make upon the character. If we were not driven by similar impulses and desires, we could not create poems and fictions and movies. On the other hand, "concerns" are not necessarily all of "consciousness."

"Is the whole thing just a whim, a choice, a defiance?" I am asked. I think of the Italian women in black, of their labors, their endurance. The poorer ones seem to know grief and patience of an exalted kind. The strong lines of their faces, the courtesies that have been bred into their bones in the effort to survive—are they a reproach to us here with our concern about powers and privileges? Some view it in that way, believe that agitation among women is a diversion, an indulgence growing out of prosperity, permissiveness.

I believe the breakdown of marriage is the historical source of the women's movement. In America the shattering seems more drastic and more dramatic than in other countries and thus the intensity of the desire for new standards, new ways of coping is naturally more acute here than elsewhere. Liberation, self-knowledge, self-reliance, training, planning—these are a sort of private investment, a savings account that acknowledges the shakiness of marriage, the shortening of family ties. In the deepest meaning of life everyone is responsible for himself and it is an illusion to imagine the pure self can ever be lived by and through anyone else. Still, we can hardly expect many to address themselves to the problem of the ultimate, the essence. To be alone, broke, with all or a part of the money to be earned, with the children to be raised, educated, supported—this is the mirror more and more women look into.

Are we so different here in America from the never-resting Florentine working women in their shops, with their market baskets, at the counters? "I think back," I write my friend, "to the clerks in Woolworth's, to old women and younger ones I remember in my hometown who had worked in stores for many decades, standing up day in and day out. Why are they not the objects of our sentiment, our purest respect? Perhaps we have never looked closely enough at them, at each other, at ourselves."

Matters between men and women will be greatly affected by the fact that we will be living longer and longer. This is a circumstance we cannot even begin to take in—longer and longer with fewer children. Will your daughter marry and live in contentment for nearly sixty years with the young man she chose just after college? Will your son be pleased to sign up for all these decades as a meal ticket, a lover, a source of life for a girl he met in his twenties? And if not, will he want to be paying alimony at seventy to a woman he left forty years ago?

To speak only from the woman's view, it is a fact that breakage does not accommodate us; separations, severances do not often take place in an atmosphere of equity. One of the hidden, brutal facts few like to think about is that young women are often fond of men older than themselves. These young women offer themselves as a substitute, a change, a renewal, and give little thought to the past the man has had, to his wife and children. Only growing older herself will teach her of the inequities of romantic life.

But this is not what the women's movement is about. It is not meant to be an ideological haven for abandoned wives. Many of its most active members are young, unmarried, or still married. Equality in society, independence of the inner life—the early life as well as the later—sense of self: these can mean many things. The meaning and urgency, however, cannot rest upon mere assertion. Ideas flower in the heart of necessity. They arrive to define changes that have already occurred, but cannot be dealt with. It is simply too uncomfortable to *think*, to *question* without the press of personal or historical need.

Longer lives, fewer children, more divorces. A terrible rain of real woe and incapacity and helplessness falls down upon many women who hadn't counted on economic and emotional disasters. Nothing is more pitiful than an older woman thrown into "freedom," lying like some wounded dragon in a paralysis of rage and embittered nostalgia.

At the present time the loosening of contracts is painful to many. The rules are not known. What are we owed by the people in our lives and what do we owe to them? The happiest and most admirable person may be one who feels he has no claim upon another except what may be voluntarily assumed. This is, perhaps, the ideal of the younger women in the liberation movement. But it seems a heavy charge to put upon frail and greedy human beings. We are not saints. Resentment is a common, if corroding, condition. With women resentment often arises out of a sudden, piercing cry that all they have felt and sacrificed is somehow not constantly foremost in the minds of those they have felt and sacrificed for. This cry represents an intolerable vulnerability. It represents the shock of learning that society does not any longer fully stand behind assertions of ownership between people, sanctity of contract, demands for static combinations immune to chance and withering.

"Who *will* do the dishes?" my friend in Italy asked me. We know who is doing them there—a kind, courageous, destitute "woman of the people." And on this so much of the sweetness of life for the well-to-do in Europe rests. Not just on the mere work and performance either but on human kindness born of poverty and resignation, the wild flowers that bloom in harsh soil.

Here the dishes are a joke, *the* joke. But jokes mean something and we laugh all the harder at those that strike at a point of intractable ordinariness. Housework and the care of children are peculiarly difficult to think about. It is wrong to imagine they are produced by simple demand. Men have less power here than they believe. Houses are dirty or neat according to something deeply graven on each person's character. So much of it is a self-propelled activity serving one's own needs and having to do with extension of oneself onto things and settings. A genuine and capable care of children cannot be ordered either. Anyone who has lived among neighbors knows all about the part played by the will and character of a particular woman in her assumption of these "natural" obligations. The poor dishes in the sink—emblematic, menacing, inert, and yet chosen for this high ideological role—perhaps have never been as cheerfully dispatched as we imagined. They have always been an obstruction and some women have moved toward them with grim and rapid resolution; others have procrastinated, idled, sighed, and finally faced them as one of the paltry vexations of life, one among, oh, so many others. The dishes are, like everything else, subject to "altered expectations."

The solution of Italy—the Italy of *our dreams*, not theirs, is gone forever. A country of madonnas and widows and no divorce and incomparable infidelities, of servants and mistresses. It is deep in the dreamlife of men, an infinitely beautiful accommodation. Yes, I write back again, the women's movement has meaning. Don't we all know that domestic relations are history itself and that they start as a response and end as a challenge? Or so I see it.

1972

SUICIDE AND WOMEN

"When I could not find her anywhere in the house or garden, I felt sure that she had gone down to the river. I ran across the fields down to the river and almost immediately found her walking-stick lying on the bank. I searched for some time and then went back to the house and informed the police. It was three weeks before the body was found when some children saw it floating in the river."

These words are from the final volume of Leonard Woolf's autobiography, *The Journey Not the Arrival Matters*, and they tell of the suicide of his wife, the great novelist Virginia Woolf. She was a beautiful woman, the daughter of a distinguished writer, possessed herself of rare talents and the creative energy to use them fully. She lived among the wittiest and most gifted people in London and her life was almost equally marked by extraordinary strains and unusual blessings.

Virginia Woolf had had bouts of madness since her youth. She had tried suicide before during periods of despair and depression. When she felt herself going mad again she weighted her skirts with stones and walked into the river—to save herself and those she loved from anguish. In a sense her suicide was cast in the heroic mold. It was a decision based upon hopelessness and with some of the Stoic's effort to act upon rational alternatives. And yet, of course, it was tragic and moving to see one so gifted and special go down so pitifully.

Recently some interesting facts about the increasing suicide rate of young women appeared in *The New York Times*. There has been, according to the new studies, an alarming rise. "In Los Angeles, the suicide rate of women under 20 went from 0.4 to 9 percent per 100,000 from 1960–1970 and from 8 to 26 for women age 20 to 30." And it is believed that the actual number is greater than that shown in the statistics.

Each suicide has its own history, its own story to tell. Suicide is always a comment upon an individual life, a particularly blurred and opaque comment in most cases. Part of the shadow a suicide casts upon the lives of those who care is just this final mystery surrounding motive and mood. We seldom ever know the details of circumstance, the scenario of the ultimate desperation. We know even less when we are confronting mere statistics. Apparently more men than women actually succeed in committing suicide. It is the attempt that is larger among women.

Suicide was previously called "self-slaughter," a more brutal and candid Anglo-Saxon word than the later Latin sibilants. In "self-slaughter" the words force a confrontation with the action, with its willed, concentrated destructiveness. The violation of self and the distance from self are tragedies only equaled by murder, homicide, which is also increasing in America. The inability to bear one's life has been felt by human beings since the beginning of time.

A. Alvarez's interesting book about suicide, *The Savage God*, shows that society has felt differently at different times about the question. When suicide was a prime legal offense, one found men being hanged for the crime of having tried to hang themselves, and in other cases there have been suicides for noble motives—rather than submit to a tyrant, for instance—and romantic suicides, a sort of fashion in melancholy and world-weariness.

There is something sacrificial in every suicide and this is what moves us. Virginia Woolf left letters to her husband and sister, saying in the suicide's characteristic way, "I can't go on spoiling your life any longer." Her own suffering together with the suffering she felt her illness would cause others combined to produce the resolution that led to the action. Of course others do not wish this sort of relief and in the end it is the suicide's own suffering and overwhelming distress that will count the most.

Suicides that come after a long struggle with recurrent depressions and mental derangement probably have some biochemical basis and can be looked at only as a bitter accompaniment to disease. It is difficult for the mind to sort out the role that general conditions in society might play. Often family histories show a disposition to suicide. Ernest Hemingway's father had killed himself in the writer's youth as had the father of the poet John Berryman. Each of these outstanding American writers died by his own hand. The sense of loss, so aching and pervasive in the scenery of the suicide's life, may of course rest upon a large number of natural deaths. Virginia Woolf's mother and father had died when she was young; her much-loved, attractive brother died suddenly; she had lost a stepsister. In addition there was the line of madness in the Stephen family. We do not know whether it is the losses, lying so heavily upon the heart, that may, even many decades later, cause the downward plunge—or whether certain families are doomed to experience suicidal despair.

Suicide is often described as a "cry for help," a way of calling out from the abyss of misery. That seems reasonable, and yet there is so often no help for the kind of pain the stricken person is feeling. The repeated attempts made by the rescued point up the endless nature of the affliction. The causes of despondency may in certain instances be too deep and too tangled or may even be unnamable, undiscoverable except as a part of the organism itself. Those who grieve for a suicide show in their grief that they have retained hope for some abatement of the pain. Had we the suicide's conviction that his condition was unalterable we would not grieve so fiercely.

Why should the suicide rate among young women be going up? Is there any way to take hold of the increase as a fact, to find some sort of explanation that includes the particular cases? With the old, poverty, isolation, and hopelessness are everywhere like a shroud. There is an isolation and hopelessness that invades the lives of the young, but it will, simply because of youth, be of a different nature. The failure of the will to live is a negation, but nevertheless an act of overwhelming force. A certain area of the will functions in any suicide and it is often remarked that the deepest pits of melancholy paralyze to such a degree that the resolution necessary for self-destruction is lacking.

Loneliness and loss. In suicide there is always a sense of loss. Many are skeptical about the notion of dying for love, but love is at the heart of suicide and at the very worst it is a loss of self-love that prompts it. But to lose a love and to be inconsolable are real emotions. The loss of love as a motive for suicide is often questioned because it is so contrary to the laws of self-interest. It says that one can indeed love another more than himself. So the cynical look beyond the love for a more self-serving hint and they claim to find it in the wish of the suicide to punish someone for the loss of love—the revenge suicide. To punish by creating an enormous guilt. If one has been rejected it is felt that the element of frustrated domination plays a part in lead- ing the rejected one to suicide. In that way even death is robbed of its purity as a statement; and yet, analyze, probe, and worry it as we will, nothing takes away the overwhelming and brutal reality of this final determination.

Frequently one reads or hears that the suicide did not appear de- spondent, but instead went about during the time before death with a convincing cheerfulness that precluded worry on the part of friends or relatives. In many suicides one can imagine that the end comes as a relief from the charade, from the pose of accepting and coping. The need to appear "cheerful" and to disguise the ravages of inner turmoil must take their toll on a beleaguered spirit. One may be forced to the wearing of masks by the indifference of others but also by a deep shame over the very feelings of weakness and desperation. Everyone would prefer not to appear helpless. Even if a suicide is responding to a rejection, imposing his will upon the future by taking his life— even then he is in despair, convinced that time can bring no upward alteration in his heavy, painful feelings.

In what way does the life we lead and the way we feel about our- selves contribute to the suicide rate? What in the situation of young women makes them more desperate than previously? The collectivity falls like water through our fingers: and this is especially true in suicide where there is so great a degree of personal anguish. Still, even though we cannot be certain, some of the assumptions of contempo- rary society suggest themselves as implicated in the loss of the will to live. One of these may be that we all feel an increasing sense of humiliation and shame about our personal failures.

With women, personal failures are manifold. They wear a thousand faces. Private relations, work, family, continuity—these are devastating challenges faced constantly by every human being. To fail without hope of recovery could hardly be exaggerated as an individual catastrophe. These things count and consolations are not inevitably convincing. Life is indeed hard. When failures of beauty, of charm, of equable nature, of temperament, of endurance come, they strike down a dejected girl with an additional force. From the cradle onward everyone has made, on behalf of girls, a demand for all things bright and beautiful. Some who start out in innocent arrears—not pretty, not charming, not lucky—know from their earliest days a sort of bankruptcy. The burden of this is as old as life, it is nothing new.

What is contemporary, perhaps, is the belief in an openness, a vast ocean of possibility, of infinite combinations, mutations, new beginnings, fresh starts. We like to think there is an endless emotional frontier ahead of us, that we are never trapped, encircled. Freedom to change, freedom from inhibition seemed to demand that we find happiness and fulfillment—or else take the blame for it. An integrated spirit, an unfettered psyche, a responsive character are not only a privilege; they are a challenge erasing alibis by which people have spared their own feelings of unworthiness. When all responsibility lies on one's own doorstep, the need for success is bitter indeed. Self-hatred, self-accusation, always so sadly pressing upon the suicide, are bound to bear down as the reasonableness of sharing blame with others diminishes. Our limitations, our chains are there for all to see—and worst of all we must look at them ourselves, without excuse or mitigation.

When everything is possible, to have little becomes unbearable. There is not only an absence then, but a cutting awareness of incapacity. Freedom has opened up new roads—and closed many of the old ones. Think of the number of respected and apparently happy spinsters in the past—school teachers, nurses, maiden aunts—and remember that their life was not always thought of as a calamity. It is not a question of marriage alone, but of renunciation, chastity, deprivation. We are no longer free to be contented old maids. The condition itself has been outlawed by critical analysis and pity.

To be left aside, or for a thousand complicated reasons to be unable, like Marilyn Monroe, to construct an existence truly satisfactory, can often be a fate, a destiny, rooted in accidents, bad luck, burdensome beginnings, or in having made bad choices. The unbearable topping to the mound of real troubles is the conviction that some unnecessary demon inside ourselves has taken control. It is the *unnecessary* that fills us with shame and guilt.

Dependence is scorned and it is natural to seek happiness by going away from the family. All of the arrangements and values of society move in that direction—our own desires lead us there, also. For young women this may be an imprudent risk and the luckiest are those who manage to keep some lifeline to the past, to their dependent days. No one to turn to, adrift, always having to earn the consideration of friends, lovers, fellow workers. Robert Frost said, "Home is where they have to take you in." Very few runaways complain of having fled too much love. Parents complain of their children's waywardness and yet many things suggest that the parents do not wish to prolong connections that require effort, compassion, sacrifice. So, when things go badly for the young there isn't much strength to draw from. The suicide is a dependent with no one to depend on.

Suicide is more a self-hatred than a protest against a narrow life. If love or marriage or motherhood disappoint, this is most likely to lead to anger, impatience, and not to the deep underground waters of self-destruction. An unwillingness to bear pain plays a role. We are not ready to accept it and scarcely know how to deal with it. Physical and emotional pain have been the lot of mankind and, in a sense, it has been the mission of America to seek the diminishment of this pain by the use of technology, raised living standards, and urbanization.

When we travel to poor countries, the pain-loaded people seem almost like another species and we stand in awe of their sheer endurance, just as we shrink from the contemplation of what they are indeed enduring. For us, it is not a mere figure of speech to use the word *unbearable*. For mental pain help is not so near at hand as for the ills of the body. Excruciations attack an organism that is unprepared defenseless. Only the assurance of being loved by someone can produce the patience necessary for survival. If more young women are committing suicide it means that they are cut off from the love of their fellow beings—or believe that to be the case.

There is something of the child in all of us that cannot accept loneliness, an abandonment to the dark. And what will the future be? The modern world places enormous demands upon the individual, requiring of him a lone, spectacular effort. You are only yourself, we say, and in some sense always alone. The question is whether we have mastered the terms of this profound singularity, this enlarging self-determination. It is clear, as the suicide figures show, that many young women have not.

1972

WHEN TO CAST OUT, GIVE UP, LET GO

THE YOUNG poet Frank O'Hara wrote,

> To be able to throw something away without yawning
> and thus make good our promise to destroy something but
> not us.

How hard it is to create maxims, design thoughts for our lives. Just when we are in need of directions there seem to be none—everything is a zigzag, either a dead-end street or a frightening new road. For every categorical yes, there is always the hovering possibility of a serious no. For every hope, a fear. The past hangs heavily upon us and we feel the weight with impatience; and yet how grave is the risk of emptiness in casting off what is behind us. I myself am inclined to the belief that change, revelation, dramatic turnings in our lives must come from within, from self-knowledge, effort, and a genuine desire for change. Nevertheless, I have seen freedom, happiness, and goodness come, finally, from what had seemed to be the wreckage of personal existence, from alterations violently resisted, from unhappiness that fell as a devastating blow. No one would wish misery surmounted as the way to peace. It is merely important to remember that it can sometimes happen.

Throwing out, giving up, casting aside: sometimes this happens naturally, as one of the benevolences of time. Again, it may have to be a decision. Accumulation goes hand in hand with inertia. The pinching shoe, the single glove—what hope makes us hang on? Of course we have been brought up to believe in the hoarded piece of string as a moral truth; it is part of the absurd, the joke of existence.

There are single gloves in our inner life also. These are the impractical, cherished memories, the longings, the clingings, the regressions that we clearly see as useless, cumbersome, and still they will not yield. We stand before these memories paralyzed, unable to go backward or forward. Mournfully we look at the glove, pick it up, cast it once more back into the drawer or box. After all, it is perfect of its kind and needs only its lost partner to assume its role: The prodigal may return.

What is real? What is important? It is almost an insult to ask these questions, especially of an unhappy person. If the questioner had an inventory of truth he would be one of those transcendent mortals— a man who could not be surprised. For most of us, today is the future, action is belief, events are character. Giving up is for others. Sermons are for friends, children; resolutions for midnight.

We set out each day with our props, costumes, gestures—our personality. These are a part of a mask, and yet the mask is real. Suddenly, you, the mask, your life, are different, violently altered by events or persons you have depended upon. We ourselves are an accumulation, and a lot of what is us has been supplied by others. When our relation to others suddenly changes, everything valuable seems to be brought into question with an unbalanced swiftness.

Memory: It is a forest. It is the sun and shade, the air current, the luminous crown, the damp root—the precious jungle of our being on earth. In memory, with its density of feeling, the treasures of human experience are preserved, just as the forest represents the aesthetic apotheosis of actual nature. And yet memory is also a menace—dark, lonely, fearful. Our rootings and clingings to memory are a sad entanglement from which one would, at certain times, free himself if he had the power to do so.

In painful memories, those that represent attachments to a lost past, the very suffering distorts the complexity of life, makes the flawed more perfect, the mixed more beautiful than it was, the doubtful more true. Memories are also the mausoleum enshrining resentments and long, futile angers. A need for rest, tranquility, for the promise of the future finally challenges the domination of painful memory. What is hoped is that in giving up the obsession with the past a new present can come into being.

Forgiveness is the goal of troubling memories. If it is possible to set aside the memories, it can then be possible to think of reliving them someday, without desperation, in a new form, kind to our souls, soothing. All the losses of life, whether accidental, inevitable, or simply cruelly thrust upon us, seek to be forgiven. Always what is most important in one's personal life is to forgive the unforgivable. The forest of memory, with its balance of light and shade, of rain and dryness, its terrors and its silences, is not under our complete control. But it accommodates us finally, if the will is there, the wish to forget, the courage to cast off.

Survival is a desert. By instinct we face it carefully, with a saving fear. Habits, expectancies, demands, vanity all disappear before the empty, unpredictable spaces, the burning and the cold, the loneliness, the sense of being utterly thrown back upon chance and one's practical valor, inner resolution. In the desert there is no hope for the selfish, the hysterical, even if those are states usually brought on by the crisis of survival. The spectacular wastes themselves are the product of disintegration, change, erosion, lunar aridity.

The idea of the desert is a negative one—to explain what we can do without. Itself a mirror, an illusion of surfaces—it destroys mirrors and illusions. Our sense of worth and of the future trembles feebly before us in the drama of survival of our ego, our egotism, our self-love. In the stripping away of false hopes and false self-hatred there is beauty, like the beauty of the Sahara, created by winds. False self-hatred is the punishing wish to take on blame, to rush to accept bad luck, to use guilt as a sort of glorification, a strangely gratifying ego-trip.

The young are the center of all things and, alas, so are the more experienced. It is natural to build the universe around our own consciousness, and difficult to do otherwise. We would be less than we are if life kept us long in a struggle for emotional survival; and the effort made, almost unconsciously, is toward the restitution of something orderly, something to be counted upon, that does not immediately threaten. In love, the despair that comes from loss, from deprivation, throws us into the desert. Sometimes it is only by stark and splendid renunciations that hurt persons can find the water in the sand.

Blame and resentment are like trunks on our backs. It is part of our nature to try to shift responsibility for ourselves to others and to condemn them when they "betray" us by refusal. Some of the greatest shocks of life are the recognition that others simply do not want always to be responsible for us. Women especially, or so it often appears, face the desert with a feeling of heartsore astonishment. The silence was meant to be filled with comforting voices. The rage they feel seems to them of a sacred order, theirs to treasure by right. One of the purposes of a more conscious and independent existence for women is to relieve them of their conviction that they will always be safe. The inclination to repeat our grievances, to insist that a payment is always due us—this is an indulgence that everyone must sooner or later give up. A hardening sets in as we go over and over the same ground. We can never be as accusing, impatient, and discourteous to anyone as we are to our own, to those we love. It is easy to see the indulgence of bad temper in others and for that reason the adversities of our friends seldom surprise us. As outsiders we had seen the blinking signs of trouble, interruption, reversal. For ourselves, vanity, habit, and rashness blind us to our follies, to the sins we commit against love.

Repetition—the motor of existence—and without it each day would begin anew in an exhausting need for discovery and experiment. Probably most of us could not bear to get up without the sigh of a blessed monotony to carry us through part of each hour. The principle of repetition is destructive, however, when it applies to our picture of things, as indeed it constantly does. To persist in a fixed idea of ourself, in a rigid evaluation of those around us who greatly matter, to think we have it all properly and finally placed forever is death.

Rearrangements, revisions, reassessments hardly occur to us at the point where they are most needed—our ideas about those closest to us. It is as if we had cast our footprints into cement and called it "our relationship." The extraordinary thing is we know well that our husbands, friends, families are capable of quite different relations with different people. By this we mean, if anything is meant, that we recognize the reciprocal quality in the manifestations of personality, the way it is modified by another—and modified most of all by the amount of courtesy, attention, trust, imagination another brings to the shifting lights and shadows of our own being.

"He is very gay and friendly at his work. It is only at home that he is a monster of gloom and ill humor." And, "To her own friends she is perfection and the life of the party. With the family—very sloppy and rude." Which is the true person? The happy daytime or the morose evening? The elated partygoer or the sullen daughter? We are trapped and we trap each other in our fixed positions.

Our unfavorable verdicts are especially dear to us. The monstrousness of superiors, the fecklessness of inferiors, the ingratitude of children, to say nothing of the world at large, the bad luck, the betrayals and treacheries, the unacknowledged generosities: these are another accumulation. To give them up is an expropriation, a sort of aggression. And yet we are imprisoned by these negatives. With them no discoveries are possible, no exhilarating freedoms welcomed.

"A sense of reality"—what does it mean? It seems to suggest some are gifted with the capacity of the willingness to see what *is* rather than what one *would like*. Apparently others have the possibility, or the misfortune, of unreality. It is not quite a choice, at least not in every instance. States of feeling, problems of value are especially elusive in their connection with reality. Fortunately, we have such a tender tie to our consciousness of things that we take the grand and practical assumption that our feelings are real, our understanding of the world about us more or less in line with the understanding of others. Naturally, there are surprises and our picture of life is challenged. Then we are hurt, angered, or simply puzzled. The very frightened will feel small, tricked; the vain will be outraged, unyielding.

Few things are more gratifying to the spirit than the meeting of a person who practices a sort of eternal vigilance, who really asks himself what his life, the life of his family and friends are truly about. This is an enormous effort, like signing on for a peculiar *régime* of calisthenics. To think about a troubled person is to ask what can his life and his problems uniquely mean to him. Where does he hurt and can it be changed? Probably these questions can only be asked in silence. They are at the least an awareness that the wishes and hopes of others are as sovereign as our own. Of course it is difficult to keep on the alert in this way. Sympathy is a gift, sometimes almost an occupation.

Love. It is strange that love for humanity, for the good, for justice, for truth is not the same as love for a boy or girl, a man or woman, for someone whose elusive affection you are seeking. I have often wondered whether there can be unilateral, unreciprocated love between men and women. There is much in love that simply cannot float alone, without an anchor or an answer. We assert the imaginary claim of the past, of the time when love was mutual. Still, if one of the two has withdrawn affection, the rapidly changing emotions of the other are more violent, more ferocious than we can easily trace. Unilateral love may be a mask for jealous resentment, for an anguish that has turned love to fear, anger, even to hatred. "I am still in love even though I am not loved." It is a puzzle. Can it be true?

One-sided love should be thrown away, if possible. It is not the impracticality, the poor "economy," that cause hesitation, but the fact that it may not be real, may only be a blurred mask for power wishes. A wish to create guilt and confusion. Sometimes by the willingness to let go of a love that has, in fact, gone, we can reach, finally, after suffering, a true condition of "loving" someone who has long ago treated us badly. Then affection is not a weird, ambivalent manipulation of the death of love, but a sort of salute to its happier beginning. Love is an ethical idea. There is always renunciation as well as possession hidden in its heart.

No one, Pascal wrote, dies so poor that he does not leave something behind. And we are never so poor that we cannot, in the interest of a kind of purity, throw away many things that are treasured without joy, held as an infernal habit, an indulgence. In the renunciation of the useless and heavy, a useful and light spirit slowly pushes up through the ground.

1973

READINGS

ON READING THE WRITINGS OF WOMEN

THE PROPER study of mankind may be man, but the subject for women is other women. This is a tiresome fate, made no more pleasing by the fact that it is a servitude to which one dooms oneself. When women think of writing an essay they seem to look out at the infinite world of art and experience and, frightened, to draw back, cozily, to women's art, women's novels, women's problems, women's place in the world, in America, in bed, at home. One's sex provides topics for a tired inspiration, something to fall back on, like growing up in India. It is a subject upon which one can speak with something like authority. I am, I say to myself, a woman after all.

Toward the achievements of women I find my own attitudes extremely complicated by all sorts of vague emotions. I take an interest in what my feminine colleagues are doing, not unlike that interest a member of a minority takes in the achievements of his group—but my reactions are not as pure and amiable as those of other minority members. (Women are a sort of minority culturally, not numerically.) As a writer I feel a nearly unaccountable attraction and hostility to the work of other women writers. Envy, competitiveness, scorn infect my judgments at times, and indifference is strangely hard to come by in this matter.

When I was younger I used to read nearly everything written by women, that is, nearly everything that aspired to seriousness or excellence. I no longer do quite that, and yet I still continue to read a great many books just because they are written by women. I am often, as I phrase it, "disappointed." This past year, for instance, I found the English novelist Iris Murdoch's book *The Bell* nearly unreadable. It seemed to me slow, unreal, with a superabundance of symbolic action that dulled the edge of the inspiration. That opinion is not outrageous, but perhaps I was unduly exercised and annoyed by the enthusiastic reviews this novel received in the British press. At the same time, under the push of this emotion, I began to read another young English writer, Doris Lessing. I first came upon a collection of her short stories, *The Habit of Loving*, published here in America last year, a volume favorably enough reviewed, but somehow unable to make itself felt in the American literary scene. I liked this book immensely. These were powerful, beautifully written stories, somewhat—and happily, I thought—influenced by the great short stories of D. H. Lawrence. Indeed this work was so interesting I ordered all the books by Doris Lessing the Holiday Bookstore would send me. Of those that arrived, I have thus far read *The Grass Is Singing*, *Martha Quest*, and an earlier collection of stories, *This Was the Old Chief's Country*. These are all superb—the works of a woman with an extraordinary gift for fiction. Doris Lessing is well known in England and very highly considered, I understand; however, my own reading of English magazines usually produces Iris Murdoch and not Doris Lessing as the most important "young" English novelist, among the women.

Again, I find that an exaggerated irritation wells up in me at any failure to concur with my own opinion on this matter because it is a matter of work by women. I don't relish disagreement, perhaps, with my opinion of the work of men, but certainly the extremity of my behavior and feeling about the writing of women does not occur when I have to think of the writing of men. I have no doubt that all this is a merely personal disease, whose origins are as obvious as they are unflattering. I do not know that other women writers feel this way, and yet I do get hints that some do, if not so strongly, not so wildly, share my unhealthy condition and that a peculiar lack of detachment marks the opinion one woman has of another's art. Competitiveness is the rule of the intellectual world to the same degree that it is the rule of any world that demands a personal exertion of the highest sort, but the competitiveness is a fleeting thing, coming only at certain moments of longing or fear. The most genuine moments of the creative life are those of passionate love and absorption in the whole stream, past and present, of culture. It could not be said that a businessman loves the great moments, or even the small, of the history of business, that the head of General Motors feels for the Ford Company and the Ford product the reverence members of the world of art may feel for each other. And so when I admit to myself the half-hostile but helplessly fascinated involvement I feel with women's writing, I excuse myself by remembering the effort I have put into reading and thinking about their work.

When I look over my library I find that I not only have all of the works of the women writers I particularly admire—women such as Virginia Woolf, Mary McCarthy, Edith Wharton—but I notice also that I own, for instance, the complete works of Elizabeth Madox Roberts and the many novels of Kay Boyle. Elizabeth Madox Roberts: two—they could not quite be called "loyalties"—two sources of addiction capture me in the case of this writer. She is a woman and also a native of my own state, Kentucky. I still have respect for her work, but I do not read it and even when I did read it my senses were not extraordinary stirred. And yet I have carried *The Great Meadow, The Time of Man, Not by Strange Gods*, and the others through a great many exhausting, costly packings and unpackings. I am unable, no matter what my practical wish, to dispose of these books. I remember that Elizabeth Madox Roberts lived for a time in Chicago, that she was a friend of Glenway Wescott, that she wrote many of her books while living in her house in Springfield, Kentucky. And then she is a woman novelist.

In the late 1940s I read a review in an English magazine that ended, in order to make some comparison I have since forgotten, with the names George Eliot, Jane Austen, and Susan Ferrier. Susan Ferrier! I was astonished that there could be a woman novelist I did not know and one of such merit as to be listed along with George Eliot and Jane Austen. With anxious energy I went around to the secondhand bookstores over and over until I was able to find *Marriage* and *The Inheritance*. Two very good books. (The flyleaf of an edition of *Marriage* says that "Walter Scott delighted in Miss Ferrier's novels and her art in dealing with Scottish life. Something of Smollett's humour, dashed with softer feeling, makes *Marriage* a delicious comedy-in-narrative.")

I can remember reading only one novel because of what I had read to be its plot. In *The New York Times* my eye fell upon the subject matter, the plot, of a novel by Elizabeth Jenkins—the author of the currently popular biography of Elizabeth the First. The title of this delightful novel, published here in 1954, is *The Tortoise and the Hare*. The hare of the title is a charming, sensitive, beautiful woman married to an attractive, successful barrister some years older; the tortoise who eventually triumphs over the hare, by stealing her husband from her, is a plain old spinster in her fifties, a plain and downright woman yes, but luxurious in her way. The spinster has money, she produces excellent dinners and her car, a Rolls, always seems to be ready and waiting whenever it is needed. She is a good judge of horses and investments; her house hasn't the taste of the poor hare's house but it is comfortable, solid, firm, and immensely reassuring. The spinster, in her expensive but dowdy clothes, has also all the pent-up energy and sexual passion of a lifetime. Even here her capability is enormous and the beautiful, introspective wife feels this odd fact as something she cannot subdue; it is a kind of strength and determination against which her own romantic nature, which needs to be admired and appreciated, is helpless. This is a very satisfactory novel; not only are the characters convincing, they are also adult, completely and thoroughly interesting.

When I read this winter in the *New Statesman* that Pamela Hansford Johnson's *The Unspeakable Skipton* showed the author to be "as good as any novelist writing in this country today," and that "it was not silly to be reminded of George Eliot," and that in this book and the one before it called *The Last Resort* Miss Johnson was "extending the territory of the novel," I naturally was filled with all that disturbing eagerness and readiness to doubt I have previously described. *The Unspeakable Skipton* turned out to be a book unusually easy to read.

"Readability" is a much-abused word, one likely to put off anyone of the slightest seriousness because it is used to praise the light, the trivial, the obvious, the easily conventional. This novel is thoroughly literary—one needs to know a good deal, to have a feeling for the literary and artistic sense to get the most from it. It is witty, perverse, and entertaining. The character of Skipton is based upon that extraordinary man, Baron Corvo, a man hard for me, at least, to like. He wrote in a most unusual, baroque style, his opinions were crackpot; his own character was his most original creation, having in itself a sort of dramatic suspense, since the real Corvo loved mystification and difficulty beyond everything else. A. J. A. Symons's *The Quest for Corvo* is more widely read, perhaps, than any of Corvo's own books.

Miss Johnson's Skipton is a writer, living in Bruges. (The real Corvo exiled himself in Venice.) There is always a danger in the use of foreign cities stuffed with attractions and romantic names. Bruges, however, is not squeezed mercilessly like a lemon for the sauce but is gently pressed for delightful comic effects. In Bruges, Skipton can invent, as a swindle, an old Flemish painter named van Brouwerts.

Skipton is starving, paranoiac, full of compulsive fears and textbook perversities. He's an awful person, redeemed by the fact that he is so terrible he never wins any kind of victory. People are suspicious or contemptuous of him. His neurotic cleanness annoys them as much as his perversity in arranging a sexual circus for tourists astonishes them. His literary pride is fascinating; it is real and arouses pity and belief because he has genuine talents. His rude letters to his publishers, begging for advances, are masterpieces of folly, insult, and madness. Skipton lives in unbearable tension. Always faced by starvation, he nevertheless goes home to the sort of literary feast he can provide himself for nothing, that is to add a few lines to his venomous portraits of his "enemies"—of such portraits are his books composed. For instance:

> Men like Billy Butterman are rarely recognized as parasites, since parasitism is associated with the minuscule; but if triple-visaged Dis gnawing the bloody heads in the bottom of Hell

were to have a louse in his armpit, that louse would be Butter-man....

There is hardly an aspect of Skipton's character that isn't repulsive; his pride is diseased, his self-absorption is so deranging that he cannot form a true idea of other people and therefore thinks a poor country cousin is a rich, miserly *rentier*. His heart seeks revenge automatically and his most usual response to life is disgust. Still Skipton is not repulsive. He is exaggerated, but the elements of his suffering and his unattractiveness are seen often in the artistic and cultural world. His vanity may be dreadful but it does not abate his poverty. His snares for his victims are always so elaborate and fantastic that he, himself, is the one at last to be trapped. His intransigence, his admirable, involved prose style, his perfection of the art of invective and ridicule have a sort of purity and beauty.

I do not know that I shall ever read this book again. I'm not sure that I won't. In the end perhaps some final, manic, mad exhilaration is lacking on the one hand, and some deep shivering identification on the other. Anyway I have read *The Unspeakable Skipton* once, and not to have done so would have been unthinkable. For it was written by a woman and that bound me to it. Had it been written by a man I might not have found time for it unless I had been assured it was first-rate. From the men, I demand only excellence.

1959

READING

READING—what sort of subject is this? There are "reading scores," and "my early reading," and "reading the future." There are neurology and pedagogy and linguistics and dyslexia and lipreading. And then there is plain reading for information and pleasure—neither very plain indeed.

In writing about reading, one is imposing more reading, a grave decision if the "worry" about reading, the decline of it, is more than a rumor. Virtue and pleasure attach to our subject. Virtue is conferred upon it from the outside, and the pleasure is to be subjective. It does not seem suitable to take a legislative tone, to invade by way of advice or censure, this solitary, private act.

I like the phrase "functional literacy." It is, apparently, a diminished, but not entirely neglected, condition. Fifth grade, we hear, and what does that mean? Fifth grade is a state with many word-blessings. Lilac and rose (lipsticks); sheer black (stockings); men and ladies (toilets); bus stop, exit, take one before meals, 80-proof, on sale, free. But if I understand the term "functional literacy," these words do not lead anywhere: fifth grade does not move to sixth, nor does *exit* to *perilous curve*. It is hard to understand a stasis, a cutoff, after the "functional literate" has arrived at "zip code," an arcane bit of interesting and useful reading. There is some perturbation in the condition, and perhaps statistics are not able to keep up with the leaps and bounds that mere function provides like a set of muscles.

Figures about illiteracy among us may stun the mind of one looking out on a street filled with automobiles, hearing the planes whining down to the airports, knowing of sonics and stereophonics and miraculous little chips. We are, in literacy, forty-ninth among the 158 members of the United Nations, and that means 60 millions among us, including 47 percent of black youth, do not, cannot read. This fact seems to call up an ancient rural folk living in brutal, repetitive isolation, centuries past, one day like the next, the hut, the unlettered darkness. But that is not true; the illiterate are of course utterly contemporary in look and experience of life, and their plight is like some crippling or myopia, personalized and yet hidden, at least in some part of its manifestation. The scandal of it, surrounded by words like priorities, tax base, overcrowding, unfortunate methods of instruction, and the easy absorption of the figures without alarm would seem to indicate one of those shiftings in our apprehension of national destiny. The sacred school, the devotional teacher, the alphabet on the wall, the cutout apple in the window—these are nostalgic, small-town images whose hold on the imagination is merely sentimental. It appears that we can "live with" our expanding illiteracy and that it is to be thought of as a handicap, individually unfortunate, but not a stain on the national psyche. Education, then, is a sort of option, a curious settling down of the American half-serious utopian claim.

To speak of a passion for reading is rather self-aggrandizing, as perhaps it would not have been in the past. This act, except for purposes of the classroom or for information, is self-propelled, unmortgaged, so to speak, not subject to obsolescence or engine trouble or the need for maintenance. It is not often that one is scolded for it, although biographies tell of the wishes of parents to interrupt on behalf of unchopped wood or expensive candles. Perhaps the love of, or the intense need for, reading is psychological, an eccentricity, even something like a neurosis, that is, a pattern of behavior that persists beyond its usefulness, which is controlled by inner forces and which in turn controls.

There seems to be a good deal of "practice" necessary to sustain the gift of genuine reading, practice being the adding of one book to another, the development of tone. Impediments to reading on the part of advanced students of literature are far from uncommon—not a reluctance before the act itself, but a sort of deafness in the matter of aesthetic tonality.

Too violent a contemporaneousness in the souls of some readers inhibits discussion and somehow infects the air, but with such subtle penetration it is hard to define. Things go on in a chatty manner, hardly to be understood as different from gossip about one's friends. This may be thought of as propitious, the current right to remove literature from too great a degree of pedagogy and to restore it to experience. And, since about works of art there is no right opinion, it is something beyond that which troubles.

Tonalities and nuances give pause. Relentless contemporaneity produces some of the same reading defects, spiritual as well as vocal, that one often notices in the American performances of classical modern drama. The actors cannot get out of their own skins, despite the period costumes, the parasols, the old serfs shuffling in with a tea tray. *Madame Bovary* is an example that comes to mind because the text does not require exegesis. The students who have chosen literature for their university study are pleased to read the novel, perhaps again and again, and nothing onerous attaches to it as a "requirement," such as might be felt in many cases about the burden of Spenser or Milton.

As the discussion goes on, we hear that Emma is "too romantic"; Ms. Homais is "just pretentious"; Charles is a "clod"; Rodolphe is "selfish"; and Léon is "weak." The adjectives are to the point, naturally arrived at as descriptive efforts. Yet something is askew in the tone of the discussion. It is too intimate, too cozy; the distance has been traversed with a disfiguring speed. A masterpiece of created "tiresome-ness," becomes "tiresome," and that is not the same thing. There is a sort of present tense of judgment that establishes a feeling of equity between author and reader.

In the latitudinarian air of the classroom, and no doubt elsewhere, there is the tendency among readers to populate works with themselves, their friends. There is too much self-esteem and too little surrender. So the students say this novel, with its diversions, "drags," and Chekhov doesn't make a "real point," and Jane Austen is often silly, meaning that, in their view, the throb of afternoon calls, the bow at the ball, cannot bear the intentions attributed to them by the characters and, along the way of course, by Jane Austen herself. The personalization of fiction, the reduction of it to the boundaries of the reading self, often one who has lived for only a few decades in the twentieth century, is an intensive democratization not quite so felicitous for the spread of literature as one might have predicted. It bears some relation to the deformations of Socialist Realism—that is, the inclination, in this case, unconscious and without ideology, to impose current conditions upon the recalcitrant past. Some feminist critics wonder why Dorothea Brooke, after the "disaster" of her marriage to Casaubon, wants to marry the vaguely nitwitted Ladislaw? Dorothea has the money to "make a new life," and in any case, she could go to work, if there was work then for women. So, psychologically nothing is to be accepted as given, created, composed, in accordance to the truth and imagination of its own terms.

On the other hand, less knowledgeable readers do not, in my view, read for a validation of their own experience. The stack of romances at the supermarket is noticeably shorter at the end of the day, showing the movements of commerce. For certain women, these seem to be a sort of daytime gift to themselves, as the washing machine growls through its cycles. It is something of an insult to ordinary people to imagine that they, for the moment, believe it possible to be as fascinating and sexy or as romantically cruel as the impossible characters on the page. They, the readers, will not experience in life a charming, interesting, detailed betrayal, but, if any, a dull, extended, paralyzing impasse. These mass-produced entertainments are rather like a glass of beer—Miller Time. They offer little instruction about the reading public for works with the claims of literature, are not in competition with them, and cannot be discussed except as items of capitalist market seduction.

One of the results of genuine power in business, in politics, in law and medicine, is that there is no time to read. Time, that curious loss in a world of time-saving, is indeed running out, we might say. It takes with it the time-consuming reading. No doubt those who address their print to the powerful adjust their psyches and perhaps their styles to the inevitable reduction to memo and summary that lies ahead—summary, the passageway of information to those whose attention is solicited for the sake of the country, the legislative plans, the conduct of wars, the dilemmas of justice. Not reading has certain benign aspects for the powerful, who are thereby spared deprecations, advice, rumors, and plain insults.

For the chic and the rich, a certain ectoplasmic culture—thought to be taste—is considered of value. A crossword puzzle familiarity with names and tags is preventive, warding off embarrassment. Names have a glow, like a pear in autumn, and are a sweetening acquisition. The list is not punitive either. Renaissance, perhaps, but not necessarily the Risorgimento; Hamlet and Macbeth, but not Laertes and Macduff; Lazarus is metaphorical and Ezekiel isn't; Dante, yes, but no shame will attach itself to a smile of confusion about Brunetto Latini, who, except for his learning, is very like one's friends. In the television program about the Duke of Windsor, Mrs. Simpson had to explain to the Prince of Wales who Emily Brontë was—all done with a tolerant smile.

This is as it must be. Knowledge of literature is an idiosyncrasy, professional sometimes, and a scarcity otherwise. The literature of history and philosophy are also little mandarin buttons worn on the caps of a few. Perhaps a certain discrete honor accompanies these accomplishments, but the large, educated, reasonably prosperous public will for the most part want to buy and read books that have elements of current interest, either in the immediacy of the subject matter or in the strength of striking ideas. Yet, a considerable number of difficult and supremely valuable books are published each year, and someone buys them for the purpose of reading, else they would not be made available. This seems all we can ask, and what education and self-education have failed to stimulate cannot be forever lamented. And of course there is always the humbling fact that even the greatly learned and devotionally pursuing will indeed care and pursue less than they might.

When one considers the nature of contemporary fiction and poetry, it would seem to deny the supposed lack of sophisticated culture and ready-reference comprehension on the part of the reader. The greatly admired authors are freely anarchic and demanding. It appears that those who read at all have read a lot. Much important contemporary writing is intensely "literary." These compositions are not addressed to a void, but rather assume a common culture out there somewhere. Skimming the pages of a book of poetry that just arrived in the mail, my eye comes upon Faustus, Uccello (followed by a single-word sentence: Bird.), Orpheus, Alcibiades, Degas, Crivelli, Bechstein, Poussin, Myshkin, Beauvais, for a beginning list in verses that might be called "open."

For a writer like Borges, the library is the landscape of human drama; it is experience, tragedy, social history. Among our own writers, satire and parody and mimicry are directed to a mind that must itself be richly aware of banalities, old movies, literary texts, conundrums, puns, a torrent of references. Ellipses, allusiveness, disconnection, are to be filled, identified, connected by the imagination and knowledge of the reader; otherwise the creative effort, so detailed, so mindful of tone, will have been in vain. "Description of physical appearance and mannerism is one of the several methods of characterization used by writers of fiction," John Barth says in an early story. "But to say that Ambrose and Peter's mother was pretty is to accomplish nothing." This asks of the reader a contemplation of physical description in narrative; it also, perhaps, asks him to smile—*knowingly*.

Proust left a short book titled *On Reading*. It says, of course, many beautiful things about himself, about decoration (William Morris), Carlyle, Ruskin, the Dutch painters, Racine, Saint-Simon—on and on. And then somewhere in the pages he notes the insufficiency of reading and says that it is an initiation, not to be made into a discipline. "Reading is at the threshold of spiritual life; it can introduce us to it; it does not constitute it."

So, perhaps we should not solicit, insist, badger, embarrass, on behalf of this almost free pleasure.

1983

SOUTHERN LITERATURE
The Cultural Assumptions of Regionalism

HENRY James, in his book on Hawthorne, speaks of the American peculiarity of finding a source of pride in one's mere length of residence in the country. There is likely to be some similar measure of aggressive assertion in the concentration on regional identity. Identity excludes, and "southernness" is a sort of opaque exclusion also. There remains, I hope, some murky distance between the South as a group of states—and not such a clear grouping as I, who was born and educated in Kentucky under the impression that I was living in the South, have reason to know—and the idea of southernness. Many persons who have been in residence in the South for years, decades even, would not describe themselves as Southern. Also, one may be a Southerner by background and deep experience and yet find himself not a creation of southernness. Not every creative mind living in the region has found itself engaged by that condition. Poe is an example. One of the greatest minds of his time—vivid, original, complicated—his years in Virginia and Maryland do not appear to have been a moral or aesthetic definition. His true home was far away: in Romantic poetry, dark landscapes, brilliant researches and puzzles.

There is culture, custom and attitude, national and personal history; and then there is the self-conscious creation by individual talents of works of the imagination. The South has produced a large, inchoate cluster of images about itself and its place in America. Bad images incline to be more concrete than consoling ones. Racism, with its overwhelming span of social, aesthetic, moral and political details, has been the central image of the South—long after the Civil War, up to our time, the time when it became clear that much of the rest of the country shared in this tragic obsession. Alongside racism in the South there were more acceptable and flattering images, sentimental themes lodged somehow in the old plantation aristocracy. These have had, even in the most unreflective dilution, an astonishing if not always distinguished endurance.

Regionalism itself is a complicated condition for art, particularly for modern art. In its folkloric aspect, it had something to teach us because it valued and honored isolated groups who had lived, spoken, created their manners. In general, for America, the folkloric is exhausted. Except for a unique talent like that of the extraordinarily gifted Zora Neale Hurston, the folkloric is not what we mean when we speak of Southern literature.

Writers must live in a place, have families, a youth, and experience in some degree of saturation. This will often, but not always, be a rich part of their creative life. Other sources are the nation, world literature, past and present thought. It is always difficult to judge the weight of the creative resources called upon by an individual talent. Region is one of them—and yet I daresay no ambitious artist wishes to be known as the best painter or novelist in Tennessee, with the mark of the amateurish shining so brightly in the claim to local fame in the arts.

For the South, the burden of fixed ideas in its own mind and in the mind of the country is a hindrance to serious thought and even to the ability to see what is around us. It is not easy to separate oneself from these conventions, conventions that are *high* and *low* we might say—some so commonplace as to be absurd and others more subtle and secretly beguiling. Southernness is more a decision than a fate, since fine talents are not necessarily under any command of place or feeling. Fidelity to place for subject matter is only the beginning of literary art and is seldom as important as the larger claims of intelligence, contemporaneity, freshness, and awareness of the long, noble challenge of literature itself. William Styron's *Sophie's Choice* is a dense and complex example of the Southern sensibility meeting modern experience at its most extreme and intractable point: the extermination camps of Germany and Poland. The aspect of this novel that concerns me is the alliance of Southern memories and themes with the making of a literary career in New York, where the action takes place, and the encounter, by way of a central character, with the meaning of the Holocaust.

The Southern young man, a writer, the first-person narrator, is close to the author himself, and part of his education from Auschwitz is the discovery of his own subject matter, in this case his novel about Nat Turner. The narrator tells us that he has not forgotten slavery and his own remaining guilt. The scene is the 1950s, and certain plot devices are "excavated" from family events that took place during slavery. The young man in New York is to be saved from bohemian down-and-outness by a legacy that survived from gold buried after an unfortunate sale of a young slave. This small drama in a large and outstandingly ambitious work interested me when I came upon it in my first reading of the book. It seemed to me a lingering refrain from an earlier cavalier tradition sounding its tones among the most urgent reflection on our own time. I use the word "cavalier" very loosely from its source in William R. Taylor's brilliant *Cavalier and Yankee: The Old South and American National Character*. I mean by the word to refer to the presumption of a highly conscious, educated, morally confused, but somehow honorable plantation mind.

Sophie's Choice is suffused with southernness is a number of ways. The guilt of slavery and the guilt of the Holocaust are brought together in the young man's mind. A very curious moment occurs when Sophie is telling of her involvement with Rudolf Franz Höss, the actual commandant at Auschwitz. Styron turns aside to instruct the reader with information about Höss: "Born in 1900, in the same year and under the same sign as Thomas Wolfe." I think it is best to let that stand as it is, a charming aside of great unlikeliness in other Auschwitz reflections.

The young Southern writer, Styron, has his Tidewater memories, his tainted legacy from slavery, but he also has ambitions in the literary world, ambitions as a writer first, and as a Southern writer in a world in which a great many vivid figures of his generation are not Southern at all but are instead Jewish. It is not, for example, Eudora Welty that serves as a challenge to his possibilities, but those *others*.

With conscious naiveté, never meant to be serious but meant instead to be amusing, there is a scene in which the young writer is asked if he has read Saul Bellow's *Dangling Man*. "Well, dog my cats," he answers. But as the conversation goes on, he begins to feel panic: "Suppose, I thought, the clever son of a bitch was right and the ancient and noble literary heritage with which I had cast my lot had indeed petered out, rumbled to a feeble halt with me crushed ignominiously beneath the decrepit cartwheels? . . . I saw myself running a pale tenth in a literary track race, coughing on the dust of a pounding fast-footed horde of Bellows and Schwartzes and Levys and Mandelbaums." I include this for its candor, its pedagogical sharpness about the melting pot which is the national literature and in which each talent, from no matter where, churns and turns as he struggles to add his own vision to that national literature.

I am led to another thought by *Sophie's Choice*, this novel so rich in moments of southernness adrift in the contemporary world. The narrator invites Nathan, the Jewish man from Brooklyn, and Sophie, the survivor of Auschwitz, to go to the South with him, to Virginia. He says to them ". . . at least Southerners have ventured North, have come to see what the North is like, while very few Northerners have really ever troubled themselves to travel to the South, to look at the lay of the land down there."

I wonder what they would see in the South today? Virginia—different indeed from Brooklyn, where the novel takes place—but then all places are different from Brooklyn. The landscape of America, from sea to sea, is lizards and moose, oranges and ice floes. The South has its landscape, but that is not what is meant by "seeing the South." The most dramatic region, Florida, is looked upon almost as an outpost of the Caribbean—this long before the Cubans settled there—not "really Southern." *Southern* is reserved for others of the former slave-holding states.

So, what will Nathan and Sophie see? "Bad temper, bad manners, poker, and treason," in Henry Adams's words? No, they would be on a journey in pursuit of fixed ideas, somehow, somewhere, to find the Southern image. Things do not have to be in existence to be imagined as visible. We see what words have told us is to be seen, what popular culture, Southern and otherwise, has created. When convention has fixed matters so firmly, even the most diverse, perverse, eccentric, and unaccountable slide into the expected. Films and popular literature will be seen in the South, with the cavalier and the violent passing on the sidewalk.

But what is defining, separating, authentic there? Southern towns have had a place in the literary imagination as vessels of southernness. But the American landscape has altered greatly; people live in such a newness of sight and assumption that the imagination can scarcely take it in without dislocation. The South has seen the same visual and psychological disintegration as the rest of the country and has accommodated the collapse by the same acceptance of the usefulness, the practicality, the inevitability, even the pleasures of the new.

Rural folk with their preserved speech and their dramas of a life with heavy roots gave a special genuineness of tone to Southern literature. They, with the rural landscape surrounding them, were there to be used, to be honored, or deplored at times. This was a fixed point. Faulkner, the supreme talent of Southern literature, the talent that almost alone gave the literature validity, made the rural South larger than life. Is the rural South still *there*, still somewhat static in its piney isolation, with some of the same woebegone ancestral memories?

It seems to me that the person who would have been in his little farm and shack, like his folks before him getting out the crop, is now in a trailer park, or in his solitary mobile home. Trailers account for almost 80 percent of low-cost new housing, I have read, and ocular evidence as one travels about the country would not dispute that. The trailer park, the mobile home, is felt by the thoughtful to represent a decline in the national imagination, to be a metallic resting place for the victims of *anomie*, to be a sort of root-killer, depriving of something deeper than the poverty of the old shack with its wisp of wood smoke drifting into the evening sky. No romance, a severing of the old relations abiding between country and town. The cavalier instinct is reduced by the absence of "good country people." Good country people do not grow up on television serials in trailer parks.

The towns of the South, the central cities, with their Main Streets, streets of the small and larger towns alike, are of great importance to the film imagination in its view and idea of the region. Cola drinking, heat, slit-eyed bigots in their pickup trucks with their shotguns on the front seat, sexy, bored young girls, menace, humor, whiskey, majorettes. This is the lower-class white South, visually and culturally a part of the sophisticated American imagination, which makes in turn liberal rejections of what is seen.

It is to the point to wonder what actually remains, whether the shifts in the small-town people have been taken in by themselves as well as absorbed imaginatively by those who would write about them, render them in films and plays. Nothing is harder to keep up with than America. We only know things do not remain the same. New vices, new pretensions, new possibilities, and an altered sense of place in the world—these come about so suddenly, or with what appears to be suddenness, that the literary imagination, slowly taking its shape, finds itself far behind. That is not a defect. Today and yesterday morning are not what literature is about. Still so much has vanished, has been gone for a long time, and to imagine it alive is to trap oneself in banalities.

For the large Southern cities, the places of business that once mingled with fine old houses and beaten alleys, the same disintegration has taken place. The rebuilding of downtown Atlanta in recent years is an astonishment. The incredible hotels—in what image are they? Their fake gold chandeliers, the raw orange of the lobbies, the schlock and kitsch of the architecture, the dead shops, the superfluous fountains dripping over plastic rocks: this creation is close to the vision that made Las Vegas out of a wasteland, and very far from the "Old South." The city fathers, the reclaimers of the hallowed "downtown," are like the rest of the country only partly in control of their landscape. But regionalism would not offer an alternative in any case, because the movement of the country is not only stronger than local will, it is stronger than local imagination. There is no way it could be otherwise, and the most refined mind would find it as difficult to create a suitable modern Southern architecture as to create a new church. Materials are what we have and what we are. Naturally, the second coming of Atlanta is, among the things one might deplore in the world, not high on the list. It means something, however; it means that the landscape and the people living in it cannot be mythologized in the old way.

The suburbanization of life is another problem for literary southernness. In a suburban world, memories are altered, new fidelities spring up from the streets, if only fidelity to the zoning laws, to the shapes the streets of the suburbs take under the dominion of income and size of building lot. This is family history. One of Peter Taylor's stories expresses a hint of this in a flowing, rhythmical ending. Suburbanization is not the point of the story's plot but rather the consequence of removals from the old ways of life. The persons have cavalier roots in their families, their excellent houses in town, their place in the community. The names, Tolliver and Lila, give the clue. The two people remove themselves from the old town in order to escape their own alcoholism, and here they are:

> . . . Tolliver and Lila just might have the bad luck to live forever
> —the two of them, together in that expensive house they bought,
> perched among other houses just like it, out there on some
> god-forsaken street in the flat and sun-baked and endlessly
> sprawling purlieus of Memphis.

One solution for the nostalgic Southern imagination as it meets a suburban world is to go duck-hunting. This endures in a number of contemporary books, just as it endures in life. Large treasures of southernness are hoarded in the hunting scene: masculinity, drinking, storytelling, memories of the past, of granddaddies and uncles, of country people in the old days, scenes of conflict and consolation. Faulkner, as in everything that relates to this scene of the literary South, is the master of the nostalgic, the historical, the tragic drama that may center upon hunting.

The sentimentalization of the modern South in Tennessee Williams, Truman Capote, and Carson McCullers has an iron hold on the popular imagination, on films and popular literature. Melodrama, memory, decay, pretension, and dreaming are combined with the tradition of sexual repression, household secrets, and longings. This is dressed up in Williams by attractive vagrants, red-light districts, old rooming houses, aging actresses, offstage strains of jazz: the appeal of the run-down and the heartbroken. For that reason it is difficult when you are thinking about the South to remove your own thoughts from the thoughts put there by the movies.

Walker Percy's *The Moviegoer* is aptly titled. In this cool and memorable novel, the region is bathed in a mist of irony and softened by an acute intelligence very alert to the follies of literary southernness. The young man who goes to movies is a gentleman, well connected, warmhearted, and amused by life. He has not done what he was expected to do, to become a doctor or a medical researcher. But, in a very offhand way, he has taken on the work of a Yankee gentleman—he makes money selling securities. He drives a battered little MG and employs a secretary, a young woman from Eufaula, Alabama. And there you have it, the key: the MG and the regional relief of Eufaula and the possibility, in the girl, of a vivacious, small-town Southern turn of speech. "I'll tell you one thing, son . . . ," she likes to say to her employer, who is also in his casual way her pursuer.

The young man knows about William Holden and Rory Calhoun, but he is a modernist, it turns out, a modernist and a Southern at once. He suffers from what he calls *malaise*, a sort of bearable alienation. He remembers *It Happened One Night*, and in his room he has one book, *Arabia Deserta*. He is very smart, with a very charming and chic volatility of taste. And he has had it with the old French Quarter and the Garden District and instead lives in a suburb called Gentilly, among "old-style California bungalows or new-style Daytona cottages." Tone and the mastery of it are everything in this remarkable book. It is a wicked, contemporary, cavalier creation, careful in detail, balancing effortlessly, or so it seems, on a very thin wire running between the old pieties and a new, fresh Southern sensibility.

In only one character does the sophistication falter, and that lies in the presentation of the aunt, with whom the young man has lived.

This lingering reminder of the "best of the South" had, we are told, worked in a settlement house in Chicago in her youth, and "embraced advanced political ideas." Further, she had served as a Red Cross volunteer in the Spanish Civil War before returning home to marry and settle down in the Garden District of New Orleans. Her early "credits" are up-to-date indeed. In that way she has, so to speak, earned her confident articulation of moral nuance, earned a certain surprising intellectuality, and can be the instrument of skeptical analysis combined with "the old forms of civility and even of humor."

In a long, final rebuke to the young man, the aunt speaks as a sort of philosopher of manners:

> "All these years I have been assuming that between us words mean roughly the same thing, that among certain people, gentlefolk I don't mind calling them, there exists a set of meanings held in common, that a certain manner and a certain grace come as naturally as breathing.... More than anything I wanted to pass on to you the one heritage of the men of our family, a certain quality of spirit, a gaiety, a sense of duty, a nobility worn lightly, a sweetness, a gentleness with women—the only good things the South ever had and the only things that really matter in this life."

Moral delicacy and discipline as a social grace, the beleaguered remnants of the old plantation heritage, the sense of *rightness* in Faulkner's lawyer-class, still haunt even the most watchful, observing Southern novelists. What may be wondered about is the fineness of the articulation, the lack of temptation to the sloth and ignorance and narrowness of so many of those others who share the presumption of class in the South. In a world where high culture is more and more a specialization, a difficult and mandarin accomplishment left to professors and to writers themselves, it is difficult to imagine the Garden District old lady spending her nights reading the *Crito*, a diversion she mentions in her long speech. I noticed in Eudora Welty's novel *The Optimist's Daughter* that when the father is miserably, restlessly dying, the daughter reads to him from *Nicholas Nickleby*. Eudora Welty and Walker Percy know the reading habits of Mississippi and New Orleans, and they are guarded, careful to include in the ornaments of life the usual popular "serious" works; but the temptation to go a little beyond, not to break the string, seems at times to represent a kind of regional cultural demand.

The Civil Rights Movement, the sharpening of the sense of identity and purpose in the black population of America, the resistance to definition by whites, makes the open use of race treacherous to the white Southern writer of fiction. In modern Southern literature, which is all that counts except for a few such as the brilliant Kate Chopin, sympathy for blacks is outstanding, with emphasis on dignity, endurance, and practical wisdom. This is Faulkner's Dilsey, McCullers's Berenice, black characters in Lillian Hellman's plays, black characters on television who seem to come out of Jack Benny's Rochester and the radio. The serving class was the source of acquaintance for the two races; but in the present time it is, for literary purposes, thick with possibilities for misadventure.

Again, Walker Percy is on the alert. In *The Moviegoer* is a butler named Mercer, who is commonly described as "devoted." But the clever young man, the modernist, observes that Mercer's face is in reality as "sulky as a Pullman porter's." Mercer wants to talk about current events, even though, having spent most of his time waiting on dinner parties, he does not know much about them. So, Mercer is a black man in transition. He is "dissolving," finding no vision of himself, either as an old retainer or as an expert in current affairs, rich enough to sustain his new idea of himself.

Wariness about the representation of black life has been constant in twentieth-century Southern literature. One of Ellen Glasgow's novels offers an example of this nervous reluctance to assume:

> ... they passed hurriedly between the crumbling houses and the dilapidated shops which rose darkly on either side of the narrow cinder-strewn walks. The scent of honeysuckle did not reach here, and when they stopped presently at the beginning

of Tin Pot Alley, there floated out to them the sharp acrid odour of huddled negroes.... The sound of banjo strumming came faintly from the dimness beyond, while at their feet the Problem of the South sprawled innocently amid tomato cans and rotting cabbage leaves.*

Ellen Glasgow is interesting in all respects and especially as an example of southernness turning into a comedy of manners open to the exercise of irony and ambiguity. She showed a positive fondness for many of the things later writers mourned, such as destruction of parts of the old landscape in order to accommodate factories.

Flannery O'Connor, asked about the abundance of freaks in Southern fiction, said Southerners at least were able to recognize them. Her work is the finest, most original to come out of the South in the last three decades. Her vision is never conventional and is instead transforming, altering the ground of expectation. Her freaks are what we may call *genuine*; they are driven by greed, blasphemy, and low cunning; they are dangerous. They assault the sentiments and the "good country people" banalities and devastate the countryside.

There is no pretension in Flannery O'Connor, as there is in Carson McCullers and Tennessee Williams, that the outlandish is filled with hidden goodness, with romantic isolation and longing. The appalling exchanges between The Misfit and the grandmother in "A Good Man Is Hard to Find" are exaggerations that are serious. The Misfit is a genuine and recognizable monster who can say, "You can do one thing or you can do another, kill a man or take a tire off his car." He has indeed taken *his* measure of the garrulous, hopeful grandmother: "She would of been a good woman ... if it had been somebody there to shoot her every minute of her life." The sourness, the angularity of the conceptions, the purity of the ear and of the style, the way things are—in Flannery O'Connor's work I think you find Southern literature that is a devastation of southernness.

Faulkner's art, with its high classical diction and its profound

Virginia (Garden City, NY: Doubleday, Doran, 1929).

absorption in his region, is nevertheless the most experimental to come out of the South. His work seems to me impossible without the avant-garde experiments of the 1920s in all the arts. The fractured view, the distortions of narrative line, the formal difficulties of his great fictions, are landmarks in twentieth-century literary art, to say nothing of Southern fiction.

Regions do not produce art. It seems to visit certain countries almost without preparation. Just as Russia was not thought by Marx and Engels to be the most likely place for the Communist Revolution, it is possible to say that Russia was not *supposed to be* the scene of an astounding outburst of nineteenth-century prose fiction. The mystery of place and art is never-ending. In our time, there is the tragic political disappointment of the South American continent, its inability to govern, to use resources wisely, to make national identities of an honorable shape, to create civilized arrangements between the citizens: out of this has come a literature of surprise and brilliance, works of art that perhaps owe more to Europe than to North America.

So it seems to me that we cannot really concern ourselves with the future of Southern literature. The conditions for all literature are unknown, accidental, and unpredictable. The South is as much a part of the television, highway world as any other part of the country. It depends upon all that we are as a nation and is in some way more quick to accept the expediencies of the moment than are other regions —and no matter the conflict with the "idea" of the South. Acceptance of the assumed and recklessly shifting pieties of American life is sometimes known in the South as patriotism.

Walker Percy, when asked how he would account for so many good Southern writers, said it was because "we" lost the War. My question would be: which war among those wars that do not capitalize the noun?

1983

MUSINGS

BASIC ENGLISHING

BALDERDASH! ETC.!
from Germinal *by Émile Zola,*
translated by Leonard Tancock. Penguin Classics, 1954

"Strikes? Balderdash!"

"Another lot of balderdash!"

"Balderdash! They'll never get anywhere with their poppycock!"

"If I walked out today they would at once grant me the hundred and fifty, the artful buggers!"

"You beastly tike!"

"Lumme! it's none too hot," said Catherine, shivering.

"Here, you, the toff!" he called to Etienne.

"Well, there's been another shemozzle...."

"Mummy, mummy, it's late!"

"Blast her!"

"Alzire, give it a bit of sponge round, will you?"

"Oh, get along with you, you ninny!"

"Right-oh, I'll catch you up."

"Good night, mate! I say, do you know that girl Roussie?"

"Past nine—well, did you ever!"

"Bloody little toad!" swore Etienne.

"Bloody hell! Aren't we nearly there?"

BUCKETS, ETC.
from The Black Sheep *by Honoré de Balzac,*
translated by Donald Adamson. Penguin Classics, 1970

"I have had my skull chipped in a duel with my legacy-hunter...
who has kicked the bucket."

"The only help the good woman can give me is to kick the bucket
as soon as possible...."

"If I stay on my pins...."

"My master will shut all your traps," Kouski replied....

"It is best to leg it to New York than moulder away in a pinewood
coffin here in France...."

HI, THERE! ETC.
from The Three Musketeers *by Alexandre Dumas,*
translated by Lord Sudley. Penguin Classics, 1952

"Hi, there!" he cried.

"Hi, there!" cried Jussac walking up to them and signing to his
men to follow him. "Hi, there, you musketeers."

"Hi, there, what's the hurry?" cried the two musketeers.

"Yes, boob's just the word for him," said Porthos.

"And I may tell you, Sir, I ran one of the blighters through with
his own sword," said Aramis.

"I saw him run two of the blighters through...."

"My wife's escaped?" cried Bonacieux. "Oh blast the woman!"

"Madame Bonacieux!" muttered d'Artagnan. "By Jove, I'm in
luck!"

"So you're frightened of that young whippersnapper, are you?"

"That's awkward," went on Athos, talking half to himself and half
to d'Artagnan. "If I kill you I shall look a bit of an ogre, shan't I?"

BYE-BYES! ETC.!
from L'Assommoir *by Émile Zola,*
translated by Leonard Tancock. Penguin Classics, 1970

"Ain't my wife daft...! Ain't she cracked to put me to bed...! Too silly, isn't it, bang in the middle of the day when you don't feel like bye-byes!"

"And don't turn your nose up at old Bazouge, because he's held much grander dames than you in his arms and they have let him deal with them without complaining, being only too glad to go on with their bye-byes in the dark."

"Have they been good boys?" she asked Madame Boche. "I hope they haven't been driving you potty."

"Of course she trusted Madame Boche, only it drove her quite potty to see a stranger taking over her room...."

It smelt jolly strong—none of your piss-and-water!

"Still it's a jolly hard way to earn it, because you risk your life more than your fair share."

Gervaise didn't even start eating, but just sent them packing with a few home truths, saying she was jolly glad she didn't have to mess about with their lousy clothes anymore.

"Blimey!" he babbled, "what a sun! It fair knocks you on the head!"

"Crikey! Wasn't it heavy?"

"If I were elected I'd go up to the rostrum and say: Bollocks!"

ETC.! ETC.!
from Pierre and Jean *by Guy de Maupassant,*
translated by Leonard Tancock. Penguin Classics, 1979

(First sentence) "Dash it!" old Roland suddenly exclaimed....

"Cripes! They're fresh, that lot!"

"Right-oh," repeated Roland....

"Look at that, and we get worked up about potty little sums of money!"

"He's a jolly handsome man!"

"Oh, these blessed doctors they're all the same: don't eat, don't drink, don't make love, cut out all fun and games. It's all naughty-naughty for your poor little health."

"Go and find that picture, duckie, as you've finished your dinner."

"By Jove! Suppose we went after lunch?"

from the summer reading of Elizabeth Hardwick

1989

PARSIFAL

WE CANNOT imagine the shape, the substance of a day in Victorian England, nor the quiet isolation of our own countryside even fifty years ago. Everything good is bought with the blood of someone's lack, someone's wretchedness. And so we are propelled onward, gaining and losing, building and destroying. Some try to hold a little here, save something there, to preserve, to remember; but the preserver is himself shaped out of losses and impatience. All of his little motors of need are running in his flesh just as they are running through the electric current in his house.

"To have time," in the personal sense, is to have an emptiness, an absence, a failure of diversion. Something is withheld from you, and this nothingness gives you time. No amount of money can buy it, and so it is fortunate that few want it. Quite the opposite: Our bodies would not be prepared, our souls and our vanity even less.

It is a jolt, not easy by any means, to find oneself suddenly at the Metropolitan Opera House for Wagner's *Parsifal*. This splendid, wonderfully successful new production is, like all the others before it since 1882, over four hours long. It is a static, contemplative work; its intensities are inward and abstract. The wound of Amfortas is not an ache, a sickness, a casualty, but the universal unhealed wound of existence. It is healed by the touch of a spear, the instrument of wounds. In a moment of dazzling modern technology, we see a flash of silvery movement—the spear, flung across the stage by Klingsor, is, with the speed of light, shining in Parsifal's hand. For the rest, we look inward, led by the music, into the cave of ourselves.

In this production, and I understand also in Bayreuth, the stage is quite dark throughout. Even the final Good Friday light is only a long, thin stream of whiteness in the shadows. In this way we are at a further remove from the usual involvement with the action on the stage. There is wisdom enough in this, since *Parsifal* can only be as it is; it is one of those works of art that will not budge to accommodate current taste. There is no way to move it. You must surrender, submit, call upon some sense of motionlessness in yourself. That is, if you want to be there for Redemption.

At *Parsifal* one must conquer time, or leave, as many do, saying with great unconscious accuracy that they must go home, they haven't time. This loss of time is not an illusion, but a fact for all of us. If, as an amateur, as a civilized person merely, one were to set out to read Shakespeare's works carefully, the Bible, Proust, or Dickens or Gibbon, it would be necessary to undergo some rare kind of discipline of withdrawal, to set up conditions very special, to work against the grain of our lives. Where will the time be found?

Wagner began *Parsifal* in 1877 and finished it in 1882, one year before his death. Nietzsche was distressed by its Christian feeling, but wrote: "It is as if someone were speaking to me again after many years about problems that disturb me...." This is still true. There in the long, pure hours we think not only of the Grail and the Sword but of ourselves and the others around us, people from space, living in a new continuum.

1971

THE ETERNAL HEARTBREAK

BILLY Budd, Foretopman, Herman Melville's mysterious, lyrical tragedy, is a contemplation of the unaccountable extremes of human character—of goodness appearing as naturally as a sunrise, and of evil inhabiting a human soul also naturally, we might say, or at least without necessity or even clear advantage. Into this curious and immensely affecting reflection on the human condition, Melville has imagined details of great and challenging singularity. He also, as a storyteller, has provided a miraculous plot that will tie the characters together on the level of action, without which the tale would be a philosophical daydream, an assertion rather than a drama. Billy Budd, a young sailor of remarkable beauty, good nature, and loyalty, is accused by the master-at-arms, a sort of naval MP, of intention to mutiny. The sailor, who under stress suffers from a stutter or speech pause, is unable to express his innocence and outrage and strikes out at the accuser, killing him by a blow. According to maritime law, he must be hanged and his body consigned to the sea.

Ah, but who is Billy Budd? He is a curiosity indeed, almost defying credible description. He is the Handsome Sailor, he is Apollo with a portmanteau, he is Baby Budd, Beauty—all of these things as he comes swinging onto the English ship *Indomitable*, wearing a silk handkerchief, a Scotch tam with a tartan band, aged twenty-one, an able-bodied seaman, fit to climb the great sails, as if ready to fly. Billy is also from the first a creature of inborn moral sweetness. He is free and innocent, a beautiful changeling from nowhere. In fact he is an orphan, an illiterate, reminding one of a freshly hatched, brilliantly colored bird. His only flaw is the one mentioned, the Englishman's stutter or pause when under stress. For the rest, he brings a glow of peace and physical perfection by his presence.

Melville gives evidence of a compositional strain to bring credibility to his extraordinary youth, to the extremity of his perfection accompanied by the purest naturalness. The pictorial Billy: "a lingering adolescent expression in the as yet smooth face, all but feminine in purity of natural complexion." And again: "Cast in the mould peculiar to the finest physical examples of those Englishmen on whom the Saxon strain would seem not at all to partake of any Norman or other admixture, he showed in his face that humane look of reposeful good nature which the Greek sculptor in some instances gave to the heroic strong man, Hercules."

John Claggart, the master-at-arms, is a mirror opposite to Billy Budd. His unaccountable but concentrated hostility to the universally loved Billy is again a conundrum, an exceptional circumstance. Claggart exhibits the strange and troubling "motiveless malignity" that Coleridge in a sort of psychological resignation falls back on as the explanation for Shakespeare's Iago. Like Billy, Claggart has no known past, no baggage of previous circumstance traveling with him. He has entered the navy at thirty-five, causing his shipmates to imagine some cloud of disrepute driving him. Once aboard, Claggart reveals a calculated adaptability that serves him well. "His constitutional sobriety, his ingratiating deference to superiors, together with a particular ferreting genius...capped by a certain austere patriotism, abruptly advanced him to the position of master-at-arms." His nature, the appalling traps he sets for Billy by the use of weak and corrupted conspirators, his sniveling denunciation of the young sailor to Captain Vere—none of this can be seen as useful to Claggart, since he has nothing to fear from Billy and nothing to gain from his destruction. In the end, Melville will need, in the absence of plausible causality, to rely upon assertion as the source of Claggart's deformation. The master-at-arms' character is said to be "not engendered by vicious training or corrupting books, or licentious living, but born with him and innate, in short, 'a depravity according to nature.'"

The third character, Captain Vere, sometimes called Starry Vere, is a rare being, but not one of as extreme definition as are the other two principals. Vere is fair-minded, bookish, decent, thoughtful, reserved. In the end he is bound by marine law, the letter and the precedent of it, to allow Billy's execution, even though the circumstances violate his sense of justice. Billy, in striking Claggart, his superior officer, has fallen into the rigorous jurisdiction of the law of the sea. That the blow should have killed Claggart is a circumstance beyond reprieve.

The Britten opera opens with a brief flash-forward of Vere as an old man lamenting with sorrow the happenings on the ship *Indomitable* in the year 1797, during the French Wars and "in the difficult and dangerous days after the Mutiny at the Nore." The mutiny referred to took place at Spithead when the crew seized the ship and sent the officers ashore in protest against the brutal conditions prevailing in the British navy. The Great Mutiny, as it was called, was a threat to Britain's sea power and also was felt to connect with the tide of revolutionary feeling spreading from France and from Napoleon's conquests. After the prologue, the opening scene of Britten's opera is a picture of the gross and cruel servitude practiced on British ships. The *Indomitable* has been called to shift from mercantile seagoing to serve as a man-o'-war in the naval battles with the French. For this purpose, men are dragged off the street or from merchant vessels and impressed into service. A novice, frightened or inexperienced, is forced on board and brutally flogged for merely slipping on the deck.

Billy Budd, not a recruit but an able-bodied seaman by choice, is sent to the *Indomitable* from a homeward-bound ship named *Rights o' Man*, referring to Tom Paine's famous radical work. Billy is willing to serve, and as he boards his new berth he cheerfully waves goodbye to his departing vessel, calling out, "Farewell, *Rights o' Man*," a harmless salutation that Claggart chooses to regard with suspicion, as if the goodbye signified a mutinous, rebellious nature.

The tragedy, the tale of dark treachery, annihilating the bright innocent, Billy Budd, takes place entirely on the ship. A ship afloat is by its very structure a profoundly resonant dramatic device. It is, first of all, a man-made intruder that sets against the elements, the winds, the storms, the calms, the uncertainty of its human and mechanical equipment. The great age of ocean explorations, centuries before the *Indomitable*—the age of, for instance, Columbus, now undergoing a vulgar and provincial downgrading—is scarcely imaginable to us today. Even the eighteenth-century vessel of Melville's fiction is under sail, without power, demanding every sort of daring and perseverance. Billy Budd, manning the great topsail, is therefore a romantic vision of strength and the spirit of adventure.

A ship against the elements is one thing, but it also contains the dangerous human drama of beings brought together in a random way, strangers of no previous acquaintance, each trapped in a void, with no exit possible until the voyage is completed. A ship at sea is, then, a prison, and as in landlocked prisons there will be a hierarchy of fixed positions, men in power over others, tempting to tyranny on the part of the powerful and to baseness as the lower orders struggle to survive. Such a base one is Squeak, a ship's corporal, a miserable creature who does Claggart's bidding.

Billy Budd is the final representation of Melville's genius. The manuscript was left in a trunk at the time of his death in 1891 and did not see publication until 1924. The early success of his seafaring novels had not prepared the public for the immense rhetorical and imaginative complexities of *Moby-Dick*, and indeed he ceased to have a public. Twenty years near the end of his life were spent as an inspector in the Customs House in New York City. Melville knew neglect and despair, and it is fitting to look at his last work of fiction as somehow a summation of the state of mind to which his experience of life had brought him. The conflict between simple, unaffected beauty and goodness and chaotic, willful destructiveness does appear to find a promising resolution that is not overwhelmed by Billy's death. His purity seems to live on and is given a transcendent force in the description of his last moments, moments that recall Christ's crucifixion. "At the same time it chanced that the vapoury fleece hanging low in the East, was shot through with a soft glory as of the fleece of the Lamb of God seen in mystical vision; and simultaneously therewith, watched by the wedged mass of upturned faces, Billy ascended; and ascending, took the full rose of dawn."

The libretto used by Benjamin Britten for the powerful opera he created out of Melville's story bears the name of Eric Crozier, a frequent collaborator of the composer's, and also the name of the distinguished novelist E. M. Forster. It is difficult to find the Forster voice in the libretto, although the novelist's attraction to this story of male beauty and innocence is easy to grant. In the original tale there is very little dialogue, and its formal dimensions are largely discursive and reflective. A libretto, with its violent condensations, its transposal of the dilatory expansiveness of prose fiction, must meet the demands of the stage and, most perplexing of all, the demands of the singing voice as the vessel of plot action, feeling, interpretation, poetry, and character. Sometimes the dialogue of the *Billy Budd* libretto is a bit more "matey" than would be true of Melville, even though here the setting is an English ship. Melville's wonderful "God bless Captain Vere!" is fixed in the mind of generations of readers and the change in the libretto to "Starry Vere, God bless you!" is a bit of a jar to the student of literature. But that is a trifle.

It must be said that the *Billy Budd* libretto works. The story is told, the tragedy unfolds, the ship is used as a powerful visual enclosure, and the work is a triumph of musical theater in the highest sense. We may note the practical dilemma of having as a hero a baritone whose outstanding feature is a striking, dominating physical beauty. Heroines in opera are offered as beautiful, fascinating, and seductive, and to achieve this, much use is made of blond wigs and flowing, concealing garments—a transformation is at hand, often quite imperfect. But a beautiful young man is something else—a beautiful young man with a superior singing voice. That we must leave to chance.

The opera is set in two acts, and the musical and dramatic tension is unrelenting, broken only by a few rhymed sea chanteys of what might be called a mixed national character, since they pair "Genoa" and "Shenandoah," "Nantucket" and "bucket"—that sort of thing. And there is a break from the dilemma of character when the ship suddenly has a chance to engage the French in battle. Due to a mist and an unsteady breeze, the chase is lost, but the scene is an interesting diversion in itself. It reveals the contrary nature of the sailors, surly and discontent at one moment but patriots eager to uphold the honor of the British navy at the next moment.

The ending of the opera is somber, as the voices of the crew rise in an ominous grumble of revulsion at the fate of Billy. But the angry, threatening voices die away, as they must, and we move to Vere's final despairing epilogue. In Melville's story, the captain is wounded in battle and dies murmuring, "Billy Budd, Billy Budd." Still, the flash-forwards to Vere as an old man, reflecting upon the curious drama on board the *Indomitable*, finally seem a proper addition. Vere is the moral center of the tragedy, an Englishman of the finest stripe, his whole being illuminated by a flame of conscience and culture. In that way he is a contrast to Billy and Claggart, who are what they are, helplessly.

At one point Melville makes an interesting conjecture, saying that only Claggart and Captain Vere truly understand the challenge represented by Billy's nature. To Claggart the amazement of the young, handsome sailor is to "be nothing more than innocent!"—just that and nothing more, an unimaginable condition to a complex and devious soul. The violent happenings on the *Indomitable* are part of the eternal heartbreak of human experience. Out of a difficult and profound moral dilemma, Benjamin Britten in *Billy Budd* created a work of great beauty and immense emotional power. A grand opera in every sense.

1993

THE HEART OF THE SEASONS

Summer—a high, candid, definite time. It may slither out of the ambiguity, hesitance, or too early ripeness of spring and edge toward the soothing peculiarities of autumn, but summer is downright, a true companion of winter. It is an extreme, a returning, a vivid comparative. It does not signify that some are cool and some are dry and sweltering; summer is a kind of entity, poetic, but not a poetic mystery. The sun is at its zenith in the Tropic of Cancer, a culmination.

Think of the yellow afternoons of the last century, such as we see in the paintings of our text, the illustrations.* Then, we believe, it was another world—quiet, perhaps not so much reflective as drowsy and wondering. A luxurious pause, an inattention except for the concentration on pleasure. A caesura to honor the sun, the warm waters, the breezes of the mountains, and the hope of some dreamlike diversion of destiny in the pause.

Here, in the paintings—all from the new Terra Museum of American Art in Chicago—is a languorous game of croquet. It appears that this game may be one too many, too much like yesterday, a routine, and nothing to surprise. And Charles Curran's bursting, voluptuous water lilies. The sun has ravished the flowers, full force,

---

*"The Heart of the Seasons" was accompanied by American Impressionist paintings from the Terra Museum collection, including Winslow Homer's *The Croquet Match* (1872), William J. McCloskey's *Strawberries* (1889), John Singer Sargent's *Dennis Miller Bunker Painting at Calcot* (1888), Frederick Carl Frieseke's *Lilies* (1912) and *Lady in a Garden* (1912), Charles Courtney Curran's *Lotus Lilies* (1888), Mary Cassatt's *Summertime: Woman and Child in a Rowboat* (1894), and James McNeill Whistler's *Note in Red: The Siesta* (1882–1883). [Editor's note.]

and how ferocious they are amid the passive, sheltered glances of the young women in the boat.

What a lot of clothes the women are dragging about in these rich-toned landscapes. Hats, sleeves, petticoats, ties at the neck, parasols—a shroud of protection, giving a somewhat fatigued femininity to these lost summer days. Sargent's summer painter must be putting the bush and the field and the reflection of the stream on canvas. He looks much as a man would today: white suit, coquettish red belt, and what appears to be a handkerchief on his head.

But she, the companion, is reading in a hat like a haystack, a dark skirt, and holding the inevitable lacy umbrella, a thing of no apparent utility unless it be a weapon against a change of his mood there in the erotic sleepiness of a full summer afternoon, and the ground dry and not even a dog in sight.

I like to remember the summer season coming to those who just stay at home the year round, that is, most of the world. The plain patterns of simple domestic life meet each year with a routine. Nothing is unexpected. An almanac of memories disputes claims of the hottest day in decades or the level of the rainfall.

The furnace is shut down and the fireplace, if there should be one, is emptied and the tiles relieved of grit and polished to an oily sienna sheen. Windows washed, everything aired; moths seeking the bedroom light bulb; grass and weeds pushing up out of the hard winter soil; leaves on the maples and elms—nothing special; doors latched back and covered by a flapping screen—with a hole in it and rusty hinges; voices calling out of the windows; perennials determined to exhibit their workhorse nature, if most a little disgruntled and with more stem than flower; insects strong as poison; the smell of chlorine in a child's hair—from the community pool across town.

The congratulation of summer is that it can make the homely and the humble if not exactly beautiful, beautifully acceptable. Such brightness at midday and then the benign pastels, blues and pinks and lavenders of the summer sky. Much may wither and exhaust, but so great is the glow and greater the freedom of the season that every extreme will be accommodated. There are great gardens filled with jewels as precious as those dug out of the earth and then the hand that planted the sparse petunias and impatiens in the window box—there's that, too.

I remember days from the summers in the upper South and sights from certain towns in the Middle West, in Ohio and Indiana, places just passed through long ago. There's something touching about the summer streets of middle-size towns: everything is a bit worn down in July, all slow and somnolent except for the supersonic humming-bird in the browning hydrangea bush at the edge of the porch. The disaster of the repetitive but solid architecture of the 1920s—once perceived as quite an accomplishment of ownership, and suitable—comfortable according to what was possible.

The front porches. That unalterable, dominating, front-face mistake left over from the time before the absolute, unconditional surrender to the automobile and to traffic. There was a time when not everyone had a car, and to children then the traffic was interesting. The brand names, the out-of-state license plates—a primitive pleasure to take note of them, like stamping your palm at the sight of a white horse. And the family on the front porch, watching the life of the street.

This porch in front and so unsightly and useless and awful in the winter with the gray of the splintered planks and the soggy sag of the furniture often left out to hibernate in public view. The old eyesores, defining the houses, many of them spacious, with gables, and bits of colored glass from a catalogue over the door, in a fan shape. If nothing else, summer redeems the dismal overhang of the porch, for a few months, and even the darkened halls and parlors within might be glad of an escape from the heat.

Somewhere there is water. Not too far away there will be an abandoned quarry, difficult to climb into and cold as a lake in Nova Scotia. There will be a stream or a river, not very deep and muddy at the banks—Middle Western water.

If there are no neighbors to be seen on the streets, they can be seen and heard at the back, there on the patio where tubs standing on tripods and filled with charcoal lumps are ready to receive marinated bits of flesh. There is pleasure in all this, in the smoke, in the luscious brown of the chicken leg—on your own little plot where you fed the chickadee last winter.

These scenes, local as the unearned wildflower, the goldenrod with its harsh cinnamon scent, are not splendid. Little of the charm of the ocean view and the table set with blue linen, and the delectable salmon, so well designed for painterly display, laid out on a platter among scattered stems of watercress. Still the American town streets—those angling off the main drag seen on the way to the airport—are a landscape of the American summer. And why should we groan with pain at the sight of the plastic flamingo on the lawn or the dead whiteness of the large inflated duck coming into its decorative own nowadays? There's not much else to buy downtown, for one thing.

These things remind me of those elders who used to go abroad every summer to the same pension, to dusty interiors and dining rooms where the wine bottle with your name on it returned every night to the table until it was empty. Perhaps in Florence or outside Siena or in the north, to the band concert in the park by a German lake.

In Russian fiction people go off to the Crimea and sigh, how dull it is here. But since there is to be a plot, the scene is not to be so dull after all. In the salon, with the violin whining and the fish overcooked, the same faces take up their posts for the same complaints and posturings. Then someone new appears to the defensive snubs of the old-timers or to the guarded curiosity of the bored. It might be a sulky young girl with a chaperone or her mother; or a woman, not a girl, to be seated on the same side of the room as the tall man from Moscow, away from his family for two weeks and subject to dreaming. And it begins to begin...

Summer romance—when the two words are brought together, each takes on a swift linguistic undercurrent. As a phrase, it is something akin to "summer soldier"—the romance carries away and the summer soldier runs away from duty or from the reality of things. Heaven is something with a girl in summer: a line of Robert Lowell's. The summer romance will have the sharpness and sweetness and the indescribable wonder of the native strawberry, raspberry, blueberry, and toward the end the somewhat gritty cling of the late blackberry.

The sun-filled romance is the dramatic background of much fiction. There is the accident of the meeting and the unreasonable heightening of the season. And classically there is often an imbalance in the lovers, an imbalance of class or situation, hard, chilly truths swept away by the soft clouds, the fields, and the urgency of the burst-open water lilies.

Edith Wharton wrote a short novel called *Summer*. In it you will find a love affair between a pretty and poor young girl from the New England hills and a clever young man from the city who likes to study the old houses of the region. As always, he is alone, happily solitary, idling about in the sunshine, and she is there, as she has always been. In the way of these sudden romances everything before and ahead seems to fade. Of course, it is not to last, at least not to last for the young man who, as it turns out, is engaged to someone of his own sort . . . and so on.

Tess of the D'Urbervilles: "Rays from the sunrise drew forth the buds and stretched them in long stalks, lifted up sap in noiseless streams, opened petals, and sucked out scents in invisible jets and breathings." This is the summer landscape that engulfs Tess and Angel Clare and finally leads to a despair of such magnitude only the genius of Thomas Hardy could imagine it and embody it in the changing seasons and the changing structure of the English countryside.

In Chekhov's story "The Lady with the Dog," the lady and the man are both married. They meet in Yalta in the summer and the romance flows along on a pitiless tide, without any possible ending except misery. When they believe the love will at last end or the devastation will have a solution, the final line says no, "it was only just beginning."

So in spite of the meadows and the picnic under the shade of the copper beech tree, the days will grow longer and there will again be buying and selling and coming and going elsewhere. The romantic ritual of the season fades, even if it will be staged again next summer with other lovers in other places. The freedom of the summer remains in the memory.

In the mountains, there you feel free...Yes. Under Mount Monadnock in New Hampshire—a storm of stars in the heavens, a pattern of gorgeous gleaming dots on the dark blue silk of the sky, all spreading down like a huge soft cloak to the edge of the field.

The mountains are perhaps not quite in such demand as they once were in summer. Too lonely and overwhelming, the pleasures offered no longer quite suitable to the extraordinary energies of those who rush to the long, long expressways on a Friday afternoon—flat roads ahead, and yet they mean getting there. The weekend, commuting distance, breads and cheeses and bottles of wine, Vivaldi on the cassette, and a lot of work to be done and gladly.

Impatience with the division of city and country, or what is more or less "country," has changed the heart of the seasons. Many face a February weekend as if it were July. There is a need for an eternal summer, some mutant need created by the demand for nature, for weekend nature, even as nature disappears along the route.

Eternal summer, kind only as a metaphor. Night is the winter of the tropics, as the saying has it. On the equator the days are twelve hours long. Withering rivers and unrelenting lassitude in the never-ending summertime. In Bombay in January, blissful for the citizens, but to those accustomed to the temperate sections of the United States, the heat of January in India spreads around like an infamous August swelter.

The gardens, the terraces, the flowers in vases. The first peas, the lettuce out of the ground, the always too greatly abundant zucchini— and at last a genuine tomato. No doubt the taste for these has grown sharper from the fact that we have them all year round in an inauthentic condition of preservation. Where the memory is never allowed to subside, according to each thing in its time, the true taste is more astonishing. One of summer's intensifications. Very much like actually swimming or sailing after the presence of the sea or lake known only as a view.

Summer, the season of crops. The concreteness of it. Not as per-
fumed and delicate and sudden as spring and not as *triste* as autumn.
Yet for the enjoyment of summer's pleasures, for the beach, the crowded
airplane to Venice, most of us consent to work all year long.

1987

NOTES ON LEONARDO AND THE FUTURE OF THE PAST

WHILE walking along 57th Street recently I wandered into an exhibition the IBM Gallery was having of models built from Leonardo's sketches. I say "wandered in" because I hardly suppose I would have gone from a simple description of the fare to be offered. I was caught by a glimpse of one of the drawings. It was not science, but the *artful* charm of the machines that drew my attention: a helicopter, a water wheel, a flying machine, a parachute which "except for its shape, resembles the modern version," as the catalogue explained, a pile driver, instruments to measure wind, humidity, distance, the degree of the incline of a slope—what could one make of them? The wonders of science have by their ever-proliferating reality lost the quality of "wondrousness." Amazement has fled the scene and we are literally prepared for anything. The real understanding of most of us does not even include the telephone and the radio, but that is no hindrance to acceptance of the most extraordinary discoveries. We cannot name anything "incredible." The astronauts and their families are just as wondrous to the television audience as their capsules; indeed, the space suits and the capsules have about them a peculiar aspect of comedy. If you think of the models from Leonardo as science, you would have to say, Oh, dear is that all? Just a little old pile driver, a dear little water wheel, and all thought of sometime in the fifteenth century.

And so it is not as science that Leonardo's inventive genius awes us. To the extraordinary achievements of the scientific imagination we can only give a blinking consent. The miraculous still lives in the personal. Niagara palls, computers compute into eternity, a universal automation changes every aspect of our lives, but we do not fall down and worship. In our age, the greatest emotion machinery can arouse is the anger we feel when it fails us in its expected functioning. Our greed, fed and fed, knows no end; but we do not feel grateful for what is in abundance. We feel that someday someone will understand everything—except the great artists. Awe clings to the total sum of genius, to Leonardo's being, not to the important fascination of the products of collective discovery.

Maxim Gorky in his brilliant memoir on Tolstoy tells of a terrifying walk with the old man along the seashore and how it appeared to Gorky that Tolstoy was really God, controlling nature. "...he was looking into the distance out to sea, and the little greenish waves rolled up obediently to his feet and fondled them as if they were telling something about themselves to an old magician....He, too, seemed to me like an old stone come to life, who knows all the beginnings and the end of things....I felt something fateful, magical, something which went down into the darkness beneath him and stretched up like a searchlight into the blue emptiness above the earth; as though it were he, his concentrated will, which was drawing the waves to him and repelling them...."

And that is how one feels about Leonardo, that if he is not God, he is at least a "god," and all things come from him. And uniquely a possible god for us. His curiosity was of such an urgent sort that it fell under Freud's suspicion. Why did he have to know everything? What was he trying to find out? We understand his dreams, too, through Freud. At least we bring him close to ourselves, whether we understand him rightly or not. (You cannot quite do that with Shakespeare. It's so hard to imagine what he was like.) Prodigiousness, sorcery, mystery, magic, Leonardo has that, of course, preeminently, and his little machines have it too, strangely more than our lonely capsules forever orbiting. For we just accept the capsule as given, something in the living room. Leonardo's drawings have come to pass, like old prophecies. You will fly in the air, like a bird.

The prophetic nature, or tendency, of art is usually of a totally different sort. Nothing of inventions, discoveries, but an unsettling apprehension, ahead of the time, of the changes in the habits of society, of the shifts in taste, of the degradations to come. Indeed the prophecies may be very small and very, very depressing, or large and tragic. We aim to frighten in our prophecies, to predict loss, diminishment. Going away from rightness, falling off, aridity, future violence: it is not the purpose of modern art to tell good news, that is, if it is concerned at all with society's future. Mary, robes flying, was lifted up to Heaven, and she smiled with joy. We would flee from the Brave New World, that is, if we could. Prediction clings even to the most banal, for banality is itself a great insistence, always there asking for its share or more than its share. Our carelessness will bear its new careless fruit, our emptiness will grow and grow. These acts of recognition please in all the arts. Ugliness and sadness reach out to us.

Design and style, without consideration for content, without visions of man's condition as it is and will be, are the usual prophetic instances in art, at least in painting; they simply predict themselves, by extension and multiplication, by strong example which, somehow, magically seize hold of the imagination at every point. And then we decide, with an odd unanimity, to call a new thing beautiful.

Beethoven said, "He who understands my music can never be unhappy again." A paraphrase can only reduce the meaning of this. In the end when you say that you have loved a novel read long ago you can only mean that it made you happy to read it. I am sure this is why art is a sacred calling; we want happiness more than we want knowledge. Indeed they are united in art, happiness and knowledge. The unexpected and the unpredictable also affirm the sacred character of art; it falls like grace upon the just and the unjust, the good man and the wayward one. We cannot ask for anything more to our sense of things than the obscure birth of Shakespeare; it satisfies our faith in the mysteriousness of nature, it tells us once more that the plan of things will never be revealed.

Those who draw near to art by possession, by extraordinary studies, by unusual acquisitiveness—what do they hope to get from it all? Salvation? Enrichment? Enrichment, that odd word just now, with respect to art, carrying with it no hint of the soul. A literal enrichment for the lucky. Can salvation dwell at the dealers, make its home at the auction block? Perhaps it can, at least if one can think of just a little salvation, a mere touch of it, a hint—that degree may indeed sometimes be bought. The sacrifice of money in the flow of things is somehow connected with the sacrifices of art. Still, one would not want to linger too long on the terms of the connection, for all manner of unlikely and uneven and incompatible things are indeed "connected."

The technology, the science rather, that fascinated Leonardo and which he thought of as a liberation for mankind, even if it was the thing itself rather than its use which he cared for, this same science seems to many artists threatening and hostile perhaps to the very existence of some art forms. Technology threatens to dry up the sources of feeling, as if they were a lake to be drained for some civic purpose. But we approach technology with fear and yet with a sort of attraction, a hint of surrender to its gorgeous power. Godard's new film, *Alphaville*, is a perfect example of this love and hatred. The message of the film is that technology kills; it destroys the sensibilities, takes meaning and joy from life. Ah, but what is the other message, the hidden one? The real care and patience and inspiration of the film have not gone into the study of the hurt human heart but into the perfect representation of the sinister technology that is so much condemned. That which we are asked to hate has, in this work, an austere, beckoning beauty. The humanist is dead, but there is a certain aesthetic satisfaction in the orderliness, the cleverness of his extermination. What fascination the film's set designers have had with the swift, bleak corridors, the dark cities and the looming skyscrapers surrounded by great bands of threatening light. And the sleek, "affectless" girls—it is hard to believe any man in the audience will find them unappealing. The exaggerations of technology are like some new and strange paradise, and one may himself feel a bit too old for them, a bit too nostalgic for the previous comforts of disorder and yet still not be able to say no.

Fear and love of technology, for the arts, seem to have replaced the fear and love of political power, of totalitarianism. It is *Alphaville* now, instead of *1984*. In an article in the *New York Herald Tribune* about the character and opinions of the young radicals it was found that most of them were not the least interested in Communism. "They're just old folks in baggy trousers who want people to write novels about tractors," one young person said. Political suppression and manipulation have taken a terrible toll in the arts of this century —suppression and war. But these repressive governments could not produce an art. It was perhaps not so much the works they feared as the vain, obsessive creators of the works. Technology, however, could produce art; a technological society might have a technological art. Literature would suffer greatly, no doubt, but painting, sculpture, and architecture could adapt—or so we think, even if some of us might regret the losses adaptation would bring. I have read somewhere that Goethe went through the Alps with the curtains of his carriage drawn.

It is astonishing how much the arts can do without. Academicians are depressed as one after another of the "essential" ingredients are simply tossed aside. And it is not accidental. We decide we can do without what we can no longer manage to create. In fiction, for instance, the construction of a satisfactory plot seems more and more difficult for writers. How to find a plot, suitable in dignity and complication, to the high degree of hope the novelist has? The sense of characters involved in a common situation, the authentic motivation, the sequence of cause and effect: there has been some interruption in our ability to produce these things in fiction. "Oh, oh, the years oh. And the rotten rose is ripped from the wall." That is fiction's province. Those sweet little towns, lying under the damp grass of their long history; the rain and the snows that wash over the graves; the lost years; the splendid plot of birth and death, mistake and punishment: we have given this up, mostly, for episode, fragments. Had to give it up. Paul Valéry felt it ignoble to have to write, "Madame put on her hat and went out the door." What we can no longer do with confidence we discard; it becomes out of date, academic, or commercial. The portrait and the aria belong here, too, perhaps.

Back to Leonardo's drawings for his inventions. I am captivated by the parachute with a figure dangling from it. The notebooks say, "If a man has a tent of linen without any apertures, twelve ells across and twelve in depth, he can throw himself down from any great height without injury." There is a sort of poetry in that. In the end, it is not Leonardo's mechanical discoveries that attract with such force; more was prophesied. The future of art, perhaps. How neatly the drawings and the models settle into the scene, find their place in our life. The tragic beauty of *The Last Supper* does not seem to be ours any longer except as the most treasured memory of our souls. But the little figure dangling from a parachute: there we are, all of us.

1966

GRITS SOUFFLÉ

To UNITE the word "grits" with the word "soufflé" is like putting a hat on a donkey. Grits, groats, grout, gruel are Old English words of a granite beauty, strength, and resonance. They tell of hard times, of rural folk, and of orphans starved by lying, fat caretakers in Dickens. Gruel, according to the O.E.D., can also mean punishment. Yet sophisticated chefs such as Lee Bailey and the late Craig Claiborne, both from the South, have given a nod to the grits soufflé while doing their cooking and writing with *haute* assurance on Long Island. For me, the word "grits," with its plebeian ring, in a defiant marriage with the pomp and puff, if it does puff, of a soufflé is the attraction of the dish.

Grits are distressingly bland and tasteless, but, light and airy, they can be souffléed, a process that even the most vivacious whipped egg whites could not accomplish with a mixture of oatmeal and water. The Deep American South is the home of grits; they are scarce in the repertoire of the Upper South of Kentucky, Tennessee, and Virginia. Rosalynn Carter in the Carters' parsimonious White House brought a bit of national exposure to Baked Cheese Grits. Sharp—very sharp— cheddar cheese is advised as a companion to the evanescent grits in baked dishes. If there were no cheese, you would be eating air with a bit of salt in it.

On a yellowing sheet of newsprint in a kitchen drawer I find Claiborne discussing grits with red-eye—sometimes called redneck— gravy. For red-eye gravy one needs to fry a piece of *country* ham, stir the leavings, and add black coffee to the pan. Country ham, of the Southern sort, is ham long hung in a smokehouse most likely to be in the back yard. It is the subject of a regional snort of superiority when sent North, perhaps as a Christmas present, only to be thrown out because it is covered with mold, as it rightly will be.

Southerners away from home practice a dip into ethnicity, memory roots, or what might be called a downscale affectation. The cuisine of the Southern states is rich in possibilities, many with a naming fortitude, such as gumbo, an okra soup. Virgil Thomson, composer, master chef, and a Southerner who spent his adult life at Harvard, in Paris, and, at last, at the Chelsea Hotel, in New York, was called on sometimes to prepare *wilted* lettuce, lettuce dressed with cooked bacon and warm grease from the frying pan. No matter the arterially threatening grease, Thomson lived past ninety. Of course, he was not thin, owing to the wilted lettuce and more refined preparations. He used to visit Montecatini to take the waters in summer, but then "I get it all back by Christmas."

1996

CHRISTMAS PAST

ORANGES and peppermint candy, fruitcake long in the making but swift enough in the eating, with a little Bourbon whiskey poured over it. A chill in the air, if not the snow of dreams, and the dusty whiffs, at that woebegone time, of soft coal burning in the grate—this was Kentucky long ago, when we sat with our father at the upright piano and each night of Christmas week sang the hymns and the old songs of Christmas, many with their dog-trot rhymes of bed and head, night and bright.

Later, in New York, I collected Christmas records, and each year I play them. The most beautiful are the oldest: Caruso singing "Cantique de Noël" in 1916, before electrical recording, and reclaimed in early mono LPs. In spite of the great tenor's range and notable volume, what we know as "O Holy Night" seems to come from a distance, from the star in the East, a pastoral world in antiquity—or perhaps it's only the hum and scratch of the twenty-six-year-old album, *A Golden Age Christmas*. Eliot's poem on the Magi begins, "A cold coming we had of it," and the sentiment is not alien to "Stille Nacht, Heilige Nacht" as sung by the matchless contralto Ernestine Schumann-Heink, in a tempo slower than that heard in the churches. She brings to the rather banal hymn a gravity and solemnity that might, if you like, foretell the strange future of the babe in the crib. My recordings of Christmas hymns sung by Elisabeth Schwarzkopf, Joan Sutherland, and others possess a jubilate accent indeed appropriate for a time of celebration, but not more fitting than the long-dead voices of a simpler, less opulent, and less spendthrift time.

In the notes to the old recording, I learned that during the twenties and thirties the tenor Giovanni Martinelli would rise up in the choir loft at St. Patrick's Cathedral during the Midnight Mass to sing, without previous announcement, "Gesù Bambino." What reciprocity can be imagined here? Perhaps the ring of a few coins tossed in the poor box.

1998

ACKNOWLEDGMENTS

WITHOUT the invaluable suggestions and extraordinary generosity of Saskia Hamilton, Harriet Lowell, and Linda Hall, this book could not have come into being. Nor could I have tracked down many of its pieces (so well hidden in back issues no search engine could find them) without the help of librarians at the Thompson Memorial Library at Vassar College, the Lucy Scribner Library at Skidmore College, Houghton Library at Harvard, and the Harry Ransom Center at the University of Texas. My gratitude to Jane Eblen Keller, Peggy Fox, Ian S. MacNiven, Darryl Pinckney, and Edwin Frank would be difficult to express, and to my most patient listeners, Marcel and Oona, impossible.

SOURCES

"The Art of the Essay" first appeared as the introduction to *Best American Essays, 1986*, edited by Hardwick. The text published here for the most part follows the version printed in the September 14, 1986, edition of *The New York Times*, under the title "Its Only Defense: Intelligence and Sparkle."

"New York City: Crash Course" first appeared in *Granta* and was later included in *Best American Essays, 1991*, edited by Joyce Carol Oates.

"Lexington, Kentucky" first appeared in *Harper's Magazine* under the title "Going Home in America: Lexington, Kentucky." Hardwick would later incorporate passages revised from this essay into her novel *Sleepless Nights*.

"Puritanical Pleasures" first appeared in *House & Garden* under the title "Puritanical Pleasures: Summer in Maine."

"The Émigré" first appeared in *Esquire*.

"Balanchine" first appeared in *Vogue* as "Balanchine: What Movement and Space Can Do for the Spirit."

"Faye Dunaway" first appeared in *Vogue* as "Faye Dunaway: The Face in the Dark."

"Knowing Sontag" first appeared in *Vogue*.

"Katherine Anne" first appeared in *Vanity Fair*.

"Things" first appeared in *House & Garden*.

"Elections" first appeared in *Vogue* as "Elections: Renewal or Just Replacement?"

"Mr. America" first appeared in *The New York Review of Books*.

"Piety and Politics" first appeared in *The New York Review of Books* under the title "The Carter Question II: Piety and Politics."

"The Kennedy Scandals" first appeared in *The New York Review of Books*.

"The Menendez Show" first appeared in *The New York Review of Books*.

"Family Values" first appeared in *The New York Review of Books*.

"Head Over Heels" first appeared in *The New York Review of Books*.

"On Behalf of the Unborn" first appeared in *The Washington Post* as "On Behalf of the Unborn: A Celibacy Amendment."

"The American Woman as Snow Queen" first appeared in *Commentary* as "The American Woman as Snow Queen: Our Self-Contemptuous Acceptance of Europe's Myth."

"The Feminine Principle" first appeared in *Mademoiselle* with the following note: "This article is based on a lecture delivered at Barnard College as part of a series of seminars in American Civilization."

"Women Re Women" first appeared in *Mademoiselle*.

"The Ties Women Cannot Shake, and Have" first appeared in *Vogue*.

"Is the 'Equal' Woman More Vulnerable" first appeared in *Vogue*.

"Suicide and Women" first appeared in *Mademoiselle*.

"When to Cast Out, Give Up, Let Go" first appeared in *Mademoiselle* under the title "When to Cast Out, Give Up, Let Go . . . Or How to Discard the Single Glove, the Strangling Memory, Even Love."

"On Reading the Writings of Women" first appeared in *The Columbia University Forum*.

"Reading" first appeared in *Daedalus*.

"Southern Literature: The Cultural Assumptions of Regionalism" first appeared in *Southern Literature in Transition: Heritage and Promise*.

"Basic Englishing" first appeared in *The New York Review of Books*.

"*Parsifal*" first appeared in *Vogue* as "Parsifal: In the Cave of Ourselves."

"The Eternal Heartbreak" first appeared in *Antaeus*.

"The Heart of the Seasons" first appeared in *House & Garden* and was later included in *Best American Essays, 1988*, edited by Annie Dillard.

"Notes on Leonardo and the Future of the Past" first appeared in *Art in America*.

"Grits Soufflé" first appeared in *The New Yorker*.

"Christmas Past" first appeared in *The New Yorker*.

OTHER NEW YORK REVIEW CLASSICS

For a complete list of titles, visit www.nyrb.com.